*The Party's Choice*

*Studies in Presidential Selection*
TITLES PUBLISHED

☆
*William R. Keech and Donald R. Matthews*
☆

# The Party's Choice

*Studies in Presidential Selection*
THE BROOKINGS INSTITUTION
*Washington, D.C.*

*Library of Congress Cataloging in Publication Data:*
Keech, William R
  The party's choice.
  (Studies in presidential selection)
  Includes bibliographical references.
    1. Presidents—United States—Nomination.
I. Matthews, Donald R., joint author.  II. Title.
III. Series.
JK521.K43    329'.022'0973    75-31757
ISBN 0-8157-4852-3
ISBN 0-8157-4851-5 pbk.

1 2 3 4 5 6 7 8 9

THE BROOKINGS INSTITUTION is an independent organization devoted to nonpartisan research, education, and publication in economics, government, foreign policy, and the social sciences generally. Its principal purposes are to aid in the development of sound public policies and to promote public understanding of issues of national importance.

The Institution was founded on December 8, 1927, to merge the activities of the Institution for Government Research, founded in 1916, the Institute of Economics, founded in 1922, and the Robert Brookings Graduate School of Economics and Government, founded in 1924.

The Board of Trustees is responsible for the general administration of the Institution, while the immediate direction of the policies, program, and staff is vested in the President, assisted by an advisory committee of the officers and staff. The by-laws of the Institution state: "It is the function of the Trustees to make possible the conduct of scientific research, and publication, under the most favorable conditions, and to safeguard the independence of the research staff in the pursuit of their studies and in the publication of the results of such studies. It is not a part of their function to determine, control, or influence the conduct of particular investigations or the conclusions reached."

The President bears final responsibility for the decision to publish a manuscript as a Brookings book. In reaching his judgment on the competence, accuracy, and objectivity of each study, the President is advised by the director of the appropriate research program and weighs the views of a panel of expert outside readers who report to him in confidence on the quality of the work. Publication of a work signifies that it is deemed a competent treatment worthy of public consideration but does not imply endorsement of conclusions or recommendations.

The Institution maintains its position of neutrality on issues of public policy in order to safeguard the intellectual freedom of the staff. Hence interpretations or conclusions in Brookings publications should be understood to be solely those of the authors and should not be attributed to the Institution, to its trustees, officers, or other staff members, or to the organizations that support its research.

# Foreword

ONE BASIC TRUTH about American politics emerged yet again from the 1972 election: presidential nominations are more important than presidential elections. In this analysis of the nominating process, William R. Keech and Donald R. Matthews examine the events leading up to the nomination of the major parties' candidates in the last ten presidential elections. They find that the crucial period for most presidential aspirants is the three years between one election and the opening of formal campaigning for the next. The search for a consensus candidate often produces a leader whom the press, the polls, and party leaders recognize as the unofficial nominee before the first primaries, and such candidates usually survive with their advantages intact. Rarely are the primaries instrumental in developing candidates who go on to win nomination. However, when no early consensus candidate is identified, when the preferences of party leaders and the rank and file differ sharply, or when political amateurs are active, the formal machinery of the selection process becomes significant in the choice of a nominee.

The mechanics of the nominating process are examined here as they affect the chances of contenders inside and outside the party in power. The informal nominating process before the primaries begin is examined first from the perspective of the incumbent president's party, then from that of the opposition party. The primaries are treated similarly. Finally, the convention's role is examined in relation to the extent of agreement that prevailed when the convention began. The authors believe that the system of nominating presidential candidates should be changed so as to lengthen the list of promising contestants in the long period of informal campaigning: the primaries should serve to narrow the choice to a few whom convention delegates could back as presidential possibilities.

This book is the seventh and final publication in the series of Studies in Presidential Selection undertaken by the Brookings Governmental Studies program, which is directed by Gilbert Y. Steiner. A bipartisan public advisory council, a list of whose members precedes this foreword, offered practical comment and assistance for the series.

The authors are grateful for comment and criticism from Jeff Fishel, Stephen Hess, Frank J. Munger, Judith H. Parris, Gilbert Y. Steiner, and James L. Sundquist. Melvin C. Smith, Timothy S. Kolly, and James Gogan provided research assistance at various stages of the project. Typing was done by Sara Sklar and Delores Burton. The volume was edited by Alice M. Carroll and indexed by Helen B. Eisenhart.

Financial support for the project of which this book is a part was furnished by a grant from the Ford Foundation. The authors' views, opinions, and interpretations are their own and should not be ascribed to other staff members, officers, or trustees of the Brookings Institution or to the Ford Foundation.

KERMIT GORDON
*President*

*November 1975*
*Washington, D.C.*

# Contents

TABLES

Contents                                                                    xi

☆

*Chapter One*

☆

# *THE PRESIDENTIAL POSSIBILITY*

ON NOVEMBER 7, 1972, some 76 million Americans exercised their most important political power—they elected a president of the United States. The ballots and voting machines on which they recorded their choices contained the names of only two men with a realistic chance of winning the office. One was George McGovern, the other Richard Nixon. Both candidates were seriously flawed. McGovern, whose capture of the Democratic party's nomination was a near miracle, proved ineffective, unconvincing, and unpopular as a candidate. And Republican President Nixon, within a few months of his landslide victory, was found to be deeply implicated in the Watergate affair, a shocking series of scandals that sent members of his administration to jail for criminal activities, seriously threatened his own impeachment, and ultimately brought about his resignation from office.

One basic lesson about American politics stands out from the 1972 election: presidential nominations are more important than presidential elections. The quality of the people's verdict depends on the quality of the options from which they chose.

Tens of millions of Americans are eligible to become president of the United States by constitutional standards.[1] Somehow, this vast number of eligibles must be narrowed to a manageable few before

1. Presidents must be native-born citizens, 35 years old, and have spent at least 14 years of their lives residing in the United States. *Constitution of the United States,* Art. 2, Sec. 1. Children of American parents who were born abroad also qualify, although some ambiguity remains on the matter. The 14 years of residence need not immediately precede election to office.

I

the electorate can make a choice. Ironically, democratic elections are impossible in large polities without eliminating almost everybody before the people decide.

While this function could be performed in a variety of ways,[2] the selection of potential presidents of the United States is carried out by the Democratic and Republican parties. With infrequent exceptions, the nation is presented every four years with a forced choice between the presidential nominees of the Democratic and Republican parties.[3] Since the selection of the American president is almost over before the election campaign even begins, the way in which presidential nominations are made and the characteristics of persons who usually win the endorsement of the major parties are matters of critical importance. Evaluation of the processes and results of presidential nominating politics can clarify the issues that should be considered if the institution is to be reformed.

## *The Complexity of Nominating Decisions*

Nominating decisions differ significantly from other collective choices, especially elections. The nomination, in the first place, is a provisional choice. The party's presidential nominee is chosen to perform not solely as president of the United States, but also as candidate for president of the United States. The qualities necessary to fill these two roles successfully are, though similar, not identical. Often, electoral considerations loom larger in nominating decisions than estimates of probable performance in the White House. But the relative weights of these two factors vary as the situation varies and from individual to individual. The two roles of the nominee considerably complicate the task of choosing between alternatives.

Of the millions of persons who are eligible for office, only a relative handful has a chance of being nominated or actively seeks the

2. See Leon D. Epstein, *Political Parties in Western Democracies* (Praeger, 1967), chap. 8; and Donald R. Matthews, ed., *Perspectives on Presidential Selection* (Brookings Institution, 1973), chaps. 2–4.

3. Daniel A. Mazmanian, *Third Parties in Presidential Elections* (Brookings Institution, 1974), presents a good analysis of the role of third parties in American presidential politics.

presidency. Ordinarily, the parties must choose among four, five, or more possible nominees. That is vastly more difficult than deciding between two possibilities; mathematically, there is no invariably satisfactory way to arrive at a group choice between more than two alternatives in a reasonably democratic way.[4]

Since both parties select their nominee on the basis of absolute majority rule, a combination of first, second, and even third choices may be necessary before a winner can emerge. Assessments of the various competitors' likelihood of winning the nomination therefore must be combined with their relative attractiveness as candidates and potential presidents in order to make a reasonable choice between them. It makes no sense to most delegates to back a first-choice candidate who has less chance of nomination than their second choice; to do so might contribute to the selection of a quite unacceptable person. Anticipated outcomes thus play a large role in nominating decisions, though they are irrelevant to decisions made in the normal American two-man, plurality election.

Some of the handy aids to reasonable decision that exist in the general election are missing from the nominating contests. Party identification, a short-cut way of deciding where to cast an election vote, is the same for all the contestants. Some nominees have been in the public eye for decades, others are not well known when the nominating contest begins. Thus presidential nominating politics is extraordinarily subtle, ambiguous, and complex.

## Patterns of the Nominating Process

Facts about presidential nominations exist in abundance. Newspapers and magazines print millions of words about them. Television and radio provide extensive public exposure to candidates and near-candidates, cover preconvention campaigns thoroughly, and broad-

---

4. See Kenneth Arrow, *Social Choice and Individual Values* (Wiley, 1963); and Duncan Black, *The Theory of Committees and Elections* (Cambridge, England: Cambridge University Press, 1959), for formal, mathematical treatment of this problem. V. O. Key, Jr.'s criticism of one-party politics in the South was based, in large part, on the view that a multiplicity of unlabeled candidates resulted in voter confusion and irrationality; *Southern Politics* (Knopf, 1949), chap. 14.

cast the proceedings of the national party conventions from gavel to gavel. Books on recent presidential campaigns regularly make the best-seller lists a few months after the winner moves into the White House.

The patterns of behavior—the recurring and sometimes commonplace events that provide structure and a degree of predictability to the process of presidential choice—are another matter. These patterns may be better understood if a set of concepts and perspectives can be defined.

The nominating process involves the political parties, the national conventions, state electoral laws, and the strategies of candidates, delegates, party leaders, and the like. How these factors affect the choice of candidates is more important than how each develops for its own sake. Who wins the nomination is of central concern, and the process of presidential nomination is fundamentally significant in terms of how it affects this result.

The election of 1936 roughly marks the beginning of a modern era of presidential nominations which differs from that of earlier days. The Democrats abandoned their time-honored two-thirds rule for convention voting in 1936, moving to the same 50-percent-plus-one-vote standard used by the Republicans. The 1936 nominations were also the first to have the benefit of public opinion polls as a measure of the popularity of potential candidates.

Since 1936 the Democratic and Republican parties have each made ten presidential nominations. The twenty nominating contests of the two parties between 1936 and 1972 provide enough experience to identify patterns in the circumstances that affect presidential candidacies. More than a hundred men (and occasional women) have emerged as potential candidates for the American presidency since 1936, offering a view of the routes to prominence within the presidential context. Crucial developments in the contest for nomination occur in the three-year period that begins at one presidential election and stretches to the start of the formal nominating process early in the next presidential year. The formal campaign for nomination begins with the approximately five-month period of the presidential primaries, culminating with the convention and its final nominating decision. Not only is each stage of the nomination process distinct, but the various stages differ from the vantage of each party—not in the usual way, by party name, but by the party's power position. For the competitive situation within the party controlling the White House ordinarily differs from that in the party out of power. The way in which presidential nominees are selected is therefore more likely to be affected by whether a party is in or out of power than by its Democratic or Republican label.

## The Good Candidate

"What a party wants is not a good president but a good candidate," James Bryce wrote near the turn of the century. "The party managers have therefore to look out for the person likely to gain most support, and at the same time excite least opposition."[5]

Most convention delegates undoubtedly want to nominate both a good candidate and a good president. But it is exceedingly difficult to define, let alone achieve widespread agreement about, what a good president ought to be. A good candidate, however, is clearly a winner. Even here there is ambiguity. The candidate who can most help a state (or local) party ticket is not necessarily the same one who has the best chance of winning the national election or of winning the struggle for a particular cause over the long haul. Winning means different things to different politicians at different times. But if the party's candidate does not win the national election, the anticipated quality of his performance in the White House becomes an altogether academic matter. To pragmatic politicians there is no sharp distinction between candidacy and performance in office: only good candidates ever have the chance to be a good president.

The search for a candidate who will attract more votes than the other party's man has been carried on in a variety of ways. While only a small segment of the total population is considered, there are still far too many possibilities to make a choice easily. Between 1936 and 1972, for example, 434 persons served as state governors and 368

5. *The American Commonwealth* (3d rev. ed., Macmillan, 1916), vol. 1, p. 187.

as U.S. senators (62 held both offices at one time or another). One hundred thirteen men and women served in the president's cabinet and eight as vice presidents.[6] Add to this list the thousands of persons who held other important positions in federal, state, and local governments and the number of experienced and reasonably successful politicians in the United States becomes quite large. And as the cases of Wendell Willkie and Dwight Eisenhower indicate, the parties do not invariably confine themselves to candidates from this rather sizable group of successful politicians.

Traditionally, potential candidates have been judged by their "availability" for the presidency, an ill-defined concept based on the attributes that were deemed necessary for a winning candidate. In 1959 Sidney Hyman listed the first of these as the candidate's official connection with the governmental process in an appointive or elective post. Nominating conventions clearly showed a preference for state governors, especially those from states with a large electoral vote and two-party voting record. Candidates from the big northern states were favored over southerners. They had to be hospitable to the claims of many economic interests in the nation. And they were expected to present an "idealized version of all that is felicitous in home and family life." Preferably, they should come from small towns and be of English stock; and, quite definitely, they should be Protestant.[7]

Such rules of thumb, liberally interpreted and by no means inviolable, have historically played an important role in presidential nominations.[8] They served as a gauge of the personal qualities of candidates that were believed to generate electoral support. More important, they were a guide to the traits to be avoided, for what made candidates unpopular was far clearer than what caused some men to be widely loved. Unless there was a candidate who was obvi-

6. Only persons who served more than one year are included in the count.

7. "Nine Tests for the Presidential Hopeful," *New York Times Magazine,* Jan. 4, 1959, p. 11. See also Sidney Hyman, *The American President* (Harper, 1954), chap. 10.

8. See M. Ostrogorski, *Democracy and the Organization of Political Parties* (Doubleday, 1964), pp. 51, 60, 70, 130–31, and 140–41, for a more traditional view. See also Albert Somit, "The Military Hero as Presidential Candidate," *Public Opinion Quarterly,* vol. 12 (Summer 1948), pp. 192–200.

ously popular like a war hero, the trick was to identify the candidate who would alienate the fewest people.

In recent years, however, the availability rules for selecting presidential candidates have eroded: A Catholic (John F. Kennedy), a divorced man (Adlai E. Stevenson), and a southerner (Lyndon B. Johnson) have been nominated. Dwight D. Eisenhower and Wendell L. Willkie became presidential candidates despite their lack of political experience. No governor since Stevenson has won the endorsement of a national convention. The leading candidates for the Democratic nomination in 1972 were from South Dakota, Minnesota, Maine, Alabama, and the State of Washington. Before 1928, three-quarters of the nominations were won by contenders who fitted the availability qualifications.[9] Since then, less than half have fitted them.

This change in the selection criteria for presidential candidates no doubt reflects numerous changes in the composition and values of the nation and its political structure. But the most significant change may have been the development of the scientific public opinion poll.

Political polls are nothing new. A number of newspapers conducted them in the nineteenth century, printing ballots which the readers clipped out and mailed in. Between 1916 and 1936 the *Literary Digest* poll, based on prepaid return postcards mailed to car owners and telephone subscribers, became a national institution. The obvious economic bias in these polls did not lead to any gross errors until the *Digest* predicted in 1936 that Alfred M. Landon would defeat Franklin D. Roosevelt in a landslide. The magazine ceased publication shortly thereafter.

A little-known market research analyst named George Gallup made a national reputation by predicting the *Literary Digest* fiasco six weeks before its ballots were sent out. Using small but scientifically chosen samples, Gallup was able to make accurate inferences about voting preference.[10] The superiority of his method was dra-

9. Gerald Pomper, *Nominating the President: The Politics of Convention Choice* (Norton, 1966), p. 127.

10. Gallup polls are taken and disseminated by the American Institute of Public Opinion, Princeton, N.J. The most complete compendium of these polls is George H. Gallup, *The Gallup Poll: Public Opinion 1935–1971* (Random House, 1972), 3 vols.

matically demonstrated in the 1936 election. No longer would politicians have to make rough guesses about the probable popularity of candidates based on their availability. Now, with the polls, they had reliable and objective measures of individual popularity.[11]

With one clear exception, the leaders in the final polls have won their party's nomination since 1936. The exception was Estes Kefauver, who had a decisive lead in the 1952 polls but lost the nomination to Adlai Stevenson (who ranked a distant third). In 1964 no single leader emerged among the Republican candidates, though Barry M. Goldwater, the ultimate nominee, was tied for first place. In 1940, Thomas E. Dewey led the last poll reported before the convention, though Willkie took a decisive lead in a poll taken during the convention. In every other case when there was enough competition to justify conducting polls, the final poll leader and the party nominee were the same.

This remarkable association between poll standings and convention victory does not mean, of course, that delegates merely read poll results and then automatically vote for the leader. But neither is the agreement between the polls and convention results coincidental. Most party leaders and convention delegates want their candidate to win the national election, and there is no more reliable and objective measure of a candidate's popularity and chances of winning than the polls.[12] Conventions must quickly agree on a single candidate for president or concede the election to the other party; the poll standings usually point to one person as the most popular solution to this problem. Poll standings are generally a sign of other important candidate advantages—press attention, popularity among party leaders, a capacity to attract massive campaign resources, expectation of victory, and the like. Furthermore, the polls are not disembodied. If a

11. A nontechnical discussion of the accuracy of polls may be found in Harold A. Mendelsohn and I. Crespi, *Polls, Television, and the New Politics* (Chandler, 1970), chap. 2. The polls' one major error in predicting the outcomes of presidential elections is thoroughly dissected in Frederick Mosteller and others, *The Pre-Election Polls of 1948*, Bulletin 50 (Social Science Research Council, 1949).

12. Trial heats between potential candidates of opposing parties are the most direct estimate of who is most likely to win. However, it is the polls of the presidential preferences of a given party's rank and file that have been most regularly taken and followed.

given candidate leads in the polls, convention delegates usually have heard similar preferences expressed by rank-and-file voters back home, by the press, and by fellow political activists. The impact of the polls is thus often subtle and indirect. They add little new to the situation except relative objectivity, reliability, and accuracy.

But by reducing uncertainty, the polls have made the traditional, mostly negative, rules of thumb about availability largely irrelevant. Candidates can now be chosen on the basis of their positive popularity as measured by the polls. The polls, for example, go far toward accounting for the astonishing success of Wendell Willkie. In the last three months of the 1940 nominating campaign, he jumped from fourth place in the polls (3 percent of the Republicans favored his candidacy) to first (with a 44 percent rating). Without authoritative measures of mass opinion, his chances of winning the nomination would have been slimmer. John Kennedy's presidential ambition seemed thwarted by his religion, but the polls showed him to be the most popular Democratic choice despite his Catholicism. The initial interest of both parties in Dwight Eisenhower as a possible presidential nominee was triggered by polls demonstrating his extraordinary popularity.[13]

The shift to poll standings as a principal criterion for selecting presidential nominees has opened up the game to aspirants who would have had little chance under the old availability rules. So long as they can demonstrate popularity, the presidential hopefuls' personal attributes do not matter much. But even this criterion of selection does not even-handedly favor all comers. The process of becoming a poll leader favors some potential presidents at the expense of others.

## The Media and Money

Mass popularity as measured by public opinion polls is today a preeminent criterion for the selection of presidential candidates. This means that if the mass communications media do not pay attention to

---

13. See Herbert H. Hyman and Paul B. Sheatsley, "The Political Appeal of President Eisenhower," *Public Opinion Quarterly*, vol. 17 (Winter 1953–54), pp. 443–60.

a person he has no chance of becoming president. Even the most
energetic of politicians cannot shake enough hands, meet enough
people, address enough audiences in person, to reach the scattered
millions he must impress favorably. Presidential nominating politics
is as a consequence conducted largely through the mass media. The
media's picture of the world matters more than reality. A serious
contender for the presidency must become a positive and prominent
part of that picture by convention time.

Not just any kind of publicity will do. If that were the case, presidential politics would be dominated by entertainers, athletes, and
other heroes, many of whom are more widely known and admired
than most presidential aspirants. In recent years such celebrities have
often sought to capitalize on their fame by entering elective politics.
Governor Ronald Reagan and Senator George Murphy of California
were both movie stars. Murphy was defeated in 1970 by the youthful John Tunney, whose claim to political prominence rested heavily
on his father Gene Tunney's immortality as a professional prize-
fighter. Jesse Helms, a popular television commentator for many
years, was elected to the Senate from North Carolina in 1972. Jack
Kemp, former quarterback for the Buffalo Bills; Wilmer (Vine-
gar Bend) Mizell, once a major league pitcher of renown; and Bob
Mathias, the decathlon champion in the 1948 and 1952 Olympic
Games, were elected to the House of Representatives. But not all
celebrities turned politician have been so successful. Shirley Temple
Black, the child movie star of the 1930s and 1940s, lost her bid for a
seat in the House. The astronaut John Glenn failed once as a senatorial candidate. Bud Wilkinson, the football coach, ran unsuccessfully for a seat in the U.S. Senate. The translation of notoriety
achieved in a nonpolitical context into votes is not invariably successful. And to date, no celebrities have attempted to move directly into
presidential contention without serving in a lesser public office first.
The publicity that makes men into presidential possibilities must be
cast in a political—preferably a presidential—context.

For the most part, this kind of publicity is not for sale. A media
blitz dependent on paid advertising can sometimes make a previously
obscure figure into a plausible candidate for governor or U.S. senator

or lesser office. Howard Metzenbaum used this approach to defeat John Glenn in an Ohio senatorial primary—although Metzenbaum lost the subsequent election to Robert A. Taft, Jr., grandson of a president and son of "Mr. Republican" Robert A. Taft. Milton Shapp, spending money on advertising in a lavish way, won election as governor of Pennsylvania on his second try. But with the possible exception of Wendell Willkie, no one has used this approach directly to become a contender for the nomination. Large expenditures of money and the use of professional public relations techniques may well be useful for reaching the Senate or a statehouse, but they are no substitute for such positions as an intermediate step in the direction of the presidency. The kind of publicity that is most useful for exposing a potential presidential candidate usually is included in the regular news and editorial content of the press and broadcasting media.

This is not to say that money is unimportant in presidential nominating politics. An effective campaign for a major party presidential nomination costs millions of dollars.[14] Even under the campaign finance reforms, a presidential aspirant must be able to raise (or appear to be able to raise) large sums in private contributions in order to be a serious contender. Those Americans who control great wealth and are interested enough in politics to invest in risky nomination contests have played a large role in choosing presidents.

But there are limits on the impact of political money and those who control it. Potential presidents who look like winners at the start discover the necessary financial resources relatively easily. All candidates complain of money problems, but no front-running candidate appears to have lost the nomination because of a lack of cash. When a leading candidate ceases to look like a winner, however, as Senator Edmund S. Muskie did in 1972, the flow of money to his campaign can dwindle so quickly that he is forced out of active contention. It is the media, not the money men, who shape mass perceptions of who is ahead, who is fading or gaining, who is hopelessly behind. These perceptions have profound effects on the raising of political money.

14. See Herbert E. Alexander, *Money in Politics* (Public Affairs Press, 1972), chap. 5.

While presidential nominating campaigns are extremely expensive, the financial resources needed to make a plausible start are only a small fraction of those needed to win. If start-up costs can be met, a strong early showing in the polls or the primaries will generate more new resources. And the successful nominating campaigns of Senator Goldwater and Senator McGovern demonstrate that candidates have not needed to rely exclusively on the traditional fat cats within their respective parties. New financial constituencies can sometimes be developed when adequate funds cannot be raised from the regular sources. Again massive coverage by the press and broadcast media is necessary in order to attract this financial constituency. Both Goldwater and McGovern were able to exploit publicity to build impressive national organizations and raise adequate funds despite the fact that the media gave neither much chance of victory. Thus compared to the media, campaign contributors have played a secondary and largely reinforcing role in screening potential presidential candidates. Their role will be reduced still further by campaign finance reforms, especially public subsidies and contribution limits.

The press that is influential in nominating politics comprises a relatively small group of individuals

representing news organizations with a commitment to coverage of national politics year in and year out, in dull seasons as well as exciting times. These organizations . . . include the three news magazines, the two wire services, the three radio-television networks, and the *New York Times*, the Washington *Post*, the Washington *Evening Star*, the *Los Angeles Times*, the *Christian Science Monitor*, the *Baltimore Sun*, the Knight newspapers, the Field papers, and the Gannett, Newhouse, Scripps-Howard, and Hearst chains . . . plus a few syndicated columnists who cover politics along with other subjects.[15]

These people write about nominating politics when no one else pays much attention, during the critical early and informal stage of the

15. David Broder, "Political Reporters in Presidential Politics," in Charles Peters and Timothy J. Adams, eds., *Inside the System* (Praeger, 1970), p. 13. See also Timothy Crouse, *The Boys on the Bus* (Random House, 1973), and James M. Perry, *Us and Them: How the Press Covered the 1972 Election* (Clarkson N. Potter, 1973), chap. 1.

nominating process. They are acknowledged experts, well connected in political circles throughout the land. Their reports appear in the nation's most prestigious newspapers and respected news broadcasts. What they write about candidates and potential candidates strongly influences what the rest of the mass media says. Collectively they are what columnist Russell Baker has called "the Great Mentioner," the source of self-fulfilling stories that a person has been "mentioned" as a possible presidential nominee.

A consensus on the characteristics and qualifications of candidates and potential candidates tends to develop within this group. In 1972, for example, they found Muskie indecisive and hot-tempered, McGovern a lightweight, Hubert Humphrey a has-been, George Wallace a demagogue. In 1968, George Romney was sanctimonious and naive, Richard Nixon secretive and untrustworthy. While reporters seek to be objective in their campaign analyses, such evaluations color their writing.[16] But this is perhaps the least consequential way the judgments of the press influence nominating outcomes. Whom the press decides to cover is often more important than what the press says. On the whole, political reporters pay the most attention to those men they consider to be serious possibilities: those with a possibility of winning the nomination, and those who appear to have the capacity to head a national campaign and to serve effectively in the White House.

As a rule, the press pays far more attention to front-running candidates and potential candidates, as indicated by the polls, than they do to longer shots. This is understandable enough, for "much of political journalism is an artful effort to disguise prediction as reporting"[17]—readers want to know what's going to happen in the future and who is going to win or lose. And why should busy reporters squander their time and attention on presidential aspirants who have little or no chance of winning?

Of course, the reporters do not rely exclusively on polls in estimating the relative chances of various contenders for the nomina-

16. See Martin F. Nolan, "Faust at the Racetrack: Let the Reader Beware," in Frederick Dutton, ed., *Playboy's Election Guide, 1972* (Playboy Press, 1972).

17. Broder, "Political Reporters in Presidential Politics," p. 15.

tion. In the last analysis, the votes of convention delegates are what matters. As the reporters move about the country talking to politicians, they learn how they feel about the potential nominees, and the bulk of the convention delegates are usually experienced state and local politicians like the ones they talk to. When there is a divergence between poll standings and the preferences of the party politicians—as there was in the Democratic party in 1952—reporters may take the polls less seriously. They also know that the candidate preferences expressed in the polls are quite shallow and subject to rapid changes as voters learn more about the candidates, as new persons join the contest and others drop out of contention, or as changing events shift campaign issues. The polls are read with such reservations in mind. And yet in a sea of subjectivity and uncertainty, the polls stand out as a hard rock of objective fact. They heavily influence the reporters' view of who is ahead, and reporters pay most attention to the leaders.

This tendency makes it difficult for new faces to get very far in presidential politics. Without extensive press coverage, it is impossible for a man to achieve a large national following and hence respectable poll standings. Yet having a large national following, as indicated in the polls, tends to be a condition for substantial press coverage.[18] It is possible to break the vicious cycle. But most of the time, the national reporters' screening of presidential possibilities tends to favor potential nominees who are already popular at the beginning of the contest.

## The Range of Choice

How "presidential possibilities" are created remains somewhat mysterious. But the results of this little understood process are clear

18. A countervailing media bias—in favor of drama, conflict, and uncertainty—becomes significant at a later stage in the nominating process. The probable outcomes of presidential primaries and conventions are frequently presented as more uncertain than they really are in order to create drama. This tends to work against the front-running candidate and in favor of his challengers. See Paul H. Weaver, "Is Television News Biased?" *Public Interest*, no. 26 (Winter 1972), pp. 57–74; and Marc F. Plattner and James R. Ferguson, *Report on Network News Treatment of the 1972 Democratic Presidential Candidates* (Bloomington, Ind.: Alternative Educational Foundation, Inc., 1972), for discussions of this and related themes.

enough: a few persons are perceived as potential presidential nominees by rank-and-file voters.

Sixty-two Democrats and forty-seven Republicans have attracted the support of 1 percent or more of their fellow partisans in Gallup polls on presidential candidate preferences since 1936. This group can serve as a rough, working definition of the people available for nomination by the two major parties.[19] Of course not all those polling this modest level of popular support seriously aspired to the office, and some not on the list at any given time emerged later with better prospects than those already included.

But no one has been nominated for the presidency who was not a member of this group. In fact, with the exception of Wendell Willkie, no one has been nominated who had not been on the list for a substantial period of time. There is always a possibility that a nominee will move quickly into public view, as Willkie did (though he was on the list for several months before his nomination). But this list errs more on the side of including too many potential candidates than too few.[20] These one hundred and nine persons have taken a necessary first step toward presidential nomination that no other Americans since 1936 have.

Considering only contested years, the number of presidential possibilities (by this definition) has varied from five to twenty within the Democratic party, from three to fourteen for the Republicans

19. A list of incumbent senators or governors would include many with no chance and leave some more realistic possibilities out. A list based on those receiving votes at party conventions would often be too narrow, since these votes often tend to unanimity, and may sometimes be too broad since it sometimes includes favorite-son governors and the like.

20. The extraordinary importance of sheer name recognition in achieving prominence as a presidential contender is underscored by the frequency with which some names appear in the polls. Among those polling 1 percent or more support for the presidential nomination since 1936 are Eleanor Roosevelt (in 1948), Franklin D. Roosevelt, Jr. (1952), and James Roosevelt (1952); John F. Kennedy (1960), Robert F. Kennedy (1968), and Edward M. Kennedy (1972); Robert A. Taft (1940–52), the son of a president, and Robert A. Taft, Jr. (1968); Theodore Roosevelt, Jr. (1936); Henry Cabot Lodge, Jr. (1940, 1952, and 1960–68); and Milton Eisenhower (1960–64). While most of these men and women displayed considerable political achievement in their own right, not all would have gotten so far or would have entered the small circle of presidential possibilities without the precious asset of a well-known political name.

TABLE I-I. *Number of Persons Who Polled at Least 1 Percent Support for Presidential Nomination, by Party and Stage of Nominating Process, 1936–72*

| Election year | Number in Democratic party | | Number in Republican party | |
|---|---|---|---|---|
| | Before primaries | Added during primaries | Before primaries | Added during primaries |
| 1936 | a | a | 8 | 0 |
| 1940 | 7 | 0 | 12 | 2 |
| 1944 | a | a | 9 | 0 |
| 1948 | 14 | 2 | 12 | 0 |
| 1952 | 15 | 5 | 12 | 0 |
| 1956 | 13 | 0 | a | a |
| 1960 | 12 | 0 | 10 | 1 |
| 1964 | a | a | 11 | 0 |
| 1968 | 5 | 0 | 12 | 1 |
| 1972 | 16 | 1 | 3 | 0 |
| Total | 82 | 8 | 89 | 4 |

Source: American Institute of Public Opinion, Gallup releases, various dates.
a. No poll taken.

(see Table 1-1). Almost all of these showed up in the polls before the formal nominating process began. Of the ninety names appearing on the Democratic lists between 1936 and 1972, eighty-two first received more than 1 percent support during the three-year period stretching from the last presidential election to the time of the first primary.[21] Eighty-nine of the ninety-three Republican names first appeared in that same period.

Not only were there few potential candidates for the presidential nomination at the beginning of the formal process, but many of them stayed around quite some time (see Table 1-2). Almost 60 percent of the Republican group were considered presidential possibilities in two or more election years. Harold Stassen's name crops up in seven different election years; Thomas Dewey, Richard Nixon, and Henry Cabot Lodge, Jr., each had measurable support in five different con-

21. The number of names is greater than the number of people on the Gallup lists because some individuals polled more than 1 percent support during several different presidential years.

TABLE 1-2. *Number of Persons Who Polled at Least 1 Percent*
*Support for Presidential Nomination in Consecutive Election*
*Years, by Party, 1936–72*

| | Persons on Republican list | | | Persons on Democratic list | | |
|---|---|---|---|---|---|---|
| Election year | Number from previous elections | For first time | | Number from previous elections | For first time | |
| | | Number | Percent | | Number | Percent |
| 1940 | 4 | 10 | 71 | a | a | a |
| 1944 | 4 | 5 | 55 | a | a | a |
| 1948 | 10 | 2 | 17 | 2 | 14 | 88 |
| 1952 | 11 | 1 | 8 | 8 | 12 | 60 |
| 1956 | b | b | b | 6 | 7 | 54 |
| 1960 | 4 | 7 | 63 | 6 | 6 | 50 |
| 1964 | 6 | 5 | 45 | b | b | b |
| 1968 | 9 | 4 | 31 | 2 | 3 | 60 |
| 1972 | 1 | 2 | 67 | 4 | 13 | 77 |

Source: Gallup releases, various dates.

a. Since the Democratic nominations of 1936 and 1944 were uncontested, and no polls were taken, it is not possible to determine the number of new and old possibilities.

b. No poll taken.

tests; Arthur Vandenberg, Robert Taft, and John Bricker in four; Herbert Hoover, General Douglas MacArthur, Earl Warren, Leverett Saltonstall, Dwight Eisenhower, Nelson Rockefeller, and Barry Goldwater in three. The Democrats displayed a noticeably higher rate of circulation, yet about a third of those showing up in the polls in an average year had been a presidential possibility in one or more previous nominating contests.

Ninety percent of the persons polling 1 percent or more support for presidential nominations between 1936 and 1972 were public officeholders.[22] Even those who had held no public office at the time they were first mentioned as possible presidents were still linked in one fashion or another to public affairs. Most of them were distinguished generals (MacArthur and Eisenhower), close relatives of presidents (Milton Eisenhower, Theodore Roosevelt, Jr., James

22. See Joseph A. Schlesinger, *Ambition and Politics: Political Careers in the United States* (Rand McNally, 1966), chap. 2, for evidence that this is not a new development.

Roosevelt), or newspaper publishers (Frank Knox, Frank Gannett). Only Wendell Willkie and Charles A. Lindbergh could claim none of these advantages, but both were active and prominent spokesmen for their political viewpoints.

The complex federal system of government in the United States results in an unusually large number of responsible public offices from which potential presidents might be expected to come. In fact, over one-third of all those persons polling at least 1 percent support for presidential nominations since 1936 were U.S. senators, almost a quarter were state governors, and nearly 20 percent were members of the president's cabinet. All the other public offices in the land contributed only a handful of presidential possibilities (see Table 1-3).

The role of different public offices in the emergence of potential presidential nominees is clearly shown in Table 1-3, where they are viewed from the perspective of all holders of each particular office. Those most frequently perceived as presidential possibilities were

TABLE 1-3. *Distribution of Nominees and Those Who Polled at Least 1 Percent Support for Presidential Nomination, by Latest Public Office Held, 1936–72*[a]

| Public office | Percent of all persons polling at least 1 percent who held office | Percent of all persons who held office polling at least 1 percent | Percent of all nominees who held office |
|---|---|---|---|
| Vice president | 2 | 100 (N = 8) | 31 |
| U.S. senator | 35 | 10 (N = 368) | 23 |
| Governor | 23 | 6 (N = 434) | 31 |
| Cabinet officer | 17 | 17 (N = 113) | 0 |
| U.S. representative | 6 | * | 0 |
| Mayor | 4 | * | 0 |
| Supreme Court justice | 2 | 6 (N = 35) | 0 |
| All others | 1 | * | 0 |
| None | 10 | * | 15 |
| Total | 100 (N = 109) | ... | 100 (N = 13) |

Source: Gallup releases, various dates.
N = total number of officeholders.
... = not applicable.
* = less than 0.5 percent.
a. Last or current office at time person *first* polled at least 1 percent support for presidential nomination among fellow partisans or was first nominated.

vice presidents—all eight vice presidents between 1936 and 1972 polled sizable support for president thereafter. No other public office comes close to this average. Seventeen percent of all cabinet members, 10 percent of all senators, 6 percent of all governors, and 6 percent of all Supreme Court justices have also broken into the presidential polls at the 1 percent level or better since 1936. Only minuscule fractions of all other types of public officials have made it into the charmed circle. The route to some prominence in presidential politics is thus not only political, but usually confined to five public offices.

But even this exaggerates the numbers of public officials with a realistic chance of winning a major party nomination. All the presidential nominees since 1936 who held public office have been either vice presidents, governors, or U.S. senators at the time of their nomination. No other public office in the United States served as the last step in the long ascent to the presidential nomination.

Only 735 persons have filled the offices of vice president, senator, and governor between 1936 and 1973. If those who are not interested in running for the presidency are subtracted along with those who have (or are felt to have) little chance of attracting the necessary resources, along with those who are too old or too obscure, there is only a handful left to contend for the two presidential nominations.

## The Structure of Political Opportunities

Political opportunities in the United States are structured; politicians tend to seek public office in patterned and roughly predictable ways.[23] At the apex of the opportunity structure for the presidency are the vice presidency, the U.S. Senate, and some state governorships (see Figure 1-1). Those who hold these offices have a much better chance for a major party nomination than anyone else. This fact both creates presidential ambitions among those who hold one of these three offices and encourages already committed presidential aspirants to contest for them. The media, party leaders, and others who regularly provide resources to would-be candidates reinforce

23. Ibid.

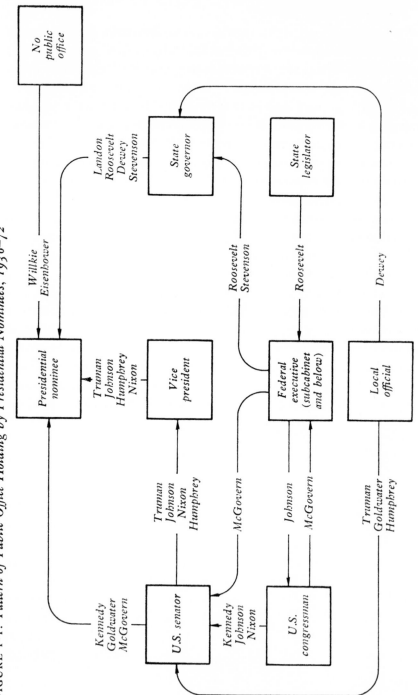

FIGURE 1-1. *Pattern of Public Office Holding by Presidential Nominees, 1936–72*

this tendency. In their continuing search for new presidential ambition and talent they tend to look where they have found them before. Thus, once begun, such a pattern of political opportunity tends to perpetuate itself.

The individual who wishes to attain the heights of a presidential nomination must first achieve sufficient prominence within a presidential context to be considered a potential nominee. Then he must translate this prominence into 50 percent plus one of the delegates' votes at his party's convention. Access to nationwide political publicity is the sine qua non of the first stage. But the ability of the incumbent of one of the offices that lead to the presidency to translate presidential prominence and popularity into a presidential nomination depends on many additional things: the institutional structure and power of the office, the backgrounds of its normal incumbents, the relationship of the office to the dominant issues of the time are among the more important of these variables. Vice presidents and U.S. senators are in especially favorable positions to succeed at both stages of the selection process; state governors are somewhat less favored. All other public offices in the land pose barriers either to achieving sufficient prominence to be considered or to winning the competition for the nomination, or both.

### THE VICE PRESIDENCY

The vice presidency is an especially advantageous position from which to receive publicity within a presidential context. While in many ways the office may not be worth a pitcher of warm spit (as Vice President John Nance Garner once observed), the incumbent automatically becomes a serious possibility for the next presidential nomination even if he has weaknesses that otherwise might bar him from serious consideration. Garner was a southerner; Alben Barkley was too old; Spiro Agnew was previously unknown nationally—yet all stood high in the polls during their tenure as vice president. Gerald Ford, never before considered a presidential contender, zoomed to the top of the polls of Republican rank-and-file preferences within days of his appointment to the vice presidency.

Vice presidents can become presidential nominees in two ways.

Both Harry Truman and Lyndon Johnson became chief executive on the death of their predecessors and then succeeded in gaining nomination while serving as president. Under more ordinary circumstances, the vice president's chances of gaining the nomination are heavily affected by the actions and inactions of the retiring incumbent. Truman preferred Governor Stevenson over the aging but more than willing Vice President Barkley; Eisenhower and Johnson apparently preferred to be succeeded by their vice presidents, although both kept them on tenterhooks until the end. Seeking a presidential nomination as vice president is an awkward business—at times the effective target is the one man who still resides in the White House, at others it must be the convention delegates and the rank-and-file partisans they represent. But the success rate of those who have lived through the ordeal is high. Usually, the vice president is the best-known party leader (short of the retiring president) and a natural candidate for the presidency.

### THE U.S. SENATE

A seat in the Senate does not automatically boost its holder toward the presidency, but it provides unique opportunities for those who wish to try. Senators are located at the heart of the nation's political communications network. Their activities are covered by a large and prestigious press corps which finds the Senate "a rich source of everything a reporter considers news."[24] The chamber's lack of control over debate and weak party discipline make it possible for a senator to become an independent national political figure if he will but try.

Not all senators can or do take advantage of these opportunities, of course. Many of them—including some of the chamber's most powerful members—are too old to be seriously considered. The senators who become prominent presidential politicians are often rather young by Senate standards. Some—for example, Johnson, Humphrey, Barkley among the Democrats and Taft and Knowland among the Republicans—have been important party leaders in the

24. Douglass Cater, quoted in Donald R. Matthews, *U.S. Senators and Their World* (University of North Carolina Press, 1960), p. 197.

Senate, but few have been among the chamber's seniority leaders. A senator need not be very powerful in the Senate in order to win wide coverage in the newspapers or on television.

But senators have other advantages in the contest for a presidential nomination. They have a better chance of becoming vice president than anyone else—ten senators have been nominated for the office since 1936, compared to only three state governors, three federal executive officials, and two U.S. representatives.[25] More members of the Senate have followed this route to the presidential nomination than have made the jump directly (see Figure 1-1), and the vice presidency is the least risky way to the White House.

Senators are proven vote-getters in statewide elections, the nearest equivalent to a national campaign. Once elected they serve for six years and frequently are reelected. Their normally long, continuous service permits them plenty of time to emerge as a presidential possibility. By contrast, most governors must achieve national acclaim quickly, get elected to the Senate, or forget about the presidency altogether (see Table 1-4). The six-year term provides Senate members with still another advantage, a chance to run for the presidency without giving up their seat in the Senate since they come up for reelection in presidential years only half the time. The only senator since 1900 to lose his seat because he sought the presidency was Barry Goldwater in 1964.[26]

Senators belong to a collegial body that conducts most of its public business Tuesdays through Thursdays. Short campaign trips are easily combined with their routine, and long periods of absence from Washington are scarcely noticed in a group of a hundred people.[27] A senator with presidential ambition can, in effect, launch a four-year campaign for the nomination; few other officials can.

Since World War II, American presidents have been preoccupied by the nation's relationships with the rest of the world. Foreign and

25. These figures include both Thomas Eagleton and Sargent Shriver for the Democratic party in 1972. Frank Knox, the Republican vice presidential nominee in 1936, had no previous office-holding experience.
26. Schlesinger, *Ambition and Politics*, p. 18.
27. They are noticed by Senate colleagues, of course, and usually deplored. See Matthews, *U.S. Senators and Their World*, especially chap. 5.

TABLE 1-4. *Distribution of Senators and Governors Who Polled at Least 1 Percent Support for Presidential Nomination, by Length of Service, 1936–72*

| Office and length of service | Percent polling at least 1 percent support[a] | | |
| --- | --- | --- | --- |
| | Democrats | Republicans | All |
| Senator | | | |
| 1–4 years | 26 | 27 | 26 |
| 5–9 years | 26 | 37 | 29 |
| 10–13 years | 22 | 18 | 21 |
| 14–17 years | 7 | 9 | 8 |
| 18 or more years | 19 | 9 | 16 |
| Total | 100 (N = 27) | 100 (N = 11) | 100 (N = 38) |
| Governor | | | |
| 1–4 years | 44 | 66 | 57 |
| 5–9 years | 56 | 34 | 43 |
| 10 or more years | 0 | 0 | 0 |
| Total | 100 (N = 9) | 100 (N = 12) | 100 (N = 21) |

Source: Gallup releases, various dates.
N = total number of officeholders.
a. At time of first mention.

military policy issues have loomed large in the news. Some association with these matters has become a valuable asset to a presidential contender; all senators can claim at least a superficial familiarity with foreign policy and national defense. Those who serve on the Senate Foreign Relations or Armed Services committees can rightly claim some measure of expertise, a fact that has not escaped the attention of the presidential aspirants in the Senate who seek assignment to these committees. Thus senators not only have tremendous advantages in attracting nationwide publicity but also are in a very favorable position, relative to others, to translate their political prominence into convention victories.

### STATE GOVERNORSHIPS

Few governors are so well advantaged. While a governor may be the focal point of his state's politics, not many state capitals are at the hub of a national communications network as Washington is. It is a great deal easier for, say, Senator Birch Bayh of Indiana to become a national figure than it is for the governor, in Indianapolis, to do so. Most governors who have become prominent as presidential possibilities since 1936 have been from large, metropolitan states. While Albany, Sacramento, and Springfield are not communications crossroads, New York, Los Angeles, and Chicago are. And the big states are politically important—in the electoral college and thus in presidential elections, at the national party conventions and thus in presidential nominating politics. The governor of a small state labors at a disadvantage that the state's senators do not have. Landon in 1936 was the last small-state governor to be nominated and the New Deal tide had wiped out almost all his opposition. Few governors of small or medium-sized states have been seriously mentioned as presidential possibilities since then (see Table 1-5).

Even governors of big states seem to have been disadvantaged recently compared to their Washington-based competitors; the last one to be nominated was Stevenson. Yet it would be a mistake to underestimate the future prospects of big-state governors as presidential nominees. They are not lacking in public prominence—an impressive 22 percent have polled 1 percent or more support for a presidential nomination, compared to 15 percent of the senators from

TABLE 1-5. *Distribution of All Senators and Governors Who Polled at Least 1 Percent Support for President among Fellow Partisans, by Party and Size of State, 1936–72*[a]

| Party and office | Percent polling at least 1 percent support | | |
|---|---|---|---|
| | Big states[b] | Other states | All states |
| Democratic senators | 13.2 (N = 38) | 12.0 (N = 183) | 12.2 (N = 221) |
| Republican senators | 16.7 (N = 36) | 4.5 (N = 111) | 7.5 (N = 147) |
| All senators | 14.8 (N = 74) | 9.2 (N = 294) | 10.3 (N = 368) |
| Democratic governors | 16.2 (N = 31) | 1.8 (N = 224) | 3.5 (N = 225) |
| Republican governors | 26.4 (N = 34) | 2.6 (N = 145) | 6.4 (N = 189) |
| All governors | 21.6 (N = 65) | 1.9 (N = 369) | 4.8 (N = 434) |

Source: Gallup releases, various dates.

N = total number of officeholders.

a. Includes only those who polled 1 percent while in service in the respective office.

b. The eight largest nonsouthern states in 1950: New York, California, Pennsylvania, Illinois, Ohio, Michigan, New Jersey, Massachusetts.

big states and 10 percent of all senators (Table 1-5). But the big-state governors have experienced greater difficulty in capitalizing on this prominence than have senators. For one thing, the gubernatorial office is one a politician cannot count on holding for very long.[28] A governor who aspires to the presidency thus has fewer chances to make his move than a senator.

For the governor chosen at the midterm elections, the first chance comes embarrassingly early (after only two years service, he is still learning the job and may have few concrete accomplishments) or distressingly late (after six years as governor, how many men still appear to be miracle workers?). Governors chosen in presidential years are badly off in another way: they must choose between seeking another term as governor (if this is permitted by their state's constitution) or running for president.

As chief executives of their respective states, governors are far less dispensable and geographically mobile than senators. Prolonged absence from the state is out of the question while the state legislature is in session—an increasingly large portion of the governor's term in the larger states. It is clearly awkward the rest of the time.

Moreover, when governors do campaign, the issues and themes that they can most authoritatively address and with which they are identified are state and local ones. The problems of New Jersey may light few fires in the hearts and minds of the residents of Iowa or Maine. And these issues are not the same as the national and international ones confronting the president. But the governors' inevitable separation from Washington politics may, under special circumstances, redound to their benefit.[29] The moral squalor of Watergate and the horror of Vietnam, for example, cannot be held against them in 1976. Almost any Washington-based politician—no matter how

28. While over a third of the states place constitutional limitations on their governors' length of service, most of them are smaller states whose governors are not likely presidential candidates anyway. On the tenure of governors, see Schlesinger, *Ambition and Politics*, chap. 3; J. Stephen Turett, "The Vulnerability of American Governors 1900–1969," *Midwest Journal of Political Science*, vol. 15 (February 1971), pp. 108–32; and Gerald M. Pomper, *Elections in America* (Dodd, Mead, 1968), chap. 6.

29. Joseph Kraft, "Governors: More Power to Them?" *Washington Post*, March 1, 1973; and Jules Witcover, "Will a Governor Lead Them?" *Washington Post*, May 19, 1973.

energetically he seeks to avoid association with both—is vulnerable to the charge that he either supported, went along with, or was ignorant of these disasters. The publication of some of President Nixon's conversations with his aides on the Watergate affair may have done more for the presidential prospects of governors than those contenders could possibly have done for themselves!

Thus despite some clear disadvantages in translating their political prominence into convention delegate votes, big-state governors are still in the running as potential presidential nominees. They may not be as numerous on the short list of possibilities as U.S. senators—but then there are two senators for every governor and only the governors of large states have the potential publicity advantages that all senators enjoy.

### OTHER PUBLIC OFFICES

Cabinet officers, especially secretaries of state, defense, and treasury and the attorney general, are among the more widely publicized officials in the land; they benefit from a relatively close association with the president and his programs. Supreme Court justices enjoy a prestige that rivals that of the president. The Court deals with some of the nation's most pressing problems and is a major source of national news. The tradition of signed Court opinions (and dissents) makes it possible for justices to establish individual reputations and followings. Both the cabinet and the Court, in fact, show up as sources of publicly perceived presidential possibilities (see Table 1-3). Indeed, a larger proportion of all cabinet members since 1936 has surfaced in the polls (17 percent) than has been true for either senators (10 percent) or governors (6 percent). Despite the traditional separation of the Supreme Court from partisan politics, both William O. Douglas and Fred Vinson have figured in modern presidential speculation; the two men make up 6 percent of the justices since 1936. Despite their visibility and prestige, no cabinet member has been nominated for the presidency by a major party since Herbert Hoover, and the Supreme Court has not furnished a presidential candidate since Charles Evans Hughes in 1916.[30] Obviously more

30. Hoover got his political start not from the cabinet, but as a relief administrator in Europe after World War I. Hughes had been governor of New York.

than political prominence explains the preeminence of vice presidents, senators, and governors over the cabinet and the Court as a source of presidential candidates.

For one thing, cabinet officers and Supreme Court justices are appointed officials; relatively few of either have been elective politicians. Given the importance and scarcity of presidential nominations, prudence suggests that the parties go with proven winners in contests as nearly like presidential elections as possible.[31]

Other factors disadvantage would-be presidents on the Court. Its insulation from partisan politics means that no justice can actively seek the presidential nomination and hold his seat on the Court, too. Trading life tenure on the Supreme Court, with its great power and prestige, for the high risks and heavy costs of a presidential nomination campaign followed by an election of uncertain outcome is not much of a bargain. Only a relatively sure race would be attractive to even the most politically minded judge.

Rather different barriers confront cabinet officials. Their average tenure is short, and dependent on the president's pleasure. Presidents tend to be suspicious of cabinet members with independent political followings, and with good reason.[32] And in recent decades the power and prestige of the cabinet has eroded. The development of an institutionalized presidency and the attendant transfer of much power and policy initiative to the White House staff have diminished the significance of the cabinet secretary. This trend has been accompanied by a sharp reduction in the proportion of cabinet officers publicly perceived as potential presidents (see Table 1-6). Before 1949, 35 percent of all inner cabinet members polled 1 percent or more support for a presidential nomination before, during, or after their service in the president's official family. Since 1949, only 17 percent have achieved that degree of prominence and popularity. Incumbents of lesser cabinet posts have suffered an equally sharp drop in their opportunities to achieve mass popularity in a presidential con-

31. The campaign for governor of New York by Arthur Goldberg, a former Supreme Court justice and secretary of labor, illustrates the point. One of the ablest and most respected men in public life proved a disaster on the hustings.
32. See Richard F. Fenno, Jr., *The President's Cabinet* (Random House, 1959).

TABLE 1-6. *Distribution of Cabinet Officers Who Polled at Least 1 Percent Support for Presidential Nomination, by Period of Service and Office, 1936–72*

| Office | Percent polling at least 1 percent support | |
|---|---|---|
| | Began service before January 1949 | Began service after January 1949 |
| *Inner cabinet* | | |
| Secretary of state | 100 (N = 4) | 40 (N = 5) |
| Secretary of defense | 22 (N = 9) | 33 (N = 9) |
| Attorney general | 20 (N = 5) | 22 (N = 9) |
| Secretary of treasury | 33 (N = 3) | 0 (N = 8) |
| Total[a] | 35 (N = 20) | 17 (N = 30) |
| *Outer cabinet* | | |
| Postmaster general | 25 (N = 4) | 0 (N = 6) |
| Secretary of agriculture | 25 (N = 4) | 0 (N = 4) |
| Secretary of commerce | 33 (N = 6) | 0 (N = 9) |
| Secretary of labor | 0 (N = 3) | 17 (N = 6) |
| Secretary of housing and urban development | ... | 33 (N = 3) |
| Secretary of health, education, and welfare | ... | 0 (N = 9) |
| Secretary of transportation | ... | 0 (N = 2) |
| Secretary of the interior | 0 (N = 2) | 0 (N = 6) |
| Total[a] | 17 (N = 18) | 4 (N = 45) |
| Entire cabinet | 26 (N = 38) | 11 (N = 75) |

Source: Gallup releases, various dates.
N = total number of officeholders.
... = not applicable.
a. Overlaps omitted in all totals.

text: before 1949, 17 percent of them surfaced on the polls at the 1 percent level or better, since then only 4 percent of them have. The cabinet has become increasingly isolated from presidential politics.

The men who now wield much of the power cabinet members once had are even more nonpolitical than cabinet secretaries; the presidential assistant is not likely ever to be thought of as presidential timber. The pool of presidential talent, ambition, and prominence to be found in the federal executive branch is drying up as an unanticipated result of efforts by recent presidents to concentrate power and initiative in the White House.

Very few members of the House of Representatives end up as presidential possibilities for a still different set of reasons. Despite coequal constitutional status with members of the Senate, the average member of the House of Representatives is a quite anonymous fellow compared to his counterpart in "the other body." He is one of four hundred and thirty-five rather than one of a hundred, and he has been elected from a smaller constituency. The important work of the House is done in committee and the tight control over debate and greater party discipline in the House provide few chances to generate publicity on the floor. Only a few members of the House—the Speaker, majority and minority party leaders, and chairmen of a handful of the more important committees—are perceived as national political figures and routinely receive national press attention. A few of these men turn up in the presidential polls, but important House positions go to senior members, often too old to be considered for the presidency and usually deeply committed to a lifetime career in the House. Ambitious younger members of the House can either seek continuous reelection until they achieve enough seniority to gain power in the House or run for the Senate or a governorship. The structure of the office predisposes the members toward staying put: their two-year term means they must abandon a career in the House in order to run for higher office. Some members take this chance every election year, of course, and three of them (Kennedy, Johnson, and Nixon) eventually became president. But increasingly, congressmen are locked into a career in the House by the relative security of House seats, the allocation of power in the House on the basis of seniority, and the specialization of members in a limited range of public policy. The route to power in the House leads away from, not toward, the presidency.

Big-city mayors preside over governmental units that equal or surpass most states in size and complexity. They have demonstrated an ability to appeal to urban electorates in a predominantly urban nation. Moreover, the mayors of New York, Chicago, and Los Angeles are better situated to obtain massive national publicity than almost any governor. And yet only Fiorello LaGuardia, John Lindsay, and Samuel Yorty polled more than 1 percent support for president between 1936 and 1972. Only Lindsay was taken at all seriously as a presidential contender.

The reasons for the mayors' poor showing as presidential possibilities are probably related to the nature of the constituencies, the politics, and the problems of the country's largest cities. The political appeals necessary to win in a metropolis may generate less enthusiasm in the suburbs, smaller cities, and rural areas. Politics and therefore politicians in central cities do not always have the highest reputation for rectitude. Also, the problems of American cities today are immense and few mayors have had the resources to attack them successfully. Few men with presidential ambitions are attracted to the office, and even fewer have much hope once they have served in it. Only one former mayor, Hubert Humphrey of Minneapolis, has achieved presidential nomination since 1936, and he only after long service as senator and vice president.

## Good Candidates and Good Presidents

Presidential candidates are a product of the nation they seek to lead. The values, prejudices, and conflicts of America, its social and economic structure, technology, political and governmental institutions all affect the kinds of people who are considered. The causal connections are numerous, subtle, indirect, and changeful. But they result in a small group of possibilities which is far from an ordinary sample of Americans.

More than the political institutions specifically designed to make presidential nominations is important to this process. The mechanical arrangements by which the major parties choose nominees may affect which specific individual wins 50 percent plus one of convention votes in a given year. But the definition of the small group from which the delegates choose is accomplished through complex and informal processes, some of which are not ordinarily thought to affect presidential politics and many of which are not susceptible to self-conscious manipulation. Just as nominations are more important than elections, so the definition of the group of presidential possibilities is more important than the formal and official stages of the nominating process.

☆

*Chapter Two*

☆

# THE INCUMBENT LEADER

THE PROCESS OF selecting presidential nominees starts well before the formal contest begins. During the period between the election of a president and the presidential primaries three years later, the competitive situation that more often than not determines nominating outcomes is defined. Much of the significant action occurs before the New Hampshire primary, which roughly marks the beginning of the formal nominating process.

The nominating process in the president's party is very different from that in the party out of power. It is often totally lacking in suspense. The presidency of the United States has become such a central and dominant office that its incumbent usually seems nearly unassailable within his own party. Even when a president's political fortunes are low, he is the party's best known and (usually) most popular figure. The prestige and publicity potential of the office and the president's capacity to manipulate events in order to further his own political fortunes are awesome barriers to would-be challengers. Moreover, a party that fails to renominate a willing president is placed in the awkward position of admitting a mistake while asking for the nation's confidence. This, more than presidential use of concrete rewards and sanctions, explains the dominant position of sitting presidents who seek renomination.

Only in 1960 was the incumbent president constitutionally ineligible to run for another term; in the other nine election years since 1936 he was the front-running candidate before the formal nominating process began. This was invariably true whether he was a Democrat or a Republican, whether or not he was popular in the country, and whether or not organized opposition to his renomination had developed since the last election. Even in 1940, 1952, and 1956, when there was substantial doubt about the president's intentions, he towered over his real or potential competitors. And every president who persisted in seeking renomination went on to win his party's endorsement.[1] The two who did not persist—Truman and Johnson, in 1952 and 1968—withdrew after the primaries began.

Not only were the eligible presidents invariably the early front-runners, but they usually faced no serious contest during the critical three years before the New Hampshire primary. Trial balloons, unofficial travels to sound out public opinion, and announcements of "availability" if the president should decide to lay down the burden were common. But politicians willing openly to take on a sitting president for the nomination were rare.

The cost of open opposition to even a seemingly vulnerable president usually outweighed the potential gains in the minds of possible challengers with a serious chance of becoming president at some point in the future. It was not Robert Kennedy but Eugene McCarthy who first took on President Johnson in 1968; it was Congressman Paul McCloskey rather than Governor Nelson Rockefeller who challenged President Nixon in 1972. President Truman was not threatened by the party's most plausible alternatives in either 1948 or 1952, despite his unpopularity in both years. If an active challenger to a president's renomination emerges, he is not characteristically the president's strongest opponent.

Presidents typically remain silent on the question of whether they will run again until the formal nominating process begins.[2] Thus ambitious candidates who do not want to challenge the incumbent are put in a difficult position.

1. The last president seeking renomination who failed to receive it was Chester A. Arthur (in 1884); he had become president on the death of Garfield. Three other vice presidents who succeeded on the death of a president were denied renomination. The only president originally nominated to that office who was denied renomination was Franklin Pierce in 1856. See Paul T. David, Ralph M. Goldman, and Richard C. Bain, *The Politics of National Party Conventions* (Brookings Institution, 1960), pp. 112–14.

2. See William Allen White, *Puritan in Babylon* (Capricorn, 1965), for an argument that Calvin Coolidge's "I do not choose to run" statement was really meant as an invitation for a draft movement.

The Twenty-second Amendment, by foreclosing the possibility of a third presidential term, may lead to more open and even competition for nominations within the president's party. Retiring presidents, however, have typically done very little to groom their successors; to do so is a risky business—it requires the sharing of power and prestige, and it reduces the president's options. Ironically, the president who tried hardest to affect the choice of his successor, Harry Truman, met with the greatest resistance. Thus the dominance of their party's nominations by incumbent presidents may have been inadvertently diminished by constitutional amendment—at least every eighth year.

But in 1960, the one instance in which the amendment has taken effect, the president's heir apparent, Vice President Nixon, was able to wrap up the nomination before the New Hampshire primary. Yet President Eisenhower did not openly and directly transfer the mantle of leadership to his young vice president; rather, Nixon was able to exploit the political and publicity potential of the vice presidency so skillfully that he became the party's natural choice despite Eisenhower's silence. Vice President Agnew seemed well along this track before his career was destroyed by scandal. Perhaps nomination of vice presidents to succeed incumbent presidents will be the normal order as a result of the Twenty-second Amendment.

In a surprising number of years the party controlling the White House has faced some unique political situation. The maneuvers of presidents and potential candidates in those years are indicative of the forces at work during the time before the primaries begin.

## Roosevelt and a Third Term: 1940

Franklin Roosevelt remained consistently the man to beat for the 1940 Democratic nomination from his massive election victory over Alf Landon in 1936 until the beginning of the next presidential election year. But uncertainty that he would run combined with growing opposition in the party led to more open maneuvering for the nomination than is normally found in the party of an incumbent president.

The main cause of doubt about Roosevelt's plans was the custom that presidents serve only two terms; until then, no president had sought a third consecutive term in office. While it had no basis in law, this unwritten rule of American politics was both ancient and popular.[3] To ignore or defy the two-term tradition would provide the Republicans (and anti-Roosevelt Democrats) with an issue of uncertain, but potentially sizable, power. As a result the President's plans for the next term—ordinarily not a subject of widespread discussion until much later—became a matter of public speculation within a few months of his swearing-in ceremony.

The President did nothing to clarify the situation. At the Democratic victory dinner in March 1937, he indicated a personal desire to step down from the presidency at the end of his second term.[4] The following June, after Governor George Earle of Pennsylvania had taken the extraordinary step of endorsing him three years ahead of time, the President refused to answer press conference questions about his plans or whether he would accept the Democratic nomination.[5] A flurry of public declarations of support and opposition to a third term followed before the issue receded somewhat from public view.[6] The President was to remain enigmatically silent on the question until the 1940 convention. This policy had the effect of leaving the President's options open while dampening the impact of the third-term issue: it was difficult to attack the President effectively for something that it was not clear he was going to do.

Landslide victories often seem to lead presidents to overestimate their power. A classic illustration of this is the series of political blunders committed by President Roosevelt in 1937 and 1938. His attempt to pack the Supreme Court was the most dramatic and damaging of these errors. But he also lost supporters by intervening in the Senate majority leadership contest following the death of Senator Joseph T. Robinson, and as a result of abortive attempts to purge the

3. See Hadley Cantril and Mildred Strunk, eds., *Public Opinion, 1935–1946* (Princeton University Press, 1951), pp. 648–53, for polling data.

4. Bernard F. Donahoe, *Private Plans and Public Dangers: The Story of FDR's Third Nomination* (University of Notre Dame Press, 1965), p. 13. His statement, however, in no way committed Roosevelt not to run.

5. Ibid., p. 14.

6. See, for example, *New York Times*, Aug. 6, 8, and 10, 1937.

party of recalcitrants in the 1938 congressional primaries. The President's inaction during the long and violent sit-down strikes in the automobile industry resulted in still more criticism.

These troubles, along with Roosevelt's silence on the matter of a third term, stimulated much speculation and no little maneuvering over the 1940 nomination. The leading alternative to Roosevelt, and the rallying point for most anti-New Dealers in the party, became Vice President John Nance Garner of Texas. A former Speaker of the House, Garner had had a sizable national following among old-line Democrats since well before the New Deal. While he had gone along with Roosevelt's policies during his first term, the vice president was not closely identified with his program. During FDR's second term, Garner's relationship with the administration cooled to the point that he was seen to be in sympathy with Roosevelt's opponents.[7] The polls showed him consistently in the lead for the nomination if Roosevelt did not run. But Garner was a southerner and would be seventy-two on taking office in 1941—two serious liabilities for a presidential contender at that time.

Two of the other leading possibilities for the nomination were also members of the Roosevelt administration: Secretary of State Cordell Hull and Postmaster General James Farley. Hull's prestige was substantial, especially on Capitol Hill where he had served with distinction for many years as a congressman from Tennessee. Not identified with the controversial New Deal domestic programs, he was relatively attractive to conservatives, while respected by the party's liberal wing. But he was a southerner, too, and only two years younger than Garner. Nor would he do anything to advance his potential candidacy—a clear indication of a lack of interest in the presidency to some, and a shrewd tactic, given the situation, to others. Farley was clearly ambitious, but a Roman Catholic. As the President's chief patronage dispenser, Farley enjoyed long-standing and warm relationships with party organization leaders across the country. But he was also seen as personifying the seamier side of politics—bosses, machines, deals, and patronage.

7. See Donahoe, *Private Plans and Public Dangers*, pp. 45–51; and Bascom M. Timmons, *Garner of Texas: A Personal History* (Harper, 1948), chap. 13.

Another prominent possible successor to Roosevelt was Paul V. McNutt. Governor of Indiana during Roosevelt's first term, he became U.S. high commissioner to the Philippines and then federal security administrator during the second. Compared to the others, McNutt was an unknown quantity. While not clearly a New Dealer, he was perhaps more likely than Garner, Hull, or Farley to continue Roosevelt's programs.[8] This suspicion, along with strikingly good looks, were major assets, for even if Roosevelt did not run for a third term, his support would be a major resource. Roosevelt's endorsement was not likely to go to anyone who promised to alter drastically the policies of the previous eight years.

Thus none of the plausible alternatives to Roosevelt who emerged during his second term were committed New Dealers. Secretary of Labor Frances Perkins, Secretary of Interior Harold Ickes, Secretary of Agriculture Henry Wallace, and Works Progress Administrator (later Secretary of Commerce) Harry Hopkins were the most prominent of the New Deal leaders. But their followers were Roosevelt's followers. So long as Roosevelt's plans were in doubt, they were unlikely to win much rank-and-file support. None of them had a firm political base in their home states and their close association with the President precluded all but the most discrete efforts to build one. And not one of them had run for elective public office before. Those Democrats who wished the New Deal to continue into the 1940s had but one reliable choice—to renominate Franklin D. Roosevelt.

That was what most Democrats seemed to want. Whenever the President's name was included in the Gallup polls of the party rank and file, he received support from 75 percent or more of all Democrats. And Roosevelt's popularity was not confined to the rank and file. As election year approached, figures like Chicago's Mayor Ed Kelly and Jersey City Mayor Frank Hague came out for a third term. Big-city machine politicians, more interested in electing aldermen than in questions of national policy, wanted the magical Roosevelt name at the top of the ticket, too.[9]

8. See *New York Times*, Aug. 26, 1937.
9. See Donahoe, *Private Plans and Public Dangers*, pp. 98 and 132.

In September of 1939 the Nazis invaded Poland. Subsequent events in Europe made a general war seem more and more inevitable. Cactus Jack Garner and Big Jim Farley were quite implausible leaders at such a moment in history. Of the alternatives to Roosevelt, only the aging Cordell Hull had any notable experience in foreign affairs.

In December of 1939, Vice President Garner announced that he would accept the Democratic nomination if it were proferred to him. The next month, Farley asked the President's permission to enter the New Hampshire and Massachusetts primaries and, in March, announced that his name would be presented to the convention. By implication at least, both men were in the race whether Roosevelt sought the nomination or not.[10] At this point none of the other possibilities were willing to become opponents of, rather than alternatives to, Roosevelt. The President remained silent. Senator Edwin C. Johnson of Colorado assessed the situation well when he said at the beginning of 1940: "If this silence continues, the Democratic nomination will be worthless to anyone other than [the President], including his favorite."[11]

## *Truman's Low Prestige: 1948*

Harry S. Truman took office on President Roosevelt's death in April 1945. The new President was greeted by massive public sympathy and support. In the first Gallup poll after Truman became President, over 70 percent of the public approved of the job he was doing. His determination, vigor, and decisiveness were a pleasant surprise; his small-town, middle-western, common-man style appealed to a streak of populism widespread among Americans. The staff of the Democratic National Committee began laying plans for the 1948 election on the assumption that Truman would be the party's candidate. Even Republican party politicians began to think the new President would be hard to beat in 1948.[12]

10. Ibid., pp. 125 and 141–43.
11. *Newsweek*, March 4, 1940, p. 14.
12. See ibid., May 7, 1945, p. 26; and *Time*, Oct. 27, 1945, p. 26.

But soon after the war ended, disenchantment with President Truman set in. Peace brought difficult new problems—"constant warfare between labor and management, a procession of strikes, slowdowns and lockouts; inflation, black markets, and a disintegrating price control apparatus; a frustrating war of nerves with the Russians over a prostrate Europe; the spectacle of a new President seemingly unable to cope with a strife torn Cabinet or a sullen and rebellious Congress."[13]

The President's prestige and popularity plummeted throughout 1946.[14] At the midterm elections the Republicans, campaigning hard on the twin themes of "Had enough?" and "It's time for a change," scored their most impressive victory since the 1920s. Republicans in the Senate increased from 38 to 51; the party's House delegation jumped from 190 to 246; for the first time in many years the GOP was in control of both houses of Congress. Also the party now controlled twenty-five of the forty-eight state houses.

The first Gallup poll after the midterm election showed Truman hitting a new low in voter support for the 1948 Democratic nomination. And yet, at 48 percent, he remained well ahead of everyone else. Truman's nearest competitor was Henry Wallace—the former vice president who had been dropped from the national ticket in 1944 and whom Truman had just fired as secretary of commerce for openly criticizing the President's policies toward the Soviet Union. Secretary of State James Byrnes was another possibility for whom some support appeared in the post midterm election poll. But Byrnes was a southerner and an ex-Catholic whose chances were not much better than Wallace's. The 1946 elections had been such a disaster for the Democrats that no new faces had emerged to serve as possible challengers to the unpopular Truman. Of the twenty-two new senators elected in 1946 only five were Democrats and three of these were from the South. Of the five new Democratic governors elected, four were from the South or border states; not one new Democratic governor was elected in the large two-party states from which presi-

13. Cabell Phillips, *The Truman Presidency* (Penguin, 1966), p. 160.
14. For an analysis of the dynamics of presidential popularity, see John E. Mueller, *War, Presidents and Public Opinion* (Wiley, 1973), chap. 9.

dential candidates usually come. Most new faces in national politics in 1946 belonged to Republicans. The Democratic party—despite its domination of national politics for twenty years—was running dangerously low on potential presidents.

One new name, however, excited politicians in both parties: Dwight D. Eisenhower. No one knew for sure what his party affiliation was, but leaders in both parties pursued the one man who appeared to insure victory at the polls. President Truman himself was apparently among the first to approach Eisenhower about the presidency. "General," Truman is reported to have said at the Potsdam Conference in 1945, "there is nothing you may want that I won't try to help you get. That definitely and specifically includes the Presidency in 1948."[15] This offer was repeated, through Secretary of the Army Kenneth C. Royall, in the fall of 1947.[16] Eisenhower declined the offers, but that scarcely ended the efforts by members of both parties to nominate him in 1948.

As 1947 began, the President's fortunes could only rise, and they did. A victorious confrontation with John L. Lewis, head of the United Mine Workers, over a coal strike, the enunciation of the Truman Doctrine, and the appointment of General George C. Marshall as secretary of state led to a resurgence in Truman's popularity. The news media agreed, as the presidential election year approached, that Truman's renomination was assured.[17]

But relatively few observers believed that the President had much chance of winning reelection. This prognosis became even gloomier for the Democrats when, in late December of 1947, Henry Wallace announced that he would run for president as an independent. While scarcely anyone thought Wallace could win, he would take votes away from Truman.

In February the President unveiled the most far-reaching set of

15. Phillips, *The Truman Presidency*, pp. 98–99.
16. Ibid., pp. 196–97. President Truman never acknowledged the first story, which appears in Eisenhower's memoirs, and he denied the second. Royall supported the story of the second offer while Eisenhower did not discredit it. Ibid., pp. 98–99 and 197.
17. See *Newsweek*, April 14, 1947, p. 28; and *Time*, Sept. 1, 1947, p. 12, and Nov. 10, 1947, p. 25.

civil rights proposals that any president had endorsed up to that time. Politically the move was designed to keep Negro voters in the Democratic fold, despite Wallace's candidacy. But this was based on the assumption that the South would support any Democratic nominee, even Truman.[18] Within weeks it became apparent that this assumption was unwise; the Truman civil rights proposals had created a serious threat of southern rebellion.[19] Nor did Truman's forthright civil rights stance result in any immediate payoff in support from what remained of the Democratic left.

President Truman officially let it be known, shortly before the New Hampshire primary in March, that he would accept nomination. No credible challenger to Truman had emerged, despite his personal unpopularity and grim electoral prospects. The Democratic party seemed to be falling apart.

## *Truman's Search for a Successor: 1952*

Harry Truman's victory over Thomas Dewey in 1948 was a personal triumph. For a time his popularity and prestige soared, approaching the height of approval he had enjoyed in 1945, but once again, Truman's popularity proved short-lived. Charges of cronyism and corruption, Senator Joseph McCarthy's investigations of alleged communist infiltration of the federal government, and the frustrating undeclared war in Korea dominated the headlines during the next four years. Truman's second term was characterized by a steady erosion of popularity and build-up of opposition, which were checked only by his withdrawal from presidential contention in late March of 1952.

The dominant question in Democratic nominating politics for 1952 was the same as for 1940: would the President seek nomination and, if not, whom would he support as his successor? The Twenty-second Amendment had been ratified in 1951, but it explicitly ex-

18. For the rationale behind the move, see Phillips, *The Truman Presidency*, pp. 17 ff.

19. Virginia Governor William Tuck's request to his state legislature that Truman's name be removed from the ballot was among the early indications of serious trouble. See *Time*, March 8, 1948, p. 20.

empted the incumbent president from its provisions. Yet since Truman had succeeded Roosevelt so early in the term, the President would have served almost eight years by 1952—reelection that year would permit him to serve almost four years longer than any future president could.

Truman, like Roosevelt before him, remained silent about his intentions. When questioned on the matter, he responded by saying he had made up his mind but would not reveal his decision until later. No matter what this decision, the longer he waited to declare his intentions, the harder it would be for an alternative candidate to challenge him or his chosen successor.

There was little doubt that the President could have the Democratic nomination, if he wanted it.[20] But, as the convention year began, most informed speculation leaned to the view that he would retire. If Truman did withdraw, the press speculated that his first choice as successor would be Chief Justice Fred Vinson, a close friend and adviser whom Truman had appointed to the Supreme Court. His second choice was likely to be Governor Adlai E. Stevenson of Illinois. Stevenson had been elected governor in 1948 with a plurality of over 500,000 votes, apparently carrying Truman on his coattails to a narrow 30,000-vote victory over Dewey in Illinois. This feat had not received much national attention at first—the big story of the 1948 election was Truman's upset victory. But speculation on possible successors to Truman placed Stevenson high on the list from then on.[21]

Subsequent reports proved these speculations to be accurate. Mr. Truman's first choice was indeed Chief Justice Vinson, who had declined to accept Truman's support on grounds of ill health. Then the President summoned Governor Stevenson to the White House in January of 1952 and offered to support him for the Democratic nomination. Much to Truman's surprise, the governor declined the offer. Stevenson's term expired in 1952, and he felt committed to

20. See, for example, *Newsweek,* July 9, 1951, p. 21; and *Time,* Feb. 4, 1952, p. 8.
21. See Alden Whitman, *Portrait: Adlai E. Stevenson* (Harper and Row, 1965), pp. 29 ff. See also *Time,* Feb. 4, 1952, p. 7; and *Newsweek,* Dec. 3, 1951, p. 29, and Jan. 28, 1952, p. 20.

seek a second. Rumors that he might abandon this course for a run for the presidency would weaken the governor's political position in Illinois. Thus Stevenson refused even to allow the President to support him publicly for the presidential nomination. Truman was left without a candidate. But, no matter how hard he tried, Stevenson was unable to stop others from beginning a draft-Stevenson movement.[22]

Not all the other possibilities were so reluctant. Senators Estes Kefauver of Tennessee and Richard Russell of Georgia declared their intentions of running for the nomination whether President Truman withdrew or not. Senator Robert Kerr of Oklahoma also declared for the nomination before the primaries, although he made it clear that he would drop out of the running if the President decided to seek four more years in the White House.[23]

The strength of the opposition, however, was not so imposing as to cause the President to reduce his optimistic estimate of his own power.[24] Senator Kerr was enormously wealthy and a major power behind the scenes in the Senate. But he was little known to the public at large and his close association with the oil and gas industry would prove to be an embarrassment in any national campaign. Russell was a regional candidate—an irreconcilable foe of civil rights legislation around whom the South could unite in an effort to achieve maximum impact on the platform and the nominee. Few saw the Georgia senator as a potential nominee.

Senator Kefauver was a different matter. The first person to become a serious presidential contender as the result of massive television publicity, Kefauver was the chairman of a special Senate committee to investigate the influence of organized crime in American life. During 1950 and 1951 this committee held sensational hearings

22. See Alfred Steinberg, *The Man from Missouri: The Life and Times of Harry S. Truman* (Putnam, 1962), pp. 409–13; Harry S. Truman, *Memoirs*, vol. 2, *Years of Trial and Hope* (Doubleday, 1956), pp. 489–95; Kenneth S. Davis, *A Prophet in His Own Country* (Doubleday, 1957), pp. 387–90; Walter Johnson, *How We Drafted Adlai Stevenson* (Knopf, 1955), chap. 2; and Phillips, *The Truman Presidency*, pp. 416–18.
23. *Time*, Feb. 25, 1952, pp. 24–25.
24. In his memoirs Truman writes that "presidential control of the convention is a principle which has not been violated in political history." *Years of Trial and Hope*, p. 492.

in fourteen major cities. From a relatively young and liberal southern senator scarcely known outside his home state and Washington, D.C., Kefauver quickly became a national figure. The hearings held in New York, carried by the national networks just as television sets were becoming standard fixtures in American homes, attracted a large and fascinated audience. They made Kefauver a celebrity. While there is no evidence that the senator planned the hearings to advance his presidential ambitions—and the idea to televise them apparently was not his—they nonetheless had the effect of making him a presidential contender.[25] On January 23, 1952, the senator announced his candidacy for the Democratic nomination, whether or not Truman stayed in the race.

Even as he announced his candidacy, it was apparent that Kefauver was not a popular figure among the organizational leaders of the Democratic party. As one news magazine put it, President Truman "would stop at almost nothing to keep [Kefauver] from getting the nomination";[26] most prominent Democratic leaders shared the aversion. The crime committee hearings had highlighted the connection between organized crime and big-city political machines, most of which were Democratic. The party had been deeply embarrassed by Kefauver's revelations and a number of Democratic politicians were destroyed as a result—unpardonable sins to party regulars. The hearings that had brought Kefauver to prominence also insured him bitter opposition from his own party's leadership. His only chance of victory was by demonstrating overwhelming popular support in the polls and primaries about to begin.

Meanwhile, President Truman continued his publicly noncommittal posture about the 1952 nomination. In private, he continued to attempt, personally and through chairman Frank McKinney of the Democratic National Committee, to persuade Stevenson to accept the role of successor. But the Illinois governor continued to refuse.[27] Time was growing short, the deadline for Truman's taking

25. Joseph B. Gorman, *Kefauver: A Political Biography* (Oxford University Press, 1971), chaps. 5–7.

26. *Newsweek*, Feb. 4, 1952, p. 17.

27. Whitman, *Portrait*, pp. 48 ff.

the steps necessary to remove his name from the New Hampshire primary was at hand. At first he was inclined to take this course, and made his famous remark about presidential primaries being "eyewash." But if he withdrew from New Hampshire, Kefauver would win the primary uncontested. And the strength of Truman's most important asset—the assumption that the nomination could be his for the asking combined with uncertainty about his intentions—would be reduced before he had chosen a successor to promote in his stead.[28] Thus the President reversed himself, apologized for the slur on primary voters, and let his name remain on the New Hampshire primary ballot. Few seem to have considered the possibility that Kefauver might win in New Hampshire.

## Eisenhower's Illness: 1956

Dwight Eisenhower's victory in the presidential election of 1952 did not make the Republicans the nation's majority party, so far as habitual party loyalties were concerned, but it did give the GOP control of the White House for the first time in more than twenty years. Suddenly, Republican presidential nominating politics took on a form familiar to Democrats.

In Eisenhower the Republicans had one of the greatest vote-getters in modern times. He was a major reason they had been able to win in 1952, and his renomination was essential to Republican prospects in 1956. As a distinct minority in the nation, the GOP was perhaps even more dependent on Eisenhower than the Democrats had been on Roosevelt. There was, therefore, never any question that the President would be renominated if he chose to be.

But there was some doubt that he would accept renomination. Eisenhower had come to politics late in life with a reluctance seldom found among presidential politicians. Clearly he enjoyed some aspects of the presidency; just as clearly, he detested other parts of the job. His place in history was assured; save for a sense of duty to his country and party, the incentives for serving as president were

28. See *Time*, Feb. 18, 1952, p. 18, for a contemporary report on this decision.

not as strong for him as for most others. Republican nominating politics between 1952 and 1956 consisted primarily of speculation about whether or not he would run. For example, Republican losses at the midterm election—the Democrats recaptured their accustomed majorities in both the House and Senate—were seen both as increasing and decreasing the chances that the President would run again.[29]

In September of 1955, President Eisenhower suffered a serious heart attack while vacationing in Denver, Colorado. The immediate reaction was to conclude that he obviously would not run for reelection. Speculation and maneuverings over a possible successor increased sharply during Eisenhower's convalescence.

While a number of names were mentioned, most attention focused on three Californians—Chief Justice Earl Warren, Vice President Richard Nixon, and Senate minority leader William Knowland, who ranked first, second, and third, respectively, in a Gallup poll of Republican preferences in the event that the President retired. Warren made some very firm statements about not running which pretty well ended talk of drafting the chief justice. Nixon seemed most likely to be the President's beneficiary in the event that Eisenhower did not run. This meant, of course, that anything other than patient waiting and visible loyalty would hurt the vice president more than help him. The situation was different for Senator Knowland, the leader of the Taft wing of the party and Taft's successor as Republican leader in the Senate. Knowland clearly wanted to be president, but was very unlikely to be designated as Eisenhower's heir. He stood to gain nothing from silence or inactivity.

Speculation focused not only on whether or not Eisenhower would run again, but also on when he would announce his decision. An early withdrawal would leave the decision relatively open by giving aspiring candidates time to organize and develop their followings. The later the withdrawal, the greater the opportunity for the President to influence the choice of his successor. Since a later decision would work to Knowland's disadvantage, his best chances lay in forcing the President's hand or in developing a campaign even

29. *U.S. News and World Report*, Nov. 12, 1954, p. 110; and *New York Times*, Nov. 7, 1954.

without the President's withdrawal. Accordingly on November 1, 1955, the press reported that Knowland intended to announce his candidacy by March 7 if Eisenhower did not run. Then on December 8 he moved the time for announcing his candidacy up to January 31 if Eisenhower had not by then revealed his intentions. The President's doctor announced soon after that a medically sound decision could not be made until the end of February.[30]

Knowland's deadline passed without a presidential announcement, though Eisenhower had by now resumed a relatively full workload, and many heart specialists believed him to be healthy enough to run again.[31] While more and more people expected the President to accept another nomination, Knowland's name was nevertheless entered in numerous primaries, with the understanding that Knowland would withdraw to back Eisenhower if he ran.

On February 29, 1956, the President announced that he would accept renomination, and Knowland immediately dropped his campaign. Nothing more was needed to determine who would be the Republican nominee in that year.

## *The Twenty-second Amendment: 1960*

In 1960, for the first time, the incumbent president was not legally eligible to run again: the eight-year limitation on presidential service of the Twenty-second Amendment had come fully in effect. Thus attention focused on the next Republican nomination even earlier than usual.

Vice President Richard Nixon was the clear and decisive front-runner throughout the entire period between the 1956 election and the 1960 convention. After President Eisenhower, Nixon was the most popular figure in the party: his poll standing among rank-and-file Republicans was never lower than 48 percent, and it ranged as high as 84 percent in January of 1960. Nixon was also very close to, and popular among, Republican leaders and party professionals.

30. See Dwight D. Eisenhower, *Mandate for Change* (New American Library, 1965), chap. 24.

31. Three out of five heart specialists polled by the *New York Times* believed he was physically able to run. *New York Times*, Jan. 10, 1956.

Nixon's potential opposition came largely from Senator William Knowland before the 1958 elections and Governor Nelson Rockefeller afterwards. Knowland's position as minority leader in the Senate, while prestigious and highly publicized, was also awkward— as the Republican leader in the Senate he was expected to be a champion of Eisenhower's legislative program, at least most of the time. This made it difficult for Knowland to establish an alternative, more conservative, posture on national and international issues. Despite his status and ambition, his poll strength stood between 9 percent and 12 percent of the rank-and-file Republicans. It seemed unlikely that he could improve on that very much so long as he remained in his Senate position. In January of 1957, Knowland announced that he would not seek reelection to the Senate but would run for governor of California instead. This decision was widely interpreted as a move to improve his presidential prospects.[32] The result, however, was to destroy his presidential chances altogether: he was defeated in the gubernatorial election by Edmund G. (Pat) Brown, who thereby became a minor presidential possibility for the Democrats.

The 1958 elections eliminated Knowland to Nixon's right, but created a new and perhaps more formidable opponent to his left— Nelson Rockefeller. After spending much of his adult life in Washington in a number of federal executive offices, Rockefeller had returned to his home state of New York to run for governor in 1958. He proved to be an unusually attractive and effective campaigner. His victory was the one big Republican triumph in an otherwise disastrous year for the GOP; Rockefeller became a nationally prominent figure overnight. Within several weeks of his election, he was the first choice of 31 percent of rank-and-file Republicans for the 1960 nomination.

The 1958 election had a mixed impact on Nixon's own fortunes. Since he had campaigned so tirelessly for Republican candidates across the nation, the heavy Republican losses were damaging to his reputation. Yet Nixon later exaggerated the situation considerably when he said that his stock after the election was at "an all time

32. *U.S. News,* Jan. 18, 1957, p. 48; *New York Times,* Jan. 8 and 9 and Aug. 9, 1957.

low."[33] His poll standing with the party rank and file dropped only to 51 percent—still far ahead of Rockefeller's.[34] And for his strenuous efforts on behalf of the Republican ticket he gained much loyalty from Republican leaders. Over the long run, this would more than make up for the temporary damage to his prestige.[35]

During the latter part of 1959, Governor Rockefeller set up a preliminary campaign organization and traveled widely to assess his prospects for the Republican presidential nomination in 1960. Testing his potential strength outside New York among voters, party professionals, and potential contributors, he found his reception chilling. Nixon seemed to have the nomination just about locked up. Rockefeller announced on December 26, 1959, that he would not run.[36]

Nixon had benefited enormously from his nearly eight years of service as vice president under Eisenhower. He was well known to the American public. The performance of many political chores on behalf of the President left him a superb set of contacts, much credit, and goodwill among Republican party politicians. The President had made him a member of the National Security Council and regularly sent him abroad as an official representative of the United States. This gave him his first significant experience in foreign affairs, thereby enhancing his stature as a potential president. The once lowly office of vice president provided him with two additional and timely boosts to his prestige in 1959 and early 1960, a trip to the Soviet Union where he held his famous kitchen debate with Nikita Khrushchev, and an opportunity to play a prominent role in the settlement of a frustrating steel strike.[37] As the election year began, and the official campaign

33. Richard M. Nixon, *Six Crises* (Doubleday, 1962), p. 301.
34. Moreover, some of the drop-off in support for Nixon resulted from the entry of Rockefeller (at 31 percent) which more than offset the withdrawal of Knowland (at 9 percent). The polls, of course, measure popularity relative to alternative candidates.
35. See the contemporary discussion in *Newsweek*, Nov. 10, 1956, p. 59; and *U.S. News*, Oct. 31, 1958, p. 42, and Nov. 14, 1958, p. 58.
36. See Theodore H. White, *The Making of the President, 1960* (Atheneum, 1961), pp. 65–77.
37. See Nixon, *Six Crises*, pp. 303–04. But see also Garry Wills, *Nixon Agonistes* (Houghton Mifflin, 1970), pt. 1, chap. 6.

for the Republican nomination commenced, Richard Nixon's nomination was almost as certain as Eisenhower's had been four years before.

## The Dump-Johnson Movement: 1968

On January 4, 1965, a triumphant President Lyndon Baines Johnson, concluding his State of the Union message, assured the Congress that "the United States has re-emerged into the fullness of its self confidence and purpose. No longer are we called upon to get America moving. We are moving. No longer do we doubt our strength or resolution. We are strong and we have proven our resolve. No longer can anyone wonder whether we are in the grip of historical decay. We know that history is ours to make." The self-confident, nearly euphoric, tone of his message seemed entirely justified. President Johnson had just won four years in the White House in his own right, in one of the largest political landslides in American history. For the first time in decades, liberal Democrats enjoyed sizable majorities in both houses of Congress. The President, acknowledged to be one of the most skillful congressional leaders in modern times, had seized the levers of presidential power upon John Kennedy's assassination with zest and effectiveness. While unflattering comparisons with his predecessor were sometimes made, Johnson was personally popular, and respect for his political ability was nearly universal.

Exploiting these circumstances, Johnson led the first session of the Eighty-ninth Congress to legislative accomplishments rarely achieved before. In 1965 a logjam of domestic reform proposals, unsuccessfully advocated for decades, was broken.[38]

But despite the auspicious beginning, Lyndon Johnson's presidency was to be marred by events that would to an unprecedented degree shake the self-confidence and purpose he had spoken of in his message to Congress. American military involvement in Vietnam coupled with the worst racial disorders in American history led to a precipitous decline in public approval of the way Johnson was han-

38. See James L. Sundquist, *Politics and Policy: The Eisenhower, Kennedy and Johnson Years* (Brookings Institution, 1968), chap. 11.

dling his job—a drop from 71 percent in January 1965 to 38 percent by October 1967. Trial-heat polls taken that same month showed his losing an election to Governor George Romney by 3 percentage points, to former Vice President Nixon by 4, and to Governor Rockefeller by 14.[39]

This much was comparable to the political depths that Harry Truman had climbed back from in 1948 and that he had faced again in 1952. But another poll finding was almost unprecedented: both Gallup and Harris showed the President trailing Senator Robert Kennedy for the presidential nomination not only among the general public, but among the Democratic rank and file as well.[40] Rivalry between Johnson and Kennedy was not at all new, but previously strained personal and political relationships had deteriorated still further because of Kennedy's growing opposition to the war. During late 1967 and early 1968 Kennedy considered running against Johnson very seriously, but rejected the possibility.[41]

But by this time there were powerful movements to dump Johnson and to end the war. Kennedy had been the first potential candidate sought to lead the anti-Johnson drive, but only Senator Eugene McCarthy was willing to become a candidate and challenge the President for the Democratic nomination.[42]

While it was far from clear that a candidate as strong as Robert Kennedy would be able to wrest the nomination from the President, few observers gave McCarthy a serious chance. In the beginning of 1968, the nominating prospects of the party in power looked like a replay of the usual: the renomination of the incumbent president.

39. *Gallup Opinion Index* (Princeton, N.J.), November 1967. See also Mueller, *War, Presidents and Public Opinion,* chap. 9, for an analysis of presidential popularity. Surprisingly, Mueller argues that the war had no independent impact on Johnson's decline in popularity; ibid., pp. 226–31.

40. See, for example, the Harris release of Sept. 26, 1966 (Louis Harris Political Data Center, Chapel Hill, N.C.); and *Gallup Opinion Index,* November 1967.

41. See Jules Witcover, *85 Days: The Last Campaign of Robert Kennedy* (Putnam, 1969), chap. 1; and Jack Newfield, *Robert F. Kennedy: A Memoir* (Dutton, 1969), pp. 189–208.

42. See Lewis Chester, Godfrey Hodgson, and Bruce Page, *An American Melodrama: The Presidential Campaign of 1968* (Dell, 1969), pp. 57–75; Theodore H. White, *The Making of the President, 1968* (Atheneum, 1969), pp. 81–101; and Eugene J. McCarthy, *The Year of the People* (Doubleday, 1969), chap. 4.

# Chapter Three

# THE STRUGGLE FOR
# A FOLLOWING

THE POLITICAL situation in a party that loses a presidential election is much more fluid and unstructured than that in the party controlling the White House. No single figure stands so automatically and authoritatively at the center of the misty scene as the president does for the party in power. The defeated presidential candidate becomes his party's titular leader, an ignominious position of uncertain duration. For a time, he is likely to remain the party's best known and most popular figure, but he is a loser, and his popularity within the party often erodes—sometimes within weeks of his defeat.

Nevertheless, by the time the formal nominating process for the next election begins, more than three years later, the situation has usually become more stable. During the period between one election and the first primaries of the next, the party through informal processes usually goes a long way toward identifying the ultimate nominee. In five of the last ten elections, the candidate who went on to win the nomination in the opposition party was clearly identified before the primaries began. Alfred Landon in 1936, Thomas Dewey in 1944, Adlai Stevenson in 1956, John Kennedy in 1960, and Richard Nixon in 1968 were acknowledged by polls, press, and party leaders as front-runners for the nomination before the first primaries. All went on to win.

In two other cases the range of candidates was narrowed to two leading prospects. In 1948 Robert Taft and Thomas Dewey seemed to be the most likely nominees, with roughly comparable chances for the nomination. In 1952 Taft and Dwight Eisenhower were in the same kind of situation. In both years one of the two went on to win.

Only three times was the outcome unpredictable at this early stage. In 1940 and 1964 in the Republican party, the preprimary situation was sufficiently cloudy that the outcome could not be foreseen. In 1972 Edmund Muskie was the acknowledged leader among Democratic possibilities but failed to win the nomination.

That early leaders usually win should not be very surprising. Anticipations of victory stimulate a flow of publicity, money, experienced staff, and other resources toward the probable winner, each new increment of one resource justifying more of them all. Politicians call this happy state of affairs "momentum"—the early leader has it.

Another factor leads to the large overlap between initial front-runners and ultimate nominees. Much the same set of skills and resources needed to become an early front-runner for the presidency are required to do well in primaries, state conventions, and the national convention itself. Indeed, the anticipation of the series of primaries and conventions has a major impact on how strong early candidacies are thought to be. The press, for example, twice rated Robert A. Taft a stronger early candidate for the Republican nomination than his poll standings justified because of his popularity among party officials and professional politicians whose influence over delegate selection and convention voting was relatively large. One reason for the weakening of Muskie's lead over the other Democrats during 1971 and early 1972 was the belief that the convention rules reforms, and the proliferation of state primaries since 1968, would give outside challengers an advantage over early front-runners. Thus while the early stages of the nominating process may be highly unstructured, the formal organization and rules of the game, which come into effect later on, have a noticeable indirect impact from the beginning. If the formal rules of the game are changed, the beginning stages of the nomination process may be changed as well.

One of the most common criticisms of presidential nominating procedures is that they consume an unconscionably long period of time. Few proposals for reforming the process are more popular than a call for shortening nominating campaigns. The period of formal decision making could be compressed merely by starting the presidential primaries and delegate selection procedures later in the presidential election year. But how can the activities that precede that period be eliminated? Maneuvering and speculation over the 1976 Republican nomination began before the 1972 election, and who is to stop it? John Kennedy began campaigning for the 1960 nomination in 1957, and who was to stop him? The only way to shorten the long period of informal and unofficial campaigning associated with contemporary presidential nominations would be to shorten the president's term of office or to hold elections at varying and unpredictable times. Few thoughtful observers advocate either one within the American context.[1]

Even if it were possible, somehow, fairly to restrict preprimary campaigning for presidential nominations, the consequences of such a reform might not necessarily be good. It usually takes time to develop and organize the massive popular support required to win a presidential nomination. The further behind a candidate is, the more time he needs. To eliminate preprimary campaigning would be to restrict the party's choice to persons already well known and popular. The infusion of new blood into the small group perceived as presidential possibilities is already slow. Franklin Roosevelt's long personal dominance of national Democratic politics, and the Republicans' long string of electoral defeats reduced the pool of prominent and experienced presidential possibilities in the late 1930s and early 1940s to dangerously low levels. It would be unwise to make it more difficult than it already is for new men to emerge as challengers to those already prominent.

While there is no sure route to becoming a front-runner, some patterns do emerge. Being titular leader—by definition a loser—is less an asset than a liability. Only two losers in the last ten campaigns won renomination the next time around (Dewey in 1948 and Steven-

1. See Elijah Ben-Zion Kaminsky, "The Selection of French Presidents," in Donald R. Matthews, ed., *Perspectives on Presidential Selection* (Brookings Institution, 1973), chap. 4.

son in 1956), and their defeats were "respectable," given the nature of the opposition. Then too, Nixon might have been more viable in 1964 but for his 1962 California defeat, and Hubert Humphrey might have been even stronger in 1972 but for the man he chose as his running mate four years earlier. Still, it is the exception rather than the rule for the titular leader to be a leading candidate to succeed himself.

On the other hand, losing candidates as well as noncandidates can gain valuable publicity in conventions that helps them in the next nominating campaign. Kennedy is the classic example, but events at the convention preceding their strongest run for the nomination made Dewey, Barry Goldwater, Muskie, and George McGovern more prominent as presidential possibilities.

Another important assist in campaigning is a strong performance in midterm elections, whether as candidate or as party spokesman. Landon, Dewey, Stevenson, Kennedy, and Nixon were able to draw on such successes to help assure early that they would be the nominees. Midterm election performances also did much for the ultimately losing campaigns of Taft (in 1950), Nelson Rockefeller (especially in 1962), George Romney (in 1966), and Muskie (in 1970).

## The Early Leader Wins the Nomination

In five of the six times an early leader was clearly identified, he went on to win the nomination. A large part of the difference between the winning and the losing front-runners has to do with the strength of their opposition.

### A PUBLIC RELATIONS SHOW: 1936

A serious liability of the party out of power in its search for a presidential nominee is loss of the last election. Not only has its leader gone down to defeat but, normally, also a number of less prominent public officials who might later have become presidential contenders. The Democratic victories of 1932 and 1934 certainly had this effect on the Republican party. Not only was Herbert Hoover discredited, but the members of his cabinet were no longer in the public limelight.

The number of Republican governors was reduced to 9 after 1934, senators to 25, members of the House to 103.

The two most prominent survivors of the Democratic sweep were Senator Arthur Vandenberg of Michigan and Governor Alfred M. Landon of Kansas; both were reelected in 1934. Senator Vandenberg, "the only Republican Senator to be re-elected on terms even mildly resembling a party victory,"[2] became "presidential timber over night."[3] Landon's triumph, however, attracted little attention—his name, for example, was not even mentioned for months after the election by *Time* or *Newsweek*. The usually thorough *New York Times* gave his reelection only a brief mention on one of its back pages.[4]

But the potential significance of Landon's victory did not go unnoticed at home. Roy Roberts and Lacy Haynes of the *Kansas City Star*, Republican national committeeman John D. M. Hamilton, and other state political leaders launched a publicity campaign to make Landon into a national figure.[5] The governor cooperated without, at first, taking their efforts very seriously.[6]

The campaign was of the "front porch" variety. Governor Landon stayed close to home and on the job; out-of-state party leaders and journalists were invited to Topeka to meet with him. Most were favorably impressed by his quiet competence and local popularity. Press releases were mailed to those who did not come in person, often stressing Kansas's balanced budget and billing Landon as "the great economizer" and the "Coolidge from the West." Photographs of Landon at his desk, with his family, riding horseback, appeared in Sunday supplements. Well-known reporters began to show up in Topeka—the Hearst organization, for example, sent both Damon Runyon and Adela Rogers St. John.[7] William Randolph Hearst's personal endorsement of Governor Landon—a mixed blessing—

2. *Time*, Nov. 19, 1934, p. 14.
3. *Newsweek*, Nov. 17, 1934, p. 9.
4. See *New York Times*, Nov. 8, 1934.
5. *Time*, May 18, 1936, pp. 15 and 18; and Donald R. McCoy, *Landon of Kansas* (University of Nebraska Press, 1966), p. 221.
6. McCoy, *Landon of Kansas*, p. 212.
7. Ibid., p. 230.

came later.[8] All this publicity had the desired snow-balling effect: Landon became a major national figure and the leading candidate for the Republican presidential nomination of 1936.[9]

While the publicity buildup for Landon is a classic example of successful public relations, it is easy to exaggerate its impact. Landon's rapid rise to national prominence owed much to the qualities of the man himself, and to a lack of competitors. Landon was a popular and effective governor; his record was moderate enough to appeal to some Democrats without alienating opponents of the New Deal. He had avoided entanglement in the factional disputes that divided the national party. Compared to the alternatives—there were not many of them—Landon possessed few major liabilities.

Former President Herbert Hoover remained the best-known Republican. But he had been badly damaged by the Great Depression and his repudiation at the polls in 1932. Even old-line Republican leaders urged him not to run again. Senator William E. Borah of Idaho had kept in the public eye by periodic loud calls for Republican party reform and a more liberal stance on public issues. But he was seventy years old, distrusted by the conservative wing of the party, and viewed as an unpredictable maverick by the party professionals. Colonel Frank Knox, publisher of the *Chicago Daily News*, was eager and relatively prominent. But the closest he had ever come to holding public office was an unsuccessful bid for the Republican nomination for governor of New Hampshire in 1924. These were scarcely impressive credentials for a man to be matched against Franklin Roosevelt. The most plausible alternative to Landon was certainly Senator Vandenberg, but he was unwilling to work for the nomination, and his chances were thus little more than those of a dark-horse compromise candidate.[10]

In the first Gallup polls, taken in November 1935, Landon was the choice of 33 percent of the Republican rank and file. While not a sensational rating, this was more strength than any other potential

8. *New York Times*, Dec. 11, 1935.

9. McCoy, *Landon of Kansas*, chap. 9; *Time*, May 18, 1936, pp. 15–18; and *New York Times*, Oct. 20, 1935.

10. *New York Times*, Dec. 16, 1935; and *Newsweek*, Feb. 15, 1936, p. 15.

candidate displayed. By March of 1936 the proportion favoring Landon had climbed to 56 percent. After almost three years of leaderless confusion, the Republicans had found their most promising challenger to Franklin Roosevelt in 1936.

### A STRONG NONCANDIDATE: 1944

Hoover and Landon had been so badly beaten by President Roosevelt that both vanished from serious presidential contention shortly after election day. Wendell Willkie, in 1940, had done better against the Democrat's champion campaigner. Even in defeat he remained the party's most colorful, dynamic, and popular leader. During 1941 and early 1942 he maintained a comfortable early lead in the polls of rank-and-file preferences for the 1944 nomination.

Yet Willkie was a controversial figure. He was an outspoken internationalist in a party with a strong isolationist wing; his views on domestic policy were too similar to Roosevelt's for the old guard. He was an amateur in politics and something of a maverick, and his behavior after his defeat did nothing to placate those among the party's established leaders who doubted that he was a true Republican. These blemishes had been temporarily overlooked by the 1940 convention, because the party was in dire need of a candidate. In 1944 things would be different.

For one thing, Thomas E. Dewey was four years older; he had won the governorship of New York at the midterm elections of 1942. Almost any New York governor figures prominently in presidential nominating politics,[11] but Dewey had been a leading presidential contender for some years before he went to Albany. Dewey took over the lead from Willkie in the first poll of rank-and-file preferences after the midterm election.

But Dewey faced a problem common to governors with presidential ambitions who are elected at midterm: he had promised in his gubernatorial campaign to devote the next four years to serving the people of New York. Thus, officially at least, he was not a candidate. By staying on the job in New York and doing it well—as he clearly

11. An exception was Governor Herbert Lehman, a Jew.

did—he remained in the public eye and continued to add to his prestige while avoiding the inevitable bruises of overt campaigning. If no other candidate was able to run away with the nomination while Dewey remained above the battle, the party might be forced to turn to the New York governor.

The likelihood that this would happen was greatly increased when both Senator Taft and Senator Vandenberg took themselves out of contention by supporting other candidates who were weaker than they were. Taft yielded to another Ohioan, Governor John W. Bricker, one of the most successful vote-getters in the state's history. While few were impressed by his ability, he looked like a president and spoke out on only noncontroversial matters in a sturdily orthodox way. He was "safe," a "real" Republican, trusted by the party professionals, colorless—nearly the antithesis of Wendell Willkie. The Bricker blandness made it difficult for him to create much popular support nationally; he ran a consistent fourth place in the polls.

Arthur Vandenberg abandoned his habitual waiting game in favor of active support for General Douglas MacArthur, the popular and charismatic chief of American forces in the Pacific. Military regulations prohibited his campaigning, or even openly acknowledging candidacy, but MacArthur let it be known that he would accept any duty his countrymen chose to give him. But unlike his onetime aide, Dwight D. Eisenhower, MacArthur was never able to translate his military prestige into massive public support. The glamorous general showed only a respectable third in the polls.

The final threat to Dewey's primacy was Harold Stassen. The "boy governor" of Minnesota, after playing a central and well-publicized role in the Willkie nomination, won reelection in 1942. Shortly thereafter he enlisted in the Navy, turning over his office to the lieutenant governor. Thus, like MacArthur, he could not campaign. But he did not object when, in October 1943, supporters entered his name in the Nebraska primary, making him, in effect, the first official candidate for the 1944 nomination.

But none of these candidates caught fire during 1943 and early 1944, while signs continued to accumulate of a growing consensus in favor of Governor Dewey. He continued to lead in the polls of rank-

and-file Republicans. A poll of the 1940 convention delegates, who had rejected him in favor of Willkie, now showed that most of them had shifted their support to Dewey.[12] He was the strongest Republican in trial-heat polls against the President.

Only Willkie and Bricker were active during this period. But the party was certainly more likely to draft Dewey than nominate Willkie—unless Willkie could demonstrate overwhelming grass-roots support. Bricker and his supporters did not even contest the assumption that Dewey could have the nomination if he wanted it; instead, they worked to reinforce Bricker's claim that he was everyone's second choice.[13]

As the election year began, Dewey was seen as the sure nominee, if he would run. But the governor neither abandoned his pledge to serve out his four-year term nor intimated that he would reject a draft. As in so many contests within the president's party, by early 1944 speculation about the Republican nomination was dominated by the question of the front-runner's intentions.[14] Would Dewey accept the nomination or wouldn't he? If Willkie's mass popularity had not eroded, if Taft or Vandenberg had campaigned hard while Dewey remained above the battle in New York, then the early lineup might have been different. But as it worked out, noncandidate Dewey was far and away the most likely nominee before the primaries began.

A STRONG TITULAR LEADER: 1956

Immediately after learning that he had lost the 1952 election by more than six million votes, Adlai Stevenson was asked, at a press conference, whether he would run again in 1956. The governor re-

12. *New York Times,* Sept. 6, 1943.
13. *Newsweek,* Sept. 27, 1943, pp. 46 and 48.
14. On May 4, 1943, the *New York Times* reported that "the general interpretation is that [Dewey] has given tacit approval" to friends organizing a draft movement. Six months later *Newsweek,* Nov. 15, 1943, p. 40, observed that few politicians took his disavowal as final. As 1944 began, *Newsweek,* Jan. 24, 1944, p. 39, said that New York's Republican national committeemen left the impression that Dewey would accept a draft. *Time,* Jan. 24, 1944, p. 16, noted that he made no pretense of being "unavailable." Most reporters, by then, surmised that Dewey wanted the nomination but was unable to avow his candidacy without seeming insincere; *Newsweek,* Feb. 7, 1944, p. 58.

plied: "1956? Examine that man's head!" Nonetheless, Stevenson was to be the Democrat's front-running presidential possibility for 1956 from the moment of his defeat in 1952 until the 1956 primaries began.

This was no mean feat. The titular leader of the losing party ordinarily starts the next election cycle as the best known and most popular man in the party but rarely is able to maintain that position for long, especially if he was badly defeated. The Democrats had accumulated a rather long queue of presidential hopefuls since 1932; now that the party was out of power, the self-starting proclivities of these ambitious men were no longer restrained by the presence of a Democratic president.

Plenty of alternatives did appear—no less than thirteen Democrats surfaced in the Gallup polls between 1952 and 1956—but no one of them was able to become a serious threat to Stevenson. The circumstances of Stevenson's nomination in 1952 probably contributed to this result. He had not campaigned for the nomination. Little known by the public at the time he was drafted, he remained a new and fresh face in national politics even after his presidential campaign. His wit and literary style had endeared him to many Democrats and had activated many enthusiastic amateurs. The fact that his opponent had been the "unbeatable" Eisenhower removed much of the stigma from his loss.

Also, Stevenson proved to be an unusually active and effective titular leader. The 1952 campaign had built up a large financial deficit for the party. Out of office, Stevenson devoted much of his time to speaking at Democratic fund-raising events. This not only helped the party, it helped Stevenson. Neither practicing law in Chicago nor running the family farm in Libertyville could attract much press attention; nor would either help in building up goodwill and credit among party leaders. Stevenson's aggressive attack on the Democratic deficit did both.[15] In 1953, Stevenson went on a five-month world tour during which he engaged in extensive talks with the leaders of many nations. Very popular and highly respected abroad,

15. Charles A. H. Thomson and Frances Shattuck, *The 1956 Presidential Campaign* (Brookings Institution, 1960), p. 8.

the defeated Democrat was warmly received—and he added further to his already wide background in foreign affairs.[16]

The 1954 midterm elections strengthened both Stevenson and some potential opponents. Stevenson campaigned long and hard on behalf of Democratic candidates. When the Democrats scored significant gains, Stevenson received some of the credit. Among the 1954 Democratic winners were a number of men who were, or as a result of their victory became, presidential possibilities: Estes Kefauver of Tennessee and Lyndon Johnson of Texas, reelected to the Senate; Governors Frank Lausche of Ohio and G. Mennen Williams of Michigan, both reelected; Averell Harriman, elected governor of New York, and George Leader, governor of Pennsylvania. Harriman's election was viewed as the most significant of these triumphs, for it removed one of his liabilities as a presidential candidate in 1952 —his lack of electoral experience.

By late 1955, two challenges to Stevenson began to take shape. Senator Kefauver launched a new series of publicity-generating congressional investigations. Insiders viewed this as his first move toward active candidacy.[17] And Governor Harriman began to hedge on his previously declared support for Stevenson, while Tammany leader Carmine DeSapio, Harriman's political mentor, began traveling widely in an effort to develop national support.[18] But both challengers had major weaknesses. Kefauver's bid for the 1952 nomination had failed, despite his decisive lead in the polls, because of opposition from party leaders. Kefauver was still unacceptable to these people in 1955[19] and he could no longer claim to be the rank-and-file Democrats' favorite. Harriman was even less popular than Kefauver, according to the polls, and he would be sixty-five years old by the time he could become president. He was, however, acceptable to the very people who had vetoed Kefauver in 1952 and were likely to do so again. Neither Harriman nor Kefauver was acceptable to the increasingly restive South. The southern racial crisis precipitated by

16. *New York Times,* July 14 and Aug. 2, 1953.
17. *Time,* July 25, 1955, p. 14.
18. Ibid., Oct. 17, 1955, p. 27.
19. *U.S. News and World Report,* Oct. 21, 1955, pp. 73–76; and *Time,* June 6, 1955, p. 27.

the *Brown* v. *Board of Education* school desegregation decision, combined with Eisenhower's extraordinary voter appeal, posed the most serious threat to traditional Democratic hegemony below the Mason-Dixon line since 1948. To nominate either Harriman or Kefauver would be, in effect, to concede the region to the Republicans. Of the leading candidates, only Stevenson had a chance of holding North and South together in an uneasy and frustrating partnership.

Governor Stevenson declared his candidacy in November of 1955; Kefauver followed with a formal announcement the next month. Harriman, apparently to avoid entering the primaries, remained silent. As the formal campaigning began, the Gallup poll reported that Stevenson was favored by 51 percent of rank-and-file Democrats to Kefauver's 18 percent and Harriman's 8 percent.[20] Stevenson was also the first choice of most party leaders and activists.[21] The prognosis was obvious: Stevenson should win the nomination, despite his defeat four years before. He would have to fight for it, for Kefauver had proven before that he could be a formidable opponent in a presidential primary. But if Kefauver should destroy Stevenson as a front-runner, Harriman rather than the senator from Tennessee would be the most likely beneficiary.[22]

A VULNERABLE LEADER: 1960

John F. Kennedy's successful campaign for the presidency began with his defeat, in a race for the vice presidential nomination, at the 1956 Democratic convention. When Governor Stevenson, upon his renomination, threw the choice of his running mate open to the convention delegates, the principal contenders were Estes Kefauver and the young, little-known senator from Massachusetts. Amid wild confusion and much vote-switching, the lead seesawed back and

20. American Institute of Public Opinion, Gallup release, March 4, 1956.
21. Stevenson led a poll of 1952 Democratic convention delegates with 38.5 percent compared to Kefauver's 23 percent, Russell's 12 percent, and Harriman's 11 percent; 65 percent thought Stevenson would win; *Time*, Sept. 19, 1955, p. 20. The Gallup poll (Dec. 7, 1955 release) showed Stevenson leading among Democratic county chairmen with 42 percent to 14 percent for Kefauver, 12 percent for Harriman, and 8 percent for Russell; 78 percent of the chairmen expected Stevenson to win.
22. See *Newsweek*, Oct. 3, 1955, p. 23.

forth through two suspenseful ballots until Kefauver won. But Kennedy came within 70 votes of winning, showing noteworthy strength in the South where distaste for Kefauver was apparently stronger than fear of a Roman Catholic candidate. Kennedy's graceful speech conceding the nomination to Kefauver was nationally televised—as his narration of a filmed history of the Democratic party and his nominating speech for Stevenson had been. Before the convention, Kennedy was an ambitious freshman senator from Massachusetts; afterwards he was the brightest young face in the Democratic party and a leading contender for the 1960 presidential nomination.[23]

For a time it appeared that the field for the 1960 nomination would consist entirely of new contenders. Stevenson announced soon after the election that he would not run again.[24] Kefauver was no longer taken seriously as a presidential candidate and did not try to be.[25] His popular following—larger than Kennedy's during 1957—gradually drifted away during 1958. Stevenson's popularity was more resilient —he either led or came close to leading every poll of rank-and-file Democrats in which his name was listed until early in 1960. While Stevenson continued to make news, he was seen not as an active candidate but as a possible compromise choice in the event of deadlock.

Kennedy, however, was running hard. As early as November 1957, *U.S. News* reported that he was leading the field.[26] *Time* followed suit the next month with a cover story on the same theme.[27] Kennedy's performance in the 1958 midterm elections solidified this position. He was reelected to his Senate seat by a three-to-one margin even though he spent much of his time campaigning for other Demo-

23. Kennedy came to the conclusion that he was fortunate to have lost to Kefauver. If he had been nominated for vice president and the Stevenson-Kennedy ticket had lost as badly as the Stevenson-Kefauver ticket did, part of the defeat might have been attributed to Kennedy's Catholicism. This might have set back the prospects of a Catholic presidential candidate for years. See Theodore C. Sorensen, *Kennedy* (Harper and Row, 1965), pp. 91–92.

24. *New York Times*, Dec. 5, 1956.

25. Joseph B. Gorman, *Kefauver* (Oxford University Press, 1971), pp. 282, 291, and 332–54.

26. November 8, 1957, p. 62.

27. December 2, 1957, p. 17.

cratic candidates across the country. Gradually Kennedy's poll ratings crept upward until, during 1959, he was running neck and neck with Stevenson.

But there were a number of other possibilities. In the Senate, Stuart Symington of Missouri, Lyndon Johnson of Texas, and especially Hubert Humphrey of Minnesota were acting like presidential contenders. Governors Pat Brown of California, Robert Meyner of New Jersey, and Mennen Williams of Michigan were also being mentioned, although none had a notable following outside his own state. The most dangerous threats to Kennedy were Symington and Johnson.

Symington was a classically available candidate—a handsome ex-businessman from a border state; not too liberal, not too conservative; acceptable to virtually every segment of the party. But he was little known and did not possess the personality and style of his competitors, especially the glamorous and articulate Kennedy. While his poll standings never exceeded 7 percent, he was a widespread second choice.

Other than Kefauver, who was not loved in the South, Lyndon Johnson was the first southerner in decades with serious prospects of becoming a genuinely national candidate. With a relatively quiescent Republican in the White House, Johnson became exceedingly powerful in the Senate as floor leader of the majority party and highly publicized outside of it. On national policy matters he was the Democratic party's most potent figure; his nearest competitor, the aging Speaker of the House, Sam Rayburn, was among Johnson's most enthusiastic supporters. Johnson's appeal as a presidential possibility was built on the brilliance he displayed in his Senate role. Thus he could not afford to resign the post, and the job precluded an active campaign. His best chance for the nomination lay in continuing to increase his national following through effective leadership in the Senate, in trying to identify himself as more a westerner than a southerner,[28] and then in attempting to cash in his Capitol Hill IOUs

28. See, for example, *Time*, Feb. 2, 1959, p. 10, and Feb. 23, 1959, p. 19.

(and Speaker Rayburn's) at the convention. One consequence of Johnson's inactive candidacy was to take away most of Kennedy's southern support.[29]

Next to Kennedy, Senator Humphrey was the most active candidate during the preprimary phase of the 1960 nomination. Despite good support from organized labor and midwestern farmers for Humphrey, his poll standings were even less encouraging than Symington's. Moreover, since he was viewed as well to the left of the other candidates, he had little chance of becoming a compromise choice.

As 1960 began, Kennedy pulled clearly in front of Stevenson in the polls for the first time. The last Gallup soundings before the New Hampshire primary showed Kennedy the first choice of 35 percent of the nation's rank-and-file Democrats to Stevenson's 23 percent and Johnson's 13 percent. He was the most popular of all the possibilities—be they active candidates or not—and seemed to be the first choice of most party leaders as well.[30] His policy appeal was centrist, with Humphrey to the left and Johnson on the right. The press had billed him as the party's front-runner for several years and he clearly had the skills and access to the plentiful resources needed to win.

And yet Kennedy was an unusually vulnerable front-runner. There were so many candidates and potential candidates that even the front-runner was the first choice of only one out of every three Democrats. Kennedy's youth and religion made some people who might otherwise have supported him hesitate. Frequently, national political conventions are presented with the choice of either nominating the front-runner or rejecting him in favor of some little-known compromise figure. In 1960 there was an unusually large array of distinguished compromise candidates—Stevenson, Symington, perhaps even Johnson—to step into the breach if Kennedy faltered.

These weaknesses of the Kennedy bid for the nomination led to much uncertainty, despite Kennedy's clear lead. Everyone expected

29. *New York Times,* Dec. 14, 1959.
30. *Chicago Daily News* poll of 1956 delegates, reported in *U.S. News,* May 4, 1959, p. 52. Gallup county chairman poll reported Oct. 21, 1959.

the senator from Massachusetts to come to the convention with more delegate votes than anyone else. But many knowledgeable observers felt that his peak strength would fall short of a majority and that he would therefore fail.[31]

## A RESURGENT CANDIDATE: 1968

The disasters of the Republican party in the 1964 election, on the presidential level and in the House of Representatives and state legislatures,[32] led to a victory in the presidential election four years later and to one of the more remarkable political comebacks of recent history. Richard Nixon seemed to have written his political obituary in 1962 after losing the California governorship. Yet he remained a possible compromise candidate at the 1964 convention, and his indefatigable campaigning for Goldwater and other Republican candidates left him very visible thereafter.[33] Indeed, he consistently led the Gallup poll of Republican preferences for the presidential nomination throughout the period before the 1966 elections. Nixon had foreseen the possibility that Barry Goldwater's nomination and defeat would enable him to play the role of elder statesman, party unifier, and architect of recovery—with himself as a candidate in 1968.[34] Nor was this possibility lost on other leaders and workers in Republican politics, many of whom, including Barry Goldwater, gravitated to the former vice president.

Nixon spent much of the next two years traveling, making speeches and campaigning for Republican candidates in the 1965 and 1966 elections. This helped keep him visible to rank-and-file Republicans while creating new political debts and solidifying old loyalties among the leadership of the party.

31. See *Newsweek*, Jan. 11, 1960, p. 14; and *U.S. News*, Dec. 7, 1959, p. 44.

32. The reverses at the state level (the Republicans completely controlled only six state legislatures) could not have come at a worse time. Many states would be required to redraw congressional district lines in the wake of the 1964 Supreme Court decision in *Wesberry* v. *Sanders* (376 U.S. 1); Democratic state legislatures could be counted on to draw congressional district lines so as to make things even more difficult for the Republicans in the future.

33. Jules Witcover, *The Resurrection of Richard Nixon* (Putnam, 1970), chaps. 4 and 5.

34. Ibid., pp. 95–96.

Nixon deserved more than a little credit for the Republican resurgence in the 1966 elections: the party gained 3 U.S. Senate seats, 47 House seats, 8 governorships, and over 500 state legislative seats, recouping virtually all its losses of 1964. But, ironically, it was President Johnson who maximized the benefits to Nixon, in a diatribe just before the elections that

was, in the memory of veteran reporters, the most brutal verbal bludgeoning ever administered from the White House by Johnson, or any other President for that matter, to a leader of the opposition party. Intentionally or not, the President's words immediately swung the national spotlight on Nixon at a time he was climaxing one of the greatest personal efforts . . . ever launched by a political leader not himself running for public office. Not only that, but the President's attack bestowed at once upon Nixon the image of *the* leader of the opposition.[35]

There were of course more direct beneficiaries of the 1966 elections. Rockefeller retained the New York governorship, but he had "completely, firmly and without reservation" ruled out his possible candidacy for president.[36] Charles Percy defeated incumbent Senator Paul Douglas of Illinois and immediately became a presidential possibility. Ronald Reagan was elected governor of California by almost a million votes, defeating incumbent Pat Brown, who eight years before had ended the presidential hopes of Senator Knowland, and four years before had humiliated Richard Nixon.

But George Romney gained the most from the 1966 elections. Reelected governor of Michigan with more than 60 percent of the vote, Romney was credited with carrying a Republican senator and five new Republican congressmen into office on his coattails. He quickly leaped ahead of Nixon in the polls of the Republican rank and file, and into the spotlight of national press attention.

The glare of this publicity was ultimately to ruin Romney. This interlude, before Nixon once again became his party's leading candidate for president, is often cited as an example of how the press can damage or destroy a candidate. But would Governor Romney have prospered as a presidential candidate if the national press had paid less attention or been less hostile? His failure is held up too as an ex-

35. Ibid., p. 165.
36. *New York Times*, May 24, 1966.

ample of how becoming a front-runner can be self-defeating. But that position is not invariably self-defeating—quite the contrary. What was it about the Romney candidacy that made this ordinarily advantageous position so self-destructive?

The transition from state governor to presidential candidate is not always easy. Issues of national and international policy must be confronted; new political complexities are posed by the need to appeal to a nationwide constituency. This transition takes place in a bright glare of publicity, and the presidential hopeful must deal not with the relatively docile representatives of the local media, but with reporters from the nation's leading newspapers and news magazines, the wire services, and broadcasting networks.

George Romney faced some unique problems in surviving this transition. First, there was the man's personality and style. Sincere, candid, aggressive, "quick to make an issue a matter of principle,"[37] he deplored the cautious equivocation of professional politicians, of whom he was generally contemptuous. His moralistic approach to politics was not one that appealed to most sophisticated reporters. "Governor Romney has a tendency to make fuzzy statements about civic virtue," Tom Wicker of the *New York Times* wrote as early as 1965, "rather than cogent remarks on live issues."[38] Second, Romney was a newcomer to politics. Unlike many governors who become presidential possibilities—Roosevelt, Stevenson, Rockefeller, Scranton, Harriman, for example—he had had no earlier experience in national politics or foreign affairs. Third, the alternative candidates in the GOP were strong enough that Romney could not afford to stay at home as Governor Landon had done in 1935 and let the reporters come to observe him in his own bailiwick.

Finally, Romney came onto the national scene at a time when the dominant national issue and the overwhelming preoccupation of the press was the Vietnam war, a problem the governor was ill prepared to handle. He had been attacked for making obtuse statements on

37. David R. Jones, "This Republican for 1968?" *New York Times Magazine*, Feb. 28, 1965, p. 75.
38. *New York Times*, July 28, 1965. See also Theodore H. White, *The Making of the President, 1968* (Atheneum, 1969), pp. 64 ff.; and Witcover, *Resurrection of Richard Nixon*, pp. 190 ff.

the topic before his 1966 election victory.[39] Once he became the Republican's front-running candidate for the presidency, the national reporters relentlessly pressed Romney for a clearer position on Vietnam.

While Romney publicly resolved not to discuss the issue until he had studied it thoroughly, he was not able to remain silent. At a press conference in February 1967, he charged that "political expediency by the Johnson administration has gotten the nation into trouble in Vietnam and elsewhere." But when challenged to give an example of what he meant, he refused to do so.[40]

The more press attention Romney received, the worse he looked.[41] His postelection poll lead over Nixon was gone by February 1967, when the percentage favoring Romney fell to 28. His percentage held fairly close to this level until early September, when Romney confessed on a Detroit television show that his position on the Vietnam issue had changed because he had been "brainwashed" during his 1965 visit to Southeast Asia. The day after the telecast the *New York Times* published on page 28 a news story based on the program.[42] That night the television networks broadcast brief clips of Romney making the statement.[43] In a single phrase, the brainwashing remark symbolized what the national press had been saying about Romney and his campaign for months; it was damaging largely because it rang true. In the weeks following the statement, Romney's poll rating fell from 24 percent to 14 percent, and he dropped from second, behind Nixon, to fourth, behind Rockefeller and Reagan as well.

All this made more emphatic what had been increasingly clear before: George Romney was no match for Richard Nixon, who was by now the clear front-runner for the Republican nomination. Private polls showed Romney so far behind in New Hampshire that he

39. See *Newsweek*, July 18, 1966, p. 21.

40. *New York Times*, Feb. 22, 1967.

41. Nixon apparently had foreseen this development. See Witcover, *Resurrection of Richard Nixon*, pp. 172–73.

42. September 5, 1967.

43. The full story of this incident may be found in White, *The Making of the President, 1968*, pp. 70 ff.

withdrew his candidacy at the end of February, before the primary. That left Nixon, far ahead in the polls, with no declared opposition. His strongest potential opponents, Governors Rockefeller and Reagan, remained noncandidates.

## Two Strong Contestants: 1948, 1952

Before 1948 the Republican party had never renominated a defeated candidate for the presidency. Hoover, Landon, and Willkie had not been able to capitalize on their titular leadership of the defeated Republicans in order to remain the front-running candidate for the next nomination very long. Governor Dewey, however, managed to retain a sometimes slim lead throughout most of the period before the 1948 primaries despite a number of imposing challengers.

The first of these to appear was Harold Stassen. On leaving the Navy at the end of the war, the young former governor of Minnesota served as an American delegate to the United Nations Conference in San Francisco. This highly publicized venture into international affairs, along with his military service, added to the already considerable luster of the Stassen name. After the San Francisco conference Stassen embarked on a speaking tour covering all forty-eight states, apparently to build himself up as a presidential candidate in 1948. Curiously, he chose not to run for the Senate in 1946, instead supporting the liberal Governor Edward Thye in the Republican primary against the aging incumbent. Thye's victory was interpreted by the national press as a boost for Stassen. But Stassen backed another liberal internationalist for the Senate in Nebraska and was embarrassed when his candidate lost. A presidential aspirant who does not hold high public office has to do something to keep in the public eye and to build a political base. But Stassen's approach to this problem seemed unorthodox and unlikely to prove effective in the long run.[44] Nonetheless, he ran a close second to Dewey in the early polls.

44. *Newsweek*, June 24, 1945, pp. 26–27, commented on the Stassen strategy under the heading "The Kiss of Stassen."

Dewey, meanwhile, continued to serve ably as governor of New York; valuable national publicity came to him more or less automatically without his campaigning for the presidency at all. With his re-election in 1946 Dewey's presidential prospects sharply improved.[45] Stassen, sensing some slippage in his relative position, formally announced his candidacy by the end of the year.

During 1947, Senator Robert A. Taft of Ohio became the leading alternative to Dewey. This was not the result of any surge in his popular support—Dewey maintained a commanding lead throughout the year while Taft consistently ran a poor third or fourth in the polls. But since last running for the presidency in 1940 Taft had become the party's acknowledged congressional leader on domestic policy; in his sphere, he was now at least as prestigious and powerful as Senator Vandenberg was in foreign affairs. In the famous 1946 "meat rationing election," the Republicans had exploited postwar frustrations to capture control of both the House and Senate. The country was preoccupied with domestic problems; the Truman administration seemed to be floundering; and Taft suddenly found himself in 1947 at the head of congressional majorities. This extraordinary opportunity, combined with the senator's long-standing popularity with the party professionals, who mildly distrusted both Dewey and Stassen, made him a potentially powerful challenger.

There remained still another threat to Dewey's early prominence. Late in 1947, speculation about General Dwight D. Eisenhower as a potential Republican nominee became widespread. If the polls were to be believed, Eisenhower could beat any candidate in either party. Strenuous efforts were made to persuade him to run, but early in 1948, after his name had been entered in the New Hampshire primary without his consent, the general took himself out of the running with a Sherman-like statement. This ended Eisenhower's possible candidacy in 1948, so far as the Republicans were concerned.

Thus as the formal nominating process began in early 1948, Governor Dewey—the defeated candidate three years before—was still ahead of the pack by such objective indicators as the polls of the

45. At the Republican National Committee meetings in December, Dewey was seen as well ahead. *Ibid.*, Dec. 16, 1946, p. 31, and Dec. 23, 1946, p. 18.

party rank and file and an early poll of state party leaders.[46] But Taft was seen as gaining, despite his weakness in the polls, while Dewey seemed to have reached the peak of his strength.[47] Numerous commentators were predicting a close race, perhaps even a deadlock between the two.[48] If anyone was in the lead, it was Dewey,[49] but there was no deep reservoir of goodwill for him in the party; he would have to demonstrate his strength clearly and win early.

Failing that, the alternatives included not only Taft, but Harold Stassen, who was running the strongest of his many campaigns and had to be taken seriously at least as a primary campaigner.[50] Senator Arthur Vandenberg and Governor Earl Warren of California, while not actively seeking the nomination, were both able and respected leaders willing to serve as compromise nominees. This time, in sharp contrast to 1944, Governor Dewey would have to fight hard for the nomination.

Dewey's upset loss at the polls in 1948 left the national leadership of the Republican party in disarray. His shocking defeat seemed to eliminate him from the presidential picture, an impression Dewey reinforced by repeated statements that he would "never again" seek the presidency.[51] At first, there was no agreement on who should succeed him. In the first Gallup poll after the election, published on July 18, 1949, eight candidates were mentioned as desirable leaders by more than 1 percent of rank-and-file Republicans; but even though some respondents mentioned more than one candidate, none had more than 21 percent support. After many years with few plausible presidential contenders, the Republicans confronted an embarrassingly large choice of them. Unless something drastically changed, the GOP would have a difficult time arriving at a consensus choice to face the faltering Democrats in 1952.

46. Ibid., April 28, 1947, p. 25.

47. Ibid., Sept. 29, 1947, p. 18.

48. See ibid., Dec. 15, 1947, p. 11, and Jan. 12, 1948, p. 12; and *New York Times*, Jan. 18, 1948.

49. *Time*, Feb. 9, 1948, p. 20.

50. "Among the rank and file of politicians, the boys who know the ropes, no one laughs at Harold Stassen." Ibid., Aug. 25, 1947.

51. Paul T. David, Malcolm Moos, and Ralph M. Goldman, *Presidential Nominating Politics in 1952* (Johns Hopkins Press, 1954), vol. 1, p. 22.

Quite a number of things happened to clarify the Republican leadership picture during the preprimary period; essentially the party's realistic choices were narrowed to General Eisenhower and Senator Taft. Before the midterm elections of 1950 and Eisenhower's designation as supreme commander of the North Atlantic Treaty Organization forces in Europe in early 1951, the general moved into place as the overwhelming first choice of the Republican rank and file. For years he had haunted both Republican and Democratic politicians—either as a dream or as a nightmare, depending on which party could succeed in attracting him as its candidate. By now, most informed observers felt that Eisenhower was a Republican—but might be prevailed on to accept a Democratic nomination if the Republicans nominated an isolationist like Taft.[52] Eisenhower, who had become president of Columbia University, made no move to clarify his position. Nonetheless, his poll standings soared during late 1949 and 1950. The last Gallup poll before the midterm elections showed him, at 42 percent, to have twice as many supporters among grassroot Republicans as his nearest competitor. Among independents and Democrats, increasingly disenchanted with the Truman administration, Eisenhower's vote-getting potential dwarfed that of any other Republican.

Eisenhower's emergence as the overwhelming poll leader was assisted by the steady drifting away of Stassen's supporters. Now president of the University of Pennsylvania, the prodigy from Minnesota found it difficult to remain in the public eye. Most departing Stassenites, attracted by Eisenhower's staunchly internationalist image, probably ended up for the general. And most Dewey supporters probably also turned to Eisenhower after the governor endorsed him in late 1950.[53]

Along with Dewey, General Eisenhower accumulated a number of other prominent supporters: Henry Cabot Lodge, Pennsylvania Senator James Duff, former national Republican chairman Hugh

52. See, for example, *Newsweek*, May 21, 1951, p. 26, and July 21, 1951, p. 15.

53. David, Moos, and Goldman date the beginning of active campaigning with Dewey's firm announcement for Eisenhower on Oct. 15 1950; *Presidential Nominating Politics*, p. 25.

Scott, and Senator Frank Carlson of Kansas. Such men do not capriciously support presidential prospects: the sheer fact of their endorsement made the idea of somehow drafting Eisenhower more conceivable; they also had the prestige, skills, and experience needed to campaign on behalf of the general until he could be persuaded to campaign on his own.

If this overwhelming trend toward Eisenhower had continued, his nomination by acclamation would have been the most likely prospect for 1952. But Eisenhower's popularity among Republicans suffered a decline starting in late 1950, while Robert A. Taft's nomination prospects surged.

The first cause of this turnabout seems to have been the midterm elections. Taft was up for reelection that year and campaigning tirelessly. As early as November 1949, Taft strategists had succeeded in pushing through a referendum changing Ohio's ballot form to one that facilitated split-ticket voting on the assumption—which proved to be correct—that this would benefit the senator.[54] Taft's reelection in a landslide was an answer to those who argued that he couldn't win a national election (his 437,000-vote margin was built up, however, against a weak challenger and with assistance from a Democratic governor). True, Taft was not a rabble-rouser, but "his intelligence, earnestness, command of facts, and unrelenting partisanship" made him an effective campaigner, especially before Republican audiences.[55] Moreover, Taft was eager to be president. He was an orthodox conservative with an active and highly professional campaign organization, and he was the acknowledged leader of the congressional Republicans' battles with the Truman administration. Eisenhower had none of these attributes. Indeed, when Eisenhower was recalled to active duty as NATO commander, the general was unable to take an active part in presidential politics even if he wanted to (which he didn't).

Under these new circumstances, the senator from Ohio experienced an uncharacteristic surge of mass popularity. The polls con-

54. Ibid., pp. 23–24.
55. Eugene H. Roseboom, *A History of Presidential Elections* (Macmillan, 1970), p. 508.

tinued to show Eisenhower a stronger potential vote-getter among independents and Democrats, but among Republicans, Taft's poll standings started climbing immediately after the midterm election. As the senator doggedly traveled the country campaigning, they began to equal those of the absent, silent, and slumping Eisenhower. In the last poll before the New Hampshire primary, Taft polled 34 percent of Republican first choices to Eisenhower's 33 percent. It was the first—and the last—time the senator ever led a presidential public opinion poll.

Traditionally, Taft's greatest strength had not been with the voters but with GOP leaders and professional politicians. As election year drew near, almost 60 percent of the nation's Republican county chairmen preferred Taft, while only about 20 percent were Eisenhower supporters.[56] Taft was the leading candidate among the party's state chairmen and national committeemen,[57] among Republican congressmen,[58] and among those who had attended the 1948 Republican convention.[59] The only leadership group within the Republican party inclined to Eisenhower were the state governors.[60]

Thus the field was effectively narrowed to two closely matched potential candidates—Eisenhower and Taft (Stassen and Warren had announced their candidacies but neither had a chance without a convention deadlock; MacArthur, after his triumphant return from Korea upon being fired by President Truman for insubordination, was another very long shot). Taft had the momentum, overwhelming support among the party leadership, and as much popularity among rank-and-file Republicans as Eisenhower. Eisenhower's far greater strength among independents and Democrats made him the more likely general election winner. But nominating contests are intramural affairs: Eisenhower's popularity outside the GOP would be of little direct benefit in gaining the nomination. Even this advantage might vanish soon if the general remained silent and abroad.

56. Gallup release, Nov. 11, 1951.

57. *New York Times*, Nov. 12, 1950, and Nov. 11, 1951; and *Time*, Feb. 5, 1951, p. 8, May 21, 1951, p. 26, and Dec. 17, 1951, p. 21.

58. *Time*, Dec. 17, 1951, p. 21.

59. David, Moos, and Goldman, *Presidential Nominating Politics*, p. 26.

60. *New York Times*, Nov. 11, 1951; and *Time*, Dec. 17, 1951, p. 21.

This was the situation when Senator Henry Cabot Lodge, just returned from a Paris conference with Eisenhower, walked into a packed press conference in Washington on January 6, 1952, and announced that he had been asked "to enter General Eisenhower as a candidate for the presidency on the Republican ticket in the New Hampshire primary. . . . General Eisenhower has personally assured me that he is a Republican."

## No Clear Leader: *1940, 1964*

The only long-established Republican leader left unscathed after Roosevelt's crushing defeat of Alfred Landon in 1936 was Michigan's Senator Arthur Vandenberg. He became the party's early leader for the 1940 nomination, by default.

Vandenberg, an imposing figure, was one of the most highly respected and powerful members of the Senate. As a possibility for the 1936 nomination, he had become better known outside the national capitol and his home state, and in 1938 he took the lead in the polls.[61] He seemed somewhat more eager for the nomination than before— but still remained unwilling to campaign actively for it. "The Senator is not lifting a finger to get the nomination," one close associate reported. "He is just working quietly to make himself the most available candidate."[62] This tactic might have worked if no new Republican leaders had emerged before 1940. But fortunately for the party if not for Senator Vandenberg's presidential prospects, several new GOP leaders appeared who were willing to fight for the dubious honor of running against Franklin Roosevelt.

The first of these was Thomas E. Dewey of New York. Beginning in 1931—as an assistant district attorney, special prosecutor, and district attorney of New York County—Dewey successfully prosecuted a series of New York racketeers, corrupt politicians, and prestigious public figures on a variety of charges. Dewey's dramatic courtroom exploits made him a national hero; his name became "as

61. *New York Times*, May 22, 1938.
62. C. David Tompkins, *Senator Arthur H. Vandenberg: The Evolution of a Modern Republican, 1884–1945* (Michigan State University Press, 1970), p. 167.

familiar to Americans . . . as that of Clark Gable, Henry Ford, Charles A. Lindbergh, Joe Louis or Joe Di Maggio."[63]

No Republican had been district attorney of heavily Democratic New York County for twenty years when Dewey, in 1937, won the office easily in his first campaign for elective position. He was mentioned as a prospective Republican presidential nominee from then on, with his chances improving if he could win the governorship of New York.[64] Virtually drafted for the 1938 governor's race, Dewey seemed such an excellent prospect that the Democrats induced the immensely popular—but reluctant—Governor Herbert Lehman to run for the governorship one more time.[65] Lehman won the election, but by only 64,000 votes out of almost 5 million.

Remarkably, Dewey's presidential stock rose after he lost the gubernatorial election. Immediately afterwards, he jumped into first place in Gallup polls of party rank and file, replacing Vandenberg. His popularity zoomed higher after the conviction of Jimmy Hines of Tammany Hall in February 1939, and he remained in first place in the polls for the rest of the preprimary season, rising as high as 60 percent in January of 1940. But Dewey was not to become the undisputed front-runner; the main reason was a second newcomer, Robert A. Taft.

Taft was elected to the U.S. Senate from Ohio in 1938. His father had been president of the United States, and the Taft name had some of the magical appeal in the Republican heartland that the Roosevelt name had in the big cities of the Northeast. Unusually outspoken for a freshman senator, Taft appealed more directly and strongly than Dewey or Vandenberg to the conservative wing of the party while remaining unassociated with recent Republican defeats. Yet Taft's popular appeal was limited compared to the racket-busting Dewey's. While manifestly able and ambitious, Taft was also "dull, prosy,

63. *Current Biography, 1940*, p. 238. See also Stanley Walker, *Dewey: An American of This Century* (McGraw-Hill, 1944); and Rupert Hughes, *The Story of Thomas E. Dewey* (Grosset and Dunlap, 1944).
64. *New York Times*, Nov. 7, 1937, and Aug. 21, 1938.
65. Governor Lehman preferred to run for the U.S. Senate.

colorless, with not a tithe of Franklin Roosevelt's great charm and personal magnetism," as *Time* bluntly put it.[66]

Yet Taft was more popular among party regulars and "the politicians who usually dominate party conventions"[67] than Dewey. One reason was Dewey's youth: if elected to the presidency, he would be thirty-eight when sworn in—only three years above the constitutional minimum. His highest responsibility had been as a local prosecuting attorney and he had been defeated in his only bid for statewide office. Taft, though not a seasoned national leader, had at least carried a big-state election; and political cartoonists did not depict him in short pants, nor did Harold Ickes crack jokes about his throwing his diaper in the ring. Dewey had a bright future in the Republican party, so the criticism went, but a 1940 bid for the presidency was premature.

Scarcely anyone in the press was predicting a Dewey win as 1940 began—both *Time*[68] and *Newsweek*[69] felt that Taft had the better chance for convention victory. The stage seemed set for a bruising convention battle between the pro-Taft party professionals and pro-Dewey rank-and-file Republicans.

But such was not to be. A third newcomer to Republican national politics would defeat both Dewey and Taft. As the primaries were about to begin, Wendell Willkie was virtually unknown to the average American. President of a large public utilities holding company, he had become something of a public figure as a spokesman for business interests in conflict with the New Deal. Because he was an acknowledged Democrat as late as 1938,[70] the substantial publicity he received during the New Deal years had not immediately led to his consideration as a potential president. The first widely noted mention of Willkie as a potential Republican nominee was by Arthur Krock in the *New York Times* on February 23, 1939. Six months

66. January 29, 1940, p. 22. See also *Newsweek*, Feb. 12, 1940, p. 16, and March 18, 1940, p. 11.
67. *Newsweek*, Jan. 8, 1940, p. 7.
68. December 18, 1939, p. 13.
69. January 1, 1940, p. 10.
70. Joseph Barnes, *Willkie* (Simon and Schuster, 1952), p. 155.

later Willkie was on the cover of *Time*. The accompanying story called him "the only businessman in the U.S. who is even mentioned as a presidential possibility for 1940." But that prospect, the news magazine concluded, was "mildly fantastic."[71]

In 1964 the Republicans again began the formal nominating period without a clear-cut choice for their candidate. They emerged from the defeat of 1960 with three obvious possibilities—Richard Nixon, Governor Nelson Rockefeller of New York, and Senator Barry Goldwater of Arizona.[72] Given his eight-year-long service as vice president, the narrow margin of his defeat in 1960, his popularity with party regulars, and his location snugly in the middle of the party's ideological spectrum, Richard Nixon initially seemed the most likely choice. The Gallup polls taken during 1961 reinforced this view: the former vice president and titular leader of the Republican party was by far the most popular potential candidate for 1964, claiming more than twice the support of either Rockefeller or Goldwater.

Out of national office for the first time in over a decade, Nixon returned to California in early 1961, indicating that he was not a candidate for the presidential nomination but not ruling out the possibility of becoming one.[73] The following September he made front-page news by announcing his candidacy for the governorship of California and adding that his move now cleared the way for the possible candidacies of Rockefeller and Goldwater.[74] This surprise move was interpreted by some, including men close to Nixon, as an indication that he felt that President Kennedy was unbeatable and therefore as Nixon's means of staying in the public eye until 1968.[75] Others pointed out that the Republican party of California was so racked by dissension that the huge state was of little value as a base from which to launch a presidential campaign. No one seemed to doubt,

71. July 31, 1939, pp. 42–45.
72. See *New York Times*, Nov. 10–15, 1960, for a number of articles speculating on the consequences for 1964 of Nixon's defeat.
73. Ibid., Jan. 20, 1961.
74. Ibid., Sept. 28, 1961.
75. Ibid., Oct. 14, 1961.

however, that the move was calculated to further Nixon's presidential ambitions at some point in the future.

The result was quite the opposite. After winning a bruising Republican primary, Nixon was soundly defeated by Democratic Governor Pat Brown. As the *New York Times* reported the next morning, this stunning defeat appeared to eliminate any possibility that Nixon would figure in the 1964 presidential race.[76] Compounding his problem, Nixon responded to defeat by bitterly attacking the press coverage of his campaign at a news conference, concluding: "You won't have Nixon to kick around any more because, gentlemen, this is my last press conference."[77] Shortly after this debacle, the former vice president abandoned his political base in California, moving to New York City to practice law.

The immediate beneficiary of Richard Nixon's misfortune was Nelson Rockefeller. As a presidential possibility, Rockefeller seemed to have almost everything in abundance—wealth, ambition, intelligence, personal charm, and extensive Washington experience in the field of foreign affairs. His performance as governor of New York was widely regarded as superior, and on the day Nixon suffered defeat, Rockefeller was reelected by a margin of more than half a million votes. Immediately after the election Republican leaders agreed that he was far in front in the race for the 1964 nomination.[78] The postelection polls seemed to confirm this view; Rockefeller had jumped into a strong lead among the party rank and file.

He was to hold this competitive advantage for only six months. After his divorce in 1961 Rockefeller's poll standings had held steady, and his reelection as governor in 1962—while by a smaller margin than in 1958—suggested that it would not bar him from the presidential nomination. But on May 4, 1963, the governor married a recently divorced woman, the mother of four young children. This, it turned out, was a serious political liability. At the time of his remarriage, Rockefeller led Goldwater by 43 percent to 26 percent among Re-

76. Ibid., Nov. 8, 1962.
77. Witcover, *Resurrection of Richard Nixon*, chap. 1.
78. See *New York Times*, Nov. 13, 1962.

publicans in the Gallup poll, but the first poll after his remarriage showed the Arizonan leading the New Yorker by 35 percent to 30 percent.[79] From that point on, Rockefeller's popularity—while always stronger when the preferences of Democrats and independents were included than among Republicans alone—continued to decline precipitously. By the beginning of 1964, only 12 percent of the Republicans listed him as their first choice for the presidential nomination. His only hope of achieving the nomination was through a series of primary victories demonstrating that the voters were less concerned about the personal lives of presidential candidates than the polls seemed to suggest. In November of 1963 he announced his candidacy. Few political observers gave him much of a chance.

Thus, by this curious process of elimination, Barry Goldwater in the spring of 1963 became the Republican's third front-running candidate for the 1964 presidential nomination. While a prominent conservative and an indefatigable party worker for years, Senator Goldwater was not considered an important contender until after the Republican convention of 1960, when he had served as the rallying point for bitter conservative objections to the Rockefeller-Nixon agreements on the platform. In the process of withdrawing his name from nomination, Goldwater delivered a fervent speech calling on his fellow conservatives to support the Nixon-Lodge ticket and challenging them to capture the party by 1964. "Let's grow up, conservatives," he said. "If we want to take the party back, and I think we can someday, let's go to work."[80]

A small group of conservative Republicans, led by F. Clifton White of New York, began organizing in 1961 to do just that, and by the spring of 1962 they had a small but growing organization.[81] At first Goldwater remained aloof from these machinations. Apparently he was not sure that he wanted to run. His Senate term would expire in 1964 and he did not wish to foreclose the possibility of run-

79. John Kessel, *The Goldwater Coalition* (Bobbs-Merrill, 1968), pp. 44–45.
80. Ibid., p. 48.
81. For the story see F. Clifton White, *Suite 3505, The Story of the Draft Goldwater Movement* (Arlington House, 1967), pp. 42–93; Robert D. Novak, *The Agony of the G.O.P. 1964* (Macmillan, 1965), chap. 9; and Theodore H. White, *The Making of The President, 1964* (Atheneum, 1965), pp. 88–97.

ning for the upper chamber again. But he did not repudiate them, either. In February of 1963 the group held a series of well-attended rallies and claimed operating campaign organizations in a majority of the fifty states.

Much of the press continued to argue that Goldwater could not win, that no leader of the conservative wing of the conservative minority party could be nominated in the face of certain electoral disaster. But the polls after Rockefeller's remarriage showing Goldwater well ahead lent an air of plausibility to Goldwater's view that the nation had a hidden conservative majority. By the time of the Kennedy assassination in November, Goldwater was nearly ready to announce his official candidacy. Shocked by the violent death of his former Senate colleague, Goldwater wavered, reconsidered his future in light of the suddenly altered political landscape, and then announced on January 3, 1964.

But Goldwater did not become the front-runner. Several months of searching press attention had for the first time widely exposed the senator's political views—including his opposition to the progressive income tax, TVA, and farm subsidies.[82] More important, the assassination of President Kennedy had made him appear a much less attractive choice than before. Lyndon Baines Johnson was now the presumed Democratic opponent. A southerner and westerner, Johnson was apparently weakest as a candidate in the industrial-metropolitan Northeast, where Goldwater himself was weakest. The Republicans' best chance of winning back the presidency in 1964 seemed to be to capitalize on Johnson's weakness. Goldwater's popularity among Republicans dropped from over 40 percent at the time of the assassination to a little over 20 percent by mid-January.

Thus all three of the most obvious Republican candidates in 1960 were seriously damaged by January of 1964. Nor had three years of searching uncovered any promising alternatives. George Romney of Michigan, mentioned as a potential contender even before he won election as governor in 1962, had pledged himself not to run for the presidential nomination in 1964 and was embroiled in a war of attrition with an unfriendly state legislature. Another first-term gover-

82. Novak, *Agony of the G.O.P.*, chap. 15.

nor, William Scranton of Pennsylvania, looked able and attractive but also sounded more convincing than most presidential possibilities when, with regularity, he flatly stated he did not wish to be a candidate.

Henry Cabot Lodge—Nixon's running mate in 1960 and ambassador to Vietnam under Presidents Kennedy and Johnson—had not been thought of as a possibility so long as President Kennedy was alive (Kennedy had soundly defeated him in a race for senator from Massachusetts). Yet as an expert on foreign affairs who could be expected to run well in the Northeast, Lodge appeared to possess strength where Johnson was most vulnerable to attack. In December, former President Eisenhower urged Lodge to return from Saigon and to make himself available for the Republican nomination,[83] but as subsequent probing by the press revealed, Eisenhower's statement did not constitute an endorsement or promise of support. Lodge remained in Saigon, and the Republicans remained leaderless.

## The Early Leader Fails: 1972

Hubert Humphrey lost the presidency in 1968 by a margin not much bigger than that by which Richard Nixon had lost eight years before. But while Nixon remained a strong prospect for the 1964 nomination until 1962, Humphrey went into political eclipse after his comparably narrow loss. The most important reason for this difference was the presence in the Democratic party of a magnetic political figure, Senator Edward Kennedy.

The first Gallup poll after the election showed Kennedy favored by twice as many rank-and-file Democrats as his nearest competitors —Muskie and Humphrey. A brief and abortive effort had been made to draft Ted Kennedy at the 1968 convention; his flat refusal to consider such a course then was viewed as the result of shock, grief, and the heavy burden of family obligations. But the tragic assassinations of his older brothers were, by now, receding into the past. The younger Kennedy seemed as attractive, able, and ambitious as John or Robert. Politically, the Kennedy name was magic. A March 1969 Gallup poll found that, six to one, Americans held favorable opinions

83. *New York Times,* Dec. 8, 1962.

of him (the ratio was even higher among Democrats) and that 80 percent of the public believed that he would win the Democratic nomination in 1972.[84] Perhaps the deeply divided party had found, at last, a leader to unite behind.

Senator Kennedy's presidential prospects were further enhanced when he scored an upset victory over Senator Russell Long of Louisiana in a race for assistant majority leader (whip) of the Senate Democrats. This position, especially since majority leader Mike Mansfield was not a dominant figure with presidential ambitions of his own, would provide a platform from which to become the leading spokesman for the Democratic party.[85] In early 1969 the presidential election of 1972 was rapidly shaping up as another Kennedy-Nixon contest.

This prognosis was shattered by Senator Kennedy's automobile accident on Chappaquiddick Island on July 19, 1969, in which a young woman riding in the car driven by Kennedy was killed. The circumstances of the accident and Kennedy's reaction to the tragedy raised serious doubts about his rectitude and about his judgment and capacity to avoid panic under pressure. A few weeks later, Kennedy announced that he would not seek the presidency in 1972, a position that he persistently reaffirmed from then on.

The senator nevertheless remained a popular figure in the Democratic party. Suspicion (or hope) that he might reenter the race remained until the closing months of the nominating contest. But he had been badly damaged by the incident at Chappaquiddick. As the pollster Louis Harris wrote a month after the accident: "Kennedy at this time is no longer the dominant prospective Democratic nominee in 1972. For the first time, with the public at least, Senator Muskie appears to be in a position to overtake the youngest of the Kennedy brothers as the front-runner."[86] Muskie was thus the initial political beneficiary of the Chappaquiddick tragedy.

In 1968, Muskie's calm, relaxed, and judicious style in his campaign

84. Gallup returns are from *New York Times*, March 9, 1969.

85. For contemporary discussion, see ibid., Jan. 4, 1969.

86. August 21, 1969 release (Louis Harris Political Data Center, Chapel Hill, N.C.). The negative impact of the accident on Kennedy's public image actually increased with the passage of time and the publication of the findings of the inquest. See Louis Harris release of June 15, 1970.

as Democratic candidate for vice president had compared favorably with the more frenetic campaigns of Humphrey, Nixon, and Agnew. One study found him to be more attractive to the voters than any other of the six candidates for president and vice president.[87] In a few short weeks, Muskie had been transformed from an able but obscure senator from a small state into a possible contender for the White House. But until Chappaquiddick, his assets were no match for Kennedy's.

The polls of the Democratic rank and file did not show a lead for Muskie until after the midterm elections. At that time he made on his party's behalf a very effective nationally televised reply to the Republican campaign. Better yet for Muskie, this reply was broadcast immediately following a technically flawed video tape of a speech by the President which "even partisan Republicans conceded . . . [was] . . . disastrous for Nixon."[88]

Throughout the period following the Chappaquiddick accident, Kennedy, Muskie, and Humphrey stayed close together in the polls, taking turns in the lead, with none achieving so much as a ten-point edge over his second-place rival. Yet Kennedy's disavowal of candidacy was taken seriously, for the time being at least. Senator Humphrey's poll standing dropped to a distinct third behind Kennedy and Muskie after the midterm elections, and unlike Muskie he did not act like a candidate for president, nor was he treated that way by the press.

Muskie, in contrast, either led the President or was very close to him in trial-heat polls; he traveled and acted like a candidate, and was viewed as the leading candidate by the press. In *Newsweek*'s description, the Democratic nominating contest had become "Ed Muskie—and The Pack."[89]

But while Muskie was clearly in front, the pack kept growing in size and diversity. The first candidate to announce seemed to be

87. David M. Kovenock, James W. Prothro, and associates, *Explaining the Vote: Presidential Choices in the Nation and the States, 1968*, pt. 3 (University of North Carolina at Chapel Hill, Institute for Research in Social Science, forthcoming).

88. Rowland Evans and Robert D. Novak, *Nixon in the White House* (Vintage, 1972), p. 344.

89. November 16, 1970, p. 33.

among the least of the threats. Senator George McGovern declared his candidacy in mid-January 1971, almost a year before Muskie declared his. Senators Hughes, Bayh, and Harris also announced early, but all three withdrew from competition before the first primaries and before their campaigns had gotten into high gear.

Yet by the time the primaries began, there were more active and declared candidates than there had ever been for any party's presidential nomination since the primaries began in 1912. In addition to Muskie, there were Senators Humphrey, McGovern, Jackson, and Hartke, Governor Wallace, Mayors Lindsay and Yorty, former Senator McCarthy, and two members of the House of Representatives, Wilbur Mills and Shirley Chisholm.

A number of factors seem to have contributed to this proliferation of Democratic candidates. First of all, President Nixon appeared beatable during late 1970 and early 1971, when most of these candidacies were launched;[90] the Democratic nomination seemed to be worth more than most presidential nominations for the party out of power. In addition, 1972 was the first year since 1960 in which the self-starting proclivities of Democratic politicians were not inhibited by the presence of an incumbent. Also important were the new rules and procedures drafted by the Democratic party's commission on party structure and delegate selection. This commission, originally chaired by Senator McGovern, was an outgrowth of the demand for reform following the bloody contest for the 1968 Democratic nomination. The new set of rules aimed to open up decision-making in the nominating process and to weaken the control of established state and local party leaders over delegate selection and voting. The new rules met with a remarkable degree of acquiescence by state parties. There were to be more presidential primaries in 1972 than in any year in recent memory, and the selection of delegates in nonprimary states was to be more open and susceptible to outside challenge than before. The "McGovern reforms" were widely expected to make it harder for early front-running candidates to sew up the nomination

90. Ernest R. May and Janet Fraser, *Campaign '72: The Managers Speak* (Harvard University Press, 1973), chap. 1.

before the convention and thus provide greater opportunities for an outside challenger to make a strong showing.[91]

Finally, while Edmund Muskie was the clear front-runner in 1971, he was not so strong a candidate that other presidential aspirants were inhibited from giving the contest a try. Chance had played a large role in thrusting Muskie to the fore. If Robert Kennedy had not been assassinated, if Hubert Humphrey had not selected him as a running mate in 1968, if the accident at Chappaquiddick had not occurred, Muskie probably would not have been the Democrats' front-runner in 1971. Even his televised speech on election eve in 1970, which had so favorably impressed the nation, was a last-minute idea conceived and promoted by partisans who were more anti-Nixon than pro-Muskie.[92] The senator from Maine had very skillfully taken advantage of his opportunities, but the fact remains that he was the man to beat primarily because the strong candidates from previous years had been eliminated by assassination, scandal, political defeat, or (apparent) withdrawal.

As a result of Muskie's unusually rapid rise to national prominence, his public image, while favorable, was dim. In December 1971 a Harris poll on public perceptions of the senator from Maine showed that most of those with opinions considered him "not too far to the left or too far to the right" (4 to 1), "an outstanding Senator" (3 to 1), a "warm, pleasing personality" (2.5 to 1), and "the kind of man you can trust" (2 to 1). A certain blandness and lack of excitement in his personality were the chief negative aspect of Muskie's public image. But, most significant, "the number who are 'not sure' about Muskie is higher in every case than the number who agree or disagree with the statement about him. Between 41 and 50 percent of the potential voters," according to Harris, "at this point do not appear certain enough of the Senator from Maine to make a definitive judgment."[93]

Thus Muskie's position was volatile. The voters' further judg-

91. For background, see Austin Ranney, "Changing the Rules of the Nominating Game," in James David Barber, ed., *Choosing The President* (Prentice-Hall, 1974), pp. 71-93.

92. *New York Times*, Nov. 4, 1970.

93. Harris release of Dec. 23, 1971.

ments about him would have to be based on information gleaned from the mass media. And the media, which tend to pay more attention to front-runners than to long-shot candidates, also hold them to a higher standard of performance. Stories began to appear dwelling on Muskie's real or alleged weaknesses—excessive caution and indecisiveness, a hot temper, a poorly staffed and managed campaign organization.[94]

During the summer of 1971, Senator Muskie's poll standings began to drop off perceptibly, not so much compared to the other Democrats in the race as compared to President Nixon. The President's dramatic imposition of wage and price controls and announcement of impending trips to China and the Soviet Union had boosted the sagging popularity of his administration. The adverse effects on Senator Muskie's standing in the poll's trial heats weakened, in turn, his claim to the Democratic nomination. In an effort to regain momentum, Muskie's campaign managers embarked on an ambitious attempt to obtain public endorsements from party leaders. The hope, of course, was to create the impression that Muskie's nomination was inevitable. But to the extent that this tactic was successful—the number of important Democratic figures endorsing Muskie was impressive—expectations about Muskie's performance in the primaries were also raised to a point difficult to meet.

On January 5, 1972, the Maine senator formally announced his candidacy for the Democratic presidential nomination in a national telecast. He was the clear front-runner for the Democratic nomination, although one whose popularity and campaign momentum seemed somewhat on the decline. None of the other candidates had succeeded in attracting much popular support in the January Gallup poll: John Lindsay was backed by 5 percent of the Democrats, Eugene McCarthy by 5 percent, George McGovern by 3 percent, and Henry Jackson by 2 percent, with a scattering of first preferences going to less serious candidates. The main threat to Muskie's

94. See, for example, "Facing Up to the Indecisiveness Issue," *Time*, May 3, 1971, p. 15; Rowland Evans and Robert Novak, "Muskie's Miscalculations," *Washington Post*, April 14, 1971; and Kevin Phillips, "Nixon's Muskie Strategy," *Washington Post*, April 19, 1971.

nomination seemed to come not from these men, but from three non-candidates: Edward Kennedy, Hubert Humphrey, and George Wallace.[95]

During the next ten days each of these men took steps that clarified his status. Senator Kennedy let it be known that he would sign the affidavits of noncandidacy required to keep his name off the Florida and Oregon primary ballots. This provided the strongest evidence yet that he meant what he said about not running in 1972. This was certainly good news for the Muskie forces. But Senator Humphrey's announcement of his active candidacy was a severe blow. Clearly the former vice president did not believe that Muskie had the nomination sewn up. Their political postures would cause the two men to divide the center of the party between them. Then Governor George Wallace announced his entry into the Florida primary—an early contest which Muskie had thought he could win. Not only was Florida now an almost hopeless cause, but Wallace could do much damage to Muskie in other states as well. The Muskie campaign was in trouble.

95. The last Gallup poll of the Democratic rank and file taken (but not published) before the New Hampshire primary showed Humphrey taking the lead from Muskie. See *Gallup Opinion Index* (Princeton, N.J.), April 1972, p. 3.

☆

*Chapter Four*

☆

# CONFIRMING THE LEADER

THE PRESIDENTIAL PRIMARY is a uniquely American institution born, after decades of agitation, in the early twentieth century.

In the post-Civil War era the party organizations in many states and cities came under plutocratic control. The elements controlling the state organizations were often the railroads, and in the cities corrupt machines allied with public utilities and other privilege seekers manipulated the convention system to suit their ends. The dominance of the party organizations and of the interests affiliated with them was simplified by the fact that in many states nomination by the major party was equivalent to election. If the party organization controlled the convention system, it controlled, in effect, the election.[1]

Under these conditions, reform was exceedingly difficult, as Lincoln Steffens and the other muckrakers documented over and over again. Their villain became the party nominating convention—large, temporary, and boisterous assemblies easily susceptible to manipulation by bosses and special interests. Robert M. La Follette in 1898 argued for radical changes:

Under our form of government the entire structure rests upon the nomination of candidates for office. This is the foundation of the representative system. If bad men control the nominations we cannot have good government. Let us start right. The life principle of representative government is that those chosen to govern shall faithfully represent the governed. To insure this the representative must be chosen by those whom he is to represent. . . .

To accomplish this we must abolish the caucus and convention by law,

---

1. V. O. Key, Jr., *Politics, Parties, and Pressure Groups* (3d ed., Crowell, 1952), p. 409.

place the nomination of all candidates in the hands of the people, adopt the Australian ballot system and make all nominations by direct vote at a primary election.[2]

Inspired by such high sentiments, plus a natural desire to change the rules of the political game to favor themselves, the Farmers Alliance, the Populists, and (somewhat later) the Progressives advocated the substitution of direct primary elections for party nominating conventions. Early in the twentieth century their agitation began to pay off, and by 1917 all but four states had adopted the direct primary method of nomination for some or all offices filled by statewide election.[3]

Extension of the primary election idea from the nomination of state, local, and congressional candidates to presidential nominations proved more difficult. President Wilson proposed substitution of a nationwide primary for the nominating conventions in a message to Congress in 1913, but his idea gained little support. Rather, most progressives advocated grafting a primary election—at which rank-and-file voters either chose delegates to the national conventions or instructed delegates as to their preferences between presidential contenders or both—onto the existing national convention method of making presidential nominations.

Florida in 1904 held a public primary election for the choice of delegates to a national party convention.[4] Wisconsin adopted a law calling for the popular election of convention delegates in 1905. The following year Pennsylvania passed a general statute on primary elections which provided for the election of district delegates to national conventions, but this feature of the law was not immediately implemented. Oregon in 1910 enacted its presidential primary law—the first to combine a vote on presidential candidates with the election of convention delegates. During the next few years, progressive

2. Quoted in V. O. Key, Jr., *American State Politics* (Knopf, 1956), pp. 95–96.

3. Key, *Politics, Parties, and Pressure Groups*, pp. 410–11.

4. Manning J. Dauer and others, "Toward a Model State Presidential Primary Law," *American Political Science Review*, vol. 50 (March 1956), p. 143. For the early history of presidential primaries, see Louise Overacker, *The Presidential Primary* (Macmillan, 1926); see also Paul T. David, Ralph M. Goldman, and Richard C. Bain, *The Politics of National Party Conventions* (Brookings Institution, 1960), chap. 10 and appendix.

forces in state after state were successful in extending the primary principle to the presidential level. By 1912 a dozen states had laws on the books requiring some form of presidential primary, while a few others had made the primary optional. By 1916, presidential primaries were held in twenty-two states and "it was freely predicted that within a short period the old-time convention would disappear and that the national convention would become like the electoral college, a mere mechanism for recording decisions already arrived at by the electorate."[5]

But policy innovation becomes widespread when the reform it proposes is considered a success and agitation for its adoption continues.[6] Neither condition held true for the presidential primary very long.

The wild and bitter Republican convention of 1912 quickly proved that a candidate—Theodore Roosevelt, in this instance—could win most of the primaries and still be denied nomination. Serious presidential contenders proved reluctant to enter the primaries under these circumstances. Voters in presidential primary states thus often found themselves confronted with a choice between trivial or parochial candidates, or no choice at all. Sometimes their delegates to the national party conventions were pledged to support hopeless or meaningless candidacies, thereby forfeiting any bargaining power and influence they might have had at the convention. Thus, the presidential primary was scarcely an unqualified success during its early years of operation. Then, too, the progressive movement collapsed after 1912 and organized campaigning for the continued spread of the presidential primary came to an end. The diffusion of this particular innovation seemed to have ended too, long before it had run its full course.

Indeed, a counter movement began. Georgia abandoned the presi-

---

5. Key, *Politics, Parties, and Pressure Groups*, p. 448.
6. See Jack L. Walker, "The Diffusion of Innovations Among the American States," *American Political Science Review*, vol. 63 (September 1969), pp. 880–99. The presidential primary is not one of the 88 policy innovations on which his study is based; however, 75 percent of the states he identifies as most innovative adopted the presidential primary before 1952, while only 50 percent of the moderately innovative and 25 percent of the least innovative had tried the experiment.

dential primary after trying it once in 1912. Iowa and Minnesota followed suit after 1916. Vermont and North Carolina gave up after 1920, Montana after 1924, and Michigan and Indiana after 1928. Two decades after the first presidential primary took place, the movement had come to "a standstill."[7] The number of presidential primary states stabilized at about fifteen. Turnout in the primaries remained low. The presidential primary, like some other progressive era reforms, seemed doomed to a slow death at the hands of popular indifference.

But the contest for the presidential nominations in 1952 reversed the trend. Both parties witnessed spirited fights for the nomination, waged, in large part, in presidential primaries. While the primary outcomes did not determine the parties' ultimate choices, they generated more interest than at any time since 1912. Television, now the principal means of nationwide communication, tended to dramatize and nationalize the previously parochial skirmishes of the primaries; with suspense, conflict, and visual appeal, the primary campaigns were an ideal subject for the medium. Turnout jumped from less than 5 million primary voters in 1948 to almost 13 million in 1952.[8] Presidential candidates began to look with greater favor on the primaries as a means of gaining national exposure and demonstrating their attractiveness to voters. The leaders of state party organizations—wheezing and toothless dragons compared to the robust machine bosses of an earlier day—found it increasingly difficult to stop them.

A final incentive to the adoption of the presidential primary was provided almost two decades later by the Democratic party's McGovern-Fraser commission.[9] In an effort to stop some of the

7. Overacker, *Presidential Primary*, p. 22.

8. Voter turnout, even in contested primaries, still remained rather low. See Austin Ranney, "Turnout and Representation in Presidential Primary Election," *American Political Science Review*, vol. 66 (March 1972), pp. 21–37.

9. Officially titled the Commission on Party Structure and Delegate Selection to the Democratic National Committee, it was chaired by Senator George McGovern of South Dakota from 1969 to 1971 and by Representative Donald Fraser of Minnesota from 1971 to 1972. See Austin Ranney, "The Line of the Peas: The Impact of the McGovern-Fraser Commission's Reform" (paper presented at the 1972 annual meeting of the American Political Science Association; processed); see also Austin Ranney, "Changing the Rules of the Nominating Game," in James David Barber, ed., *Choosing the President* (Prentice-Hall, 1974), chap. 3.

abuses and injustices apparent at the Democrats' ill-starred 1968 convention, the commission prepared eighteen guidelines intended to insure that the state Democratic parties' procedures for selecting delegates to the 1972 convention were open, fair, and timely. One relatively easy way for a state party to comply with these rules without disturbing its traditional ways of conducting other business was to adopt a presidential primary law. In the period 1969–72, seven states adopted primaries, yielding a total of twenty-three, including eleven of the twelve largest states, and involving about two-thirds of all convention delegates.

But a nationally coordinated system of primaries has not been achieved. Each state decides for itself whether to have a primary, what form it will take, and when to have it. Not all states with primaries list the names of presidential candidates on the ballot. Not all of those that allow the names of presidential candidates on their ballots make an effort to assure that all serious candidates are included. Furthermore, not all of the states that allow voters to express a presidential preference insure that those preferences will be reflected in the state delegates' votes at the national convention. The result is a set of primaries that vary in so many ways that they virtually defy classification.[10]

If primaries were merely a means by which states selected their delegates to national party conventions, this chaotic picture would be of little concern. However, in the last twenty years, state presidential primaries have become national events. The press would not descend on New Hampshire, and other states, if the primary outcome had no more impact than that state's proportional weight in the national convention.

State primary outcomes are watched carefully for evidence about the relative strengths and weaknesses of candidates. A strong performance in one state can bring publicity that makes a previously un-

10. See, for example, David, Goldman, and Bain, *Politics of National Party Conventions*, chap. 10. See also Richard D. Hupman and Robert L. Thornton, comps., *Nomination and Election of the President and Vice-President of the United States, Including the Manner of Selecting Delegates to National Political Conventions* (Government Printing Office, 1972); a similar volume has been published every presidential year since 1936.

promising candidate a serious threat nationwide. Similarly, a disappointing performance can knock a previously viable candidate effectively out of the race. Outcomes of delegate selection contests in states without primaries almost never have this multiplier effect. The uncoordinated sequence of primaries is capable of altering greatly the relative strengths of candidates on the national scene.

## The Impact of the Primaries

Viewed quantitatively, the impact of the presidential primaries on nominations within the party in power is not impressive. In eight of the last ten nominations the dominant position of the front-runner before the primaries remained essentially unchanged at the end of the series. In seven of these elections (1936, 1940, 1944, 1948, 1956, 1964, 1972) the president sought renomination; in one instance (1960) the front-runner entering the primaries was the heir apparent to a president ineligible to succeed himself. In all eight cases the candidate maintained the lead throughout the primary period and was ultimately nominated.

More often than not there was some kind of challenge during the primary period (the exceptions being 1944, 1956, and 1960). Most of these look quixotic in retrospect, and even more of them seemed so at the time they were launched. Only two can claim some measure of success. The Kefauver challenge in 1952 and the McCarthy challenge in 1968 were followed by the withdrawal of the incumbent, but the evidence does not support the argument that Presidents Truman and Johnson withdrew because of their poor showing in primaries. Both claim that they had previously intended to withdraw (though Truman's contention is more convincing than Johnson's). And it seems unlikely that either would have been denied the nomination had he continued to seek it.

But there is no doubt that Truman and Johnson were embarrassed in the New Hampshire primaries, and that their opponents were strengthened and encouraged (in Johnson's case, the outcome led to the entry of Robert Kennedy, the President's strongest potential opponent, into the race). This in turn affected the presidents' incentives. Whatever either president's true intentions, these embarrassments added to the costs of securing the nomination at the same time that they reduced its value by insuring that it could be secured only by an open struggle.

Though there were many challenges of one sort or another, only in 1952 and 1968 did they seriously affect the incumbents' incentives to run again. It appears that if a challenge is to become dangerous, both the political vulnerability of the president and the prestige of the challenger must be extraordinary.

Vice President Garner was surely the most prestigious challenger to a president, but he entered the 1940 primaries against an incumbent whose popularity and prospects of reelection were both high. When President Truman's prestige was at a nadir in 1948, his numerous opponents could not mobilize a single plausible challenger to him. However, in both 1952 and 1968 the incumbents' popularity ratings were low, their prospects of reelection uncertain, and each faced a challenger with manifest prestige, ambition, and talent.

When the incumbent has withdrawn, as in 1952 and 1968, the primaries themselves have not identified his successor for the nomination. Senator Kefauver was able to use the 1952 primaries to build massive public support, but the influence of party leaders and regular organizations denied him the nomination in favor of a candidate who had not entered the primaries at all. The 1968 nomination went to a man who had contested no primaries, though in this case Humphrey led each of the polls of Democratic rank and file between April and the time of the convention. Thus, the primaries did more to reduce the president's incentives to run again than they did to identify the next nominee. Playing giant killer may well be self-defeating in terms of the aggressor's presidential prospects.

## *Present and Future President: 1936, 1940, 1944, 1956, 1972*

While opposition to President Roosevelt had developed within the Democratic party by 1936, and had grown significantly by 1940, it was not reflected in any serious challenge to him in the presidential primaries. In 1936, with no illusions about beating the President, Colonel Henry Breckenridge, assistant secretary of war under Woodrow Wilson, ran in several primaries in order to offer "a rallying point" for anti-New Deal Democrats. The rally was not impressive. Nor was the 1940 challenge to Roosevelt from Vice President Garner's candidacy in the Wisconsin, Illinois, California, and Oregon primaries. The Garner slate received almost a quarter of the vote in the Wisconsin primary, which was interpreted as a good showing and just cause for some alarm among Roosevelt backers. But Garner's subsequent showing in Illinois, California, and Oregon was much less strong—he netted between 10 percent and 15 percent of the vote in each. The end result of the primaries was thus to reduce the credibility of Garner, Roosevelt's most prestigious opponent. By 1944, in wartime, a challenge to Roosevelt from within the Democratic party was unthinkable. Unopposed, he swept every Democratic primary in which his name was entered.

Similarly, once President Eisenhower announced his willingness to accept renomination for a second term in 1956, his selection by the Republicans was assured. Senator William Knowland immediately dropped his campaign—although his name remained on the ballot in several primary states with filing dates preceding the President's announcement. Altogether some 81,000 Republican primary participants voted for Knowland in these states; 5 million indicated their support for Eisenhower by voting for him in uncontested primaries.[11]

Richard Nixon was challenged from both his right and his left in the 1972 primary campaigns, but neither challenger seriously weakened the President. Congressman Paul McCloskey, attacking Nixon from the left, emphasized an antiwar perspective. His main campaign was in New Hampshire, where he received 20 percent of the vote to Nixon's 69 percent. Though 20 percent was the threshold he had once set as a condition for continuing the campaign, McCloskey withdrew from active campaigning soon after the New Hampshire result.

Congressman John Ashbrook of Ohio took on the President from the right. While Ashbrook had received 10 percent of the votes in

11. James W. Davis, *Presidential Primaries: Road to the White House* (Crowell, 1967), p. 300.

New Hampshire, he received only 9 percent in Florida, where he had campaigned more extensively. Florida Republican voters gave the President 87 percent of their ballots and for the most part ended any speculation that Nixon might be denied renomination.[12]

## Confirming the Inheritance: 1948, 1964

The nominations of former Vice Presidents Truman in 1948 and Johnson in 1964 illustrate the political potency of incumbency from two extremes. Johnson was near his political zenith, and Truman was at one of his nadirs.

As the primary season began in early 1948, President Truman was in deep political trouble.[13] His prestige and popularity were shockingly low. The South was in a state of alarm over his civil rights proposals. His former secretary of commerce, Henry Wallace, had announced his presidential candidacy as an independent. Few thought Truman could win an electoral contest against almost any foreseeable Republican opponent.[14] And yet no major candidate challenged President Truman in the presidential primaries!

The reason was simply this: Truman's Democratic opponents had no candidate with enough political appeal to have a chance against an incumbent president—except General Dwight D. Eisenhower. The challenge to President Truman thus took the form of a futile effort to draft Eisenhower despite his firm withdrawal from presidential politics after Republican efforts to draft him earlier in the year.[15]

12. See Ernest R. May and Janet Fraser, *Campaign '72: The Managers Speak* (Harvard University Press, 1973), pp. 76–90; and Lou Cannon, *The McCloskey Challenge* (Dutton, 1972).

13. See Alfred Steinberg, *The Man from Missouri: The Life and Times of Harry S. Truman* (Putnam, 1962), pp. 300–09.

14. *Newsweek*, June 7, 1948, p. 14. All but one of fifty political writers polled by *Newsweek* believed that Truman would be renominated, and all believed that he would be defeated in November. But when asked who was best qualified to be president, they rated Vandenberg first, then Dewey, Taft, Stassen, Eisenhower, Justice William O. Douglas, and Senator Harry Byrd, in that order. The first Democrat was in sixth place, while the President of the United States was an also-ran, receiving only one vote.

15. Eisenhower had responded to the Republican effort: "My decision to remove myself completely from the political scene is definite and positive. . . . I could not accept the nomination even under the remote circumstances that it were tendered to me." *Time*, Feb. 2, 1948, p. 9.

This effort to create an Eisenhower boom attracted active support from an extraordinarily wide variety of Democrats. The South was represented by both the liberal Senator Claude Pepper of Florida and the leader of the region's conservatives, Senator Richard Russell of Georgia. (Only six of the forty-five Democratic senators publicly supported Truman; thirteen publicly opposed him.[16]) Big-city machine politicians such as Jacob Arvey and Mayor Edward Kelly of Chicago and Mayor Frank Hague of Jersey City were sympathetic. Such prominent New Deal–Fair Deal leaders as Leon Henderson, Senator Paul Douglas of Illinois, and Mayor Hubert Humphrey of Minneapolis were active in the efforts to dump Truman for Eisenhower. Walter Reuther of the United Auto Workers took part in the move, too. Even Franklin Roosevelt's sons were for Eisenhower.[17]

This quixotic movement finally died shortly before the convention when Eisenhower once again stated that he would not accept the 1948 nomination "under any conditions, terms, or premises."[18] Some erstwhile Eisenhower supporters switched to Supreme Court Justice William O. Douglas and sought to draft him. Senator Pepper, unwilling to give up, suggested that Eisenhower run as a national candidate and that the Democratic party confine its activities to state, local, and congressional races. When this modest proposal evoked no enthusiasm, the senator from Florida announced that he, himself, would yield to a draft.[19] But the challenge to Truman's renomination was over.

In 1964 the Democratic presidential primaries had no effect on President Johnson's prospect for nomination. The only semblance of opposition to emerge was Governor George Wallace of Alabama, who was seen as seeking to prove a point more than to challenge the President. Wallace campaigned in Wisconsin, Indiana, and Mary-

16. *Newsweek*, April 5, 1948, pp. 19–20.
17. See Cabell Phillips, *The Truman Presidency* (Penguin, 1966), pp. 210–11; Jules Abels, *Out of the Jaws of Victory* (Holt, 1959), p. 74; Irwin Ross, *The Loneliest Campaign: The Truman Victory of 1948* (New American Library, 1968), pp. 72–75. For a regretful retrospective look by one of the participants, see Chester Bowles, *Promises to Keep: My Years in Public Life, 1941–1969* (Harper and Row, 1971), pp. 172–75.
18. Phillips, *Truman Presidency*, p. 211.
19. *Newsweek*, July 19, 1948, p. 48, and July 26, 1948, p. 19.

land against stand-in candidates pledged to support LBJ. The votes polled by the Alabama governor in these three nonsouthern states (34 percent in Wisconsin, 30 percent in Indiana, and 43 percent in Maryland) were imposing but not enough to win. Wallace's stature as a potential presidential candidate was considerably enhanced by these returns, but the prospect of Johnson's nomination at Atlantic City was not affected at all.

## Confirming the Heir: 1960

In all of the presidential elections between 1936 and 1972, only in 1960 was an incumbent ineligible to succeed himself because of the constitutional prohibition ratified in 1951. Governor Nelson Rockefeller's announcement, in late December 1959, that he would not be a candidate for the Republican nomination eliminated the possibility that the primaries would be used in 1960 to challenge the front-runner. Even though there was no contest, Vice President Nixon allowed his name to be entered in several primaries to help keep his candidacy in the news during the more active Democratic nominating campaign, and to prevent any possible opponents from picking up delegate votes by default. In the absence of opposition, the results had little meaning.

## Primaries Can Matter: 1952, 1968

The Democratic primaries of 1952 were significantly different from those in the four previous elections, for they were the first to alter the competitive situation of a presidential nomination within the party in power. Despite uncertainty about his intentions, President Truman seemed the most likely Democratic nominee as the primaries began. He had sought, since January, privately to persuade Governor Stevenson to run as his successor. When these efforts failed, he had decided, after some vacillation, to allow his name to be entered in the New Hampshire primary, presumably to deny his challengers a chance to build themselves up unopposed by either the President or his political heir. This course also kept Truman's options open; if he was unable to find a satisfactory successor, he could always run himself rather than let Senators Kefauver, Russell, Kerr, or someone else win by default.

None of the active alternatives to Truman were thought to be very serious presidential possibilities in advance of the primaries. Kefauver enjoyed a bright public image as a crime fighter, but he had earned it in a way that alienated the party professionals, including President Truman. His only chance for the nomination, a faint hope at best, was to demonstrate such vast popular strength in the primaries that the party leadership would feel compelled to nominate him anyway. Senator Russell was a regional figure, in the race to enhance the South's bargaining power at the convention. Senator Kerr had announced that he would run only if the President withdrew.

This situation was drastically altered when Senator Kefauver defeated President Truman, by a 55–45 percent margin, in the New Hampshire primary. Quite unexpected, Kefauver's victory was called a "sensational success."[20] Kefauver's television-created image and his tireless handshaking tours of the little state had dealt the unpopular President another serious blow. On March 29, at a Jefferson-Jackson day dinner, President Truman announced that he would not be a candidate for reelection. His withdrawal, combined with Stevenson's adamant refusal to run, insured the Democrats an open nominating contest.

It would be a mistake, however, to say that the Democratic voters of New Hampshire caused this significant shift in the course of events. President Truman had preferred not to run for reelection before the primary.[21] But the New Hampshire results must have increased his already substantial incentives to retire. To remain in contention without launching a personal campaign—his posture in New Hampshire—would run the risk of further public humiliation. The New Hampshire defeat made the prospects of general election victory by either Truman or his chosen successor more remote than ever. The costs of staying in the race had been significantly increased

20. *Time*, March 24, 1952, p. 21.
21. Harry S. Truman, *Memoirs*, vol. 2, *Years of Trial and Hope* (Doubleday, 1956), chap. 31.

while the benefits for doing so—control over the next nomination or another chance to run, as an underdog, for four more years in the White House—had been devalued.

The New Hampshire primary and Truman's withdrawal made Kefauver into a serious presidential contender. His poll standings shot upward (see Figure 4-1); his chronic lack of funds and staff was alleviated. And yet Kefauver's basic weakness—the adamant opposition of the President and the party's professional politicians—was scarcely helped by his public humiliation of Truman. Kefauver's only chance was to keep on winning primaries. One news magazine likened his situation to that of a professional burglar: "a good average isn't enough—he has to win every time."[22]

This Kefauver just about managed to do. Two days after Truman's announcement, Kefauver won two more primaries, in Wisconsin and Nebraska. In Wisconsin Kefauver was unopposed, but in Nebraska the senator from Tennessee defeated Senator Kerr by a 6 to 4 margin. Kerr was sufficiently lacking in other assets that this outcome was viewed as fatal. *Time* called him a 72-hour candidate: serious only from Saturday night (when Truman withdrew) to Tuesday night (when the Nebraska returns were in).[23]

Kefauver continued his string of primary victories in Illinois, New Jersey, Massachusetts, and elsewhere. But in all these primaries he was unopposed, and his victories were scarcely noticed in the national press. Florida would be a significant contest, for there Kefauver would be matched against Richard Russell, perhaps the South's most popular and prestigious figure, supported by Governor Fuller Warren (who had been personally embarrassed by Kefauver's crime hearings) and the party establishment. Russell got the most votes (55 percent to Kefauver's 42 percent), but it was not seen as a Russell victory by the press. *Newsweek* even headlined its story on the primary results with "Kefauver Keeps Rolling."[24]

For one thing, while Russell's margin over Kefauver might well have been considered a landslide in a regular election, presidential

22. *Time*, March 24, 1952, p. 24.
23. April 14, 1952, p. 14.
24. May 19, 1952, p. 28.

FIGURE 4-1. *Preferences of Democratic Rank and File for 1952 Presidential Candidates*

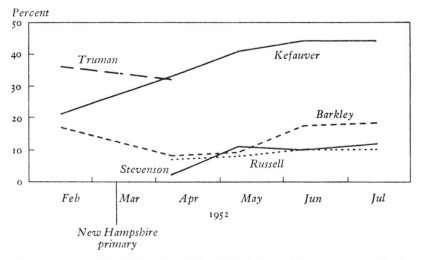

Source: George H. Gallup, *The Gallup Poll: Public Opinion 1935–1971* (Random House, 1972).

primary returns are evaluated in terms of expectations. Knowledge-able observers had expected Russell to do better than he did, and early predictions from the Georgia senator's camp had Russell lead-ing 2 to 1.[25] And Russell had won because of his great strength in northern and central Florida—the "old South" parts of the state. Kefauver carried the cities and the sections of the state populated by transplanted northerners. The pattern of the voting underscored the futility of Russell's national candidacy.[26]

All told, Kefauver entered thirteen state primaries and won twelve, and his sole loss, in Florida, was widely viewed as something of a moral victory.[27] This remarkable record made him into the most popular leader among the Democratic rank and file. He had trailed Truman in the polls before New Hampshire, but by the end of his marathon primary campaign Kefauver was the first choice of 45 per-cent of all rank-and-file Democrats (see Figure 4-1). His nearest

25. Ibid.
26. *Time*, May 19, 1952, p. 29.
27. He also lost the District of Columbia primary to Harriman.

competitor, Vice President Alben Barkley, was supported by 18 percent. He had shown that a politician could use this series of seemingly local contests to become the party's popular choice nationwide.

Even so, the nomination remained wide open as the convention began. The party's leaders, from the President on down, were overwhelmingly opposed to Kefauver. Yet every alternative to the Tennessee senator also had major liabilities—except Adlai Stevenson, who continued to resist nomination.

In 1968, for the second time since 1936, the primaries altered the competitive situation in the party in power. As in 1952 a wartime president was challenged in the New Hampshire primary by a senator who was not previously thought to be one of the party's most likely future presidents. As in 1952 the unexpectedly strong showing of the challenger was for the president at best a moral defeat, and as in 1952 the president would withdraw from the nominating contest at the end of March. And as in 1952 the challenging candidates then would fail to win the nomination.

At first, the Republican contest in the 1968 New Hampshire primary had seemed to be the more interesting one, but after Romney's withdrawal at the end of February, attention switched to the Democratic race. Only Senator Eugene McCarthy had actually filed for a place on the ballot, but the New Hampshire regular Democratic organization, led by Governor John King, launched an extensive campaign for President Johnson as a write-in candidate and on behalf of delegates pledged to support Johnson at the national convention.

McCarthy had been the first choice of only 12 percent of New Hampshire Democrats in January,[28] but since then his campaign had caught fire. This was partly the result of McCarthy's personal style, but more important were the hundreds of college students who poured into New Hampshire to work for the Minnesota senator. Without regular jobs or family responsibilities, they were able to mount an impressive grass-roots campaign for McCarthy's anti-Vietnam war stance.

The New Hampshire primary results came in two parts. In the

28. Theodore H. White, *The Making of the President, 1968* (Atheneum, 1969), p. 101.

nonbinding presidential preference poll, President Johnson won by
49.5 percent to 42.4 percent. In the separate election of delegates, the
McCarthy slate swept twenty of the twenty-four slots.

In purely arithmetical terms the primary resulted in a win for the
President, and a split decision when the delegate contests were also
considered. But expectations are more important than arithmetic in
interpreting primary results and McCarthy had done far better and
Johnson far worse than knowledgeable observers had expected them
to do. From then on, the press and the public had to take Eugene
McCarthy's bid for the nomination seriously.

Four days after the New Hampshire primary Robert Kennedy
announced his candidacy for the presidential nomination, pledging
an aggressive campaign in the late primaries. He had been vacillating
over the decision for months; the Tet offensive and the New Hampshire primary results apparently tipped the balance in favor of his
running.[29] Suddenly, anti-Johnson Democrats had two champions.
Of the two, Kennedy was far the better known and more popular—
the March Gallup poll showed him running a dead heat with the incumbent President among rank-and-file Democrats, while Johnson
was preferred over McCarthy 2 to 1. Kennedy's strength lay at the
core of the traditional Democratic coalition—working class and minority group voters—while McCarthy's appeal was to students and
affluent, educated suburbanites, a vital but far less numerous segment
of the party.[30] But even given their different constituencies, it seemed
unlikely that the two anti-Johnson candidates together could block
the President's renomination. The bulk of the professional party
leadership, fearing a disastrous party split, were still behind the President, in spite of the New Hampshire primary.[31] Indeed a post-New
Hampshire *New York Times* survey of Democratic leadership in
all fifty states estimated that the President could count on more than
65 percent of the Democratic convention votes. Only in New En-

29. Ibid., pp. 194–207; and Jules Witcover, *85 Days: The Last Campaign of
Robert Kennedy* (Putnam, 1969), chaps. 1 and 2.

30. See Louis Harris release, April 11, 1968 (Louis Harris Political Data Center,
Chapel Hill, N.C.).

31. See the Associated Press survey of Democratic state chairmen, in *New York
Times,* March 16, 1972, and of Democratic governors in ibid., March 28, 1972.

gland and in the Pacific Coast states were the combined Kennedy-McCarthy forces in a majority.[32] And if the two anti-Johnson candidates persisted in their plans to slug it out in two-way primary races in Indiana, Nebraska, Oregon, and California, one of them was likely to be seriously damaged, if not destroyed, as a viable candidate before the convention began.

But Johnson was not willing to pay the price of renomination under these circumstances. On March 31st the President concluded a nationwide television speech on Vietnam by stating, "I shall not seek and I will not accept nomination of my party as your President." The announcement was a shocking surprise, even to the President's close associates.

It is clearly wrong to ascribe his withdrawal solely to his defeat in New Hampshire and anticipated poor showing in the Wisconsin primary scheduled two days later—the President had been seriously considering the move for months.[33] But the two primaries did demonstrate that his renomination could not be won without a bitter fight and a sharply divided party; this would diminish the President's chances for a victory in November. The Kennedy and McCarthy candidacies thus simultaneously increased the costs and reduced the value of the nomination for President Johnson.

Johnson's withdrawal, coming only two weeks after Robert Kennedy declared his candidacy, resulted in extraordinary confusion within the Democratic party. To allow the nomination to go by default to either Kennedy or McCarthy was unthinkable to the more conservative, prowar wing of the party. But starting at this late date, primary campaigns in the two states (New Jersey and South Dakota) and the District of Columbia whose filing dates had not already passed would be risky. Thus Lyndon Johnson's apparent heir, Vice President Hubert Humphrey, remained noncommittal for almost a month, formally announcing his candidacy only after primary deadlines were safely past. In the meantime the bulk of the party's leaders, who were in neither Kennedy's nor McCarthy's camp, were left

32. Ibid., March 24, 1968.
33. Lyndon Baines Johnson, *The Vantage Point* (Holt, Rinehart and Winston, 1971), chap. 18; and White, *Making of the President, 1968*, chap. 4.

without a candidate. Many sought hurriedly to organize favorite-son candidacies to hold their state delegations together until the situation stabilized.

In the midst of the political confusion occasioned by the rapidly changing list of candidates and by the Tet offensive, Reverend Martin Luther King, Jr., was assassinated in Memphis, Tennessee. The murder of the most prestigious figure of the civil rights movement provoked violent demonstrations which degenerated into looting and arson in more than a hundred cities. Thousands of troops were summoned to quell the disorder; thousands were arrested and thirty-nine people died.[34]

It would be difficult to envision a less propitious time than the spring and summer of 1968 for a huge and divided American party to arrive at agreement on a candidate for the highest office in the land. Yet American elections—and hence nominations—are run by the calendar. It is not possible to postpone the choice of nominees until emotions have calmed and greater stability has been achieved. Time moves on—and so must the nominating process.

Senator McCarthy won the Wisconsin primary—two days after Johnson's withdrawal and two days before the King assassination— by a substantial margin. But his 56 percent of the popular vote was not viewed as a massive triumph; Johnson polled 35 percent despite his withdrawal statement. The Pennsylvania and Massachusetts primaries were next. McCarthy's was the sole name on the ballot in both states. Despite substantial write-in votes for Kennedy and Humphrey, the senator from Minnesota won both primaries easily (71.5 percent in Pennsylvania, 42 percent in Massachusetts).

The Indiana and Nebraska primaries, scheduled for May 7 and May 14, were the first that Robert F. Kennedy could enter. The Kennedy campaign, while showing signs of improvisation, was operating at a frenetic pace. The New York senator's ability to evoke an emotional response from a crowd—especially in black ghettos after the assassination of Martin Luther King—was impressive, even frightening. Even so, Kennedy's campaign did not improve his national poll standings. The April Gallup poll found him ahead of

34. White, *Making of the President, 1968*, p. 261.

McCarthy and Humphrey in the race for approval among Democratic partisans. By May, he had lost 4 points and fallen behind the vice president in the percentages of Democrats' preferences for presidential candidates: [35]

|            | Kennedy | McCarthy | Humphrey | No opinion |
|------------|---------|----------|----------|------------|
| April 1968 | 35      | 23       | 31       | 11         |
| May 1968   | 31      | 19       | 40       | 10         |

Kennedy clearly needed primary victories, not so much to best Senator McCarthy as to stay in contention with the surging vice president.

In Indiana, Kennedy came in first in a three-way race against Senator McCarthy and Governor Roger D. Branigan, a proadministration stand-in. The results seemed to hurt McCarthy, who came in third with 27 percent of the vote, more than it helped Kennedy, whose 42 percent was somewhat below expectations. Two weeks later in Nebraska—scarcely favorable terrain for a liberal—Kennedy was a more impressive victor, polling 51 percent to McCarthy's 31 percent. But on May 28 the Democratic voters of Oregon gave McCarthy a solid primary victory over Kennedy, 45 percent to 39 percent. [36] The aura of Kennedy invincibility—the Oregon primary was the first election defeat suffered by any of the Kennedy brothers—was damaged. Kennedy's last chance to regain momentum and to prove that he was a winner via the primaries was the California primary scheduled for June 4. It was an exhaustive, expensive, and intemperate campaign capped by a televised debate between the two candidates. As is frequently the case in such televised events, both sides thought they had won. [37] The primary returns were less ambiguous—Robert Kennedy, 46 percent; Eugene McCarthy, 42 percent; the slate pledged to Attorney General Thomas Lynch (a Humphrey stand-in), 12 percent. Kennedy had won, though by no means overwhelmingly, in the nation's largest state. Along with the psychological victory went 170 delegate votes. Combined with the delegates Kennedy expected to

35. *Gallup Opinion Index* (Princeton, N.J.), May 1968, p. 9.

36. See John M. Orbell, Robyn M. Dawes, and Nancy J. Collins, "Grass Roots Enthusiasm and the Primary Vote," *Western Political Quarterly*, vol. 25 (June 1972), pp. 249–59.

37. Lewis Chester, Godfrey Hodgson, and Bruce Page, *An American Melodrama: The Presidential Campaign of 1968* (Dell, 1969), p. 389.

garner in his home state of New York, they would stand him in good stead at the Chicago convention. In South Dakota, whose primary was held the same day as California's, the Kennedy slate of delegates had won a smashing victory, polling as many votes as the two slates favoring Senator McCarthy and Vice President Humphrey combined.

Upon leaving the public celebration of the most important political victory of his life, Robert F. Kennedy was killed by a madman in a Los Angeles hotel. Humphrey was the immediate political beneficiary of the Kennedy assassination. Many, perhaps most, of the delegates pledged to Kennedy would probably end up in his camp.[38] Kennedy's rank-and-file supporters in the party seemed to divide up rather evenly between the two surviving candidates—Humphrey's poll standings jumped 16 points to 56 percent after Kennedy's assassination in June; McCarthy now stood at 37 percent, an 18-point increase.[39] At the last moment, Senator George McGovern of South Dakota announced his candidacy in the hope that former Kennedy supporters might rally around him rather than drifting, dispiritedly, to Vice President Humphrey. But as the summer progressed toward late August and the Chicago convention, almost everyone agreed that the stop-Humphrey movement had failed.

38. See *New York Times* survey, June 10, 1968.
39. *Gallup Opinion Index,* July 1968, p. 5.

☆

*Chapter Five*

☆

# THE IMPACT OF THE PRIMARIES

PRESIDENTIAL PRIMARIES are preliminary elections in which the voters of a state select delegates to represent them at their national party convention, or express their preferences between the presidential candidates, or do both. Thus, directly or indirectly, party voters affect the votes of their state's convention delegates.

Recently presidential primaries have done much more than that. A primary can have a multiplier effect far beyond the borders of the state in which it takes place. The massive national publicity that the presidential primaries receive makes it possible for a little-known politician to become a national figure by a strong showing in a single state and go on to capture convention delegates in other states, whether they hold primaries or not. Similarly, a candidate's support across the entire nation can erode if his primary performance falls well below expectations. The solution of an essentially parochial question—who shall represent state $X$ at party $A$'s nominating convention—has been transformed into a test of strength between presidential contenders that can affect convention outcomes.

The states decide, on their own initiative, whether to hold presidential primaries or to select convention delegates in some other way. They also decide when the primary shall be held and how the contest will be organized. The result of this decentralized and uncoordinated control over presidential primaries is a bewildering variety and complexity in the rules of the primary game. And yet the primaries have in a quite unplanned way evolved into a national system with two critically important properties: these preliminary contests take place over a period of three to four months, and the later primaries have tended to be held in larger states than the earlier ones.

As a consequence, the significance of inequalities in resources between presidential contenders is reduced. The start-up costs of a primary campaign are not high. One or two early victories in states like New Hampshire and Wisconsin can generate enough publicity, and enough plausibility as a potential winner, to make the accumulation of the vast resources needed to contest later primaries in big states much easier. If the California primary came first and the New Hampshire primary last, an early long shot like George McGovern would have had much less chance of winning. The basic properties of the primary system enhance the chances of long-shot candidates for the presidency.

But there is a countervailing consequence of the serial nature of today's primary system: victories scored in the late primaries can make up for early defeats. This works to the advantage of candidates who enter the primary season in or near the lead. Marginal challengers who suffer early defeats rarely survive as viable candidates long enough to attempt a comeback. But early leaders who are defeated in one or more of the early primaries—like Dewey in 1948 and Stevenson in 1956—usually have a second chance. What Dewey lost in Wisconsin and Nebraska in 1948 he was able to recoup in Oregon; what Stevenson lost in Minnesota in 1956 he overcame in California.

The primary system thus both encourages competition for the opposition party's nomination and gives the leading contenders a second chance. But the primary system rarely changes the competitive situation within the party very much. In six of the last ten nominating battles (1936, 1944, 1956, 1960, 1968, 1972) there was a single front-running candidate for the opposition party's nomination as the primary season began, and five of these leaders before New Hampshire remained the leader at the end of the primaries. Muskie is the only clear front-runner since 1936 to have been destroyed by the primaries. The number, variety, and strength of the challengers to Muskie in 1972 were, of course, quite unusual.

While typically the party out of power has a single front-runner at the beginning of the primary season, this is not always the case.

What impact does the primary system have when there is no single "man to beat"?

Even though Dewey was the popular leader before the 1948 primaries began, it was not clear that his chances for the nomination were much better than those of Taft, who avoided primary competition. While Stassen nearly deprived Dewey of his main asset as the party's popular leader, the New Yorker was able to recoup his losses, leaving the situation after the primaries much as it had been before March.

The Republicans entered the 1952 primary season with two equally matched candidates—Robert A. Taft and Dwight D. Eisenhower—well ahead of other presidential possibilities. While the sources of these two men's strength were radically different, it was not possible to say that one man's prospects were notably better than the other's. At the end of a long series of primary skirmishes, the situation remained essentially the same; Taft and Eisenhower had pretty well split the primaries down the middle. While Eisenhower had gone ahead of Taft in the polls, the primaries had done very little to clarify who would be, or who ought to be, the party's nominee.

Even more confusing situations prevailed within the Republican party in 1940 and 1964. While Dewey led in the polls in 1940, he was not generally considered a front-runner in the usual sense of the term. In fact, few observers felt that any of the prominent Republican prospects would make a strong presidential candidate. Wendell Willkie emerged, seemingly out of nowhere, to fill this void. But Willkie won the nomination without entering a single primary. When no one emerges from the primary system as a plausible presidential nominee, such a publicity blitz can work as it did for Wendell Willkie in 1940. When Nelson Rockefeller attempted a similar campaign in 1968, bypassing the primaries in favor of a massive publicity campaign, he failed to shake Nixon's firm control of the party.

Finally, in 1964, the Republicans experienced one of the most bizarre nominating contests in recent American history. They began the primary season with several potential candidates of apparently comparable strength (or weakness); after the primaries the strategic situation was little clarified. There were still several candidates—

Goldwater, Nixon, Scranton, and Lodge—now within 2 percentage points of one another in the polls. But Goldwater had enough pledged delegates to make him unstoppable at the convention.

The record of the presidential primary system as it has operated in the opposition party since 1936 can thus be summed up as follows: When the party has a single front-runner, the primaries rarely change the situation. When the competitive situation within the party is more confused (1940, 1948, 1952, 1964), the primary system does little to facilitate the emergence of a single leader of the party.

The modesty of this impact of the presidential primaries on the competitive situation—especially when compared to the quite extravagant claims sometimes made on their behalf—should not lead to the hasty conclusion that they are exercises in futility. The primaries are more than a mechanism for clarifying the relative popularity of candidates; they are also one of several ways convention delegates are chosen. And these delegates, when assembled, make the official nominating decision.

## The Early Leader Wins the Nomination

In the five elections in which the initial leader in the primary went on to become the party's nominee, his active competition in the primaries was rather weak. Borah (in 1936), Kefauver (in 1956), and Humphrey (in 1960) were quite unlikely nominees, but they were the most active primary challengers of early leaders. In 1968 Nixon, the early leader, had no significant primary opposition at all. While Wendell Willkie was an internationally prominent figure when he challenged Dewey in 1944, he was weak enough within the Republican party by then that a single primary defeat destroyed his campaign.

### SURVIVAL BY INACTION: 1936

Before the first primaries Governor Alfred Landon of Kansas was the leading contender for the Republican presidential nomination. Continuing his earlier strategy, he refused to campaign personally in any of the primaries and sought, with nearly total success, to avoid even indirect involvement in them. His success in the primaries suggests that at that time the candidate in the lead before the primaries did not have to win; he merely needed to avoid losing.

The limited number and manifest weakness of Landon's challengers made Landon's strategy sensible. Only the maverick Senator William E. Borah of Idaho tried to use the 1936 primaries offensively, as a way of furthering his own candidacy. But Borah either had to seek out the opposition in their home states or run against nobody at all;[1] neither is a promising way to build a strong presidential candidacy.

In Illinois he was able to force a confrontation with Frank Knox. Borah lost—54 percent to 46 percent—but gained credit for "a fair-to-middling" moral victory.[2] He was even able to claim that though Knox, who was supported by the party leaders of his home state, carried Chicago, "I carried Illinois."[3]

Borah's victories in states where he faced no serious opposition did not significantly strengthen his candidacy, but his defeats were taken seriously. In South Dakota, an organization slate believed to be favorable to Landon narrowly defeated a slate of delegates pledged to Borah;[4] favorite-son Robert A. Taft defeated him 2 to 1 in Ohio; in New Jersey, Landon, whose name was entered without his consent, defeated the Idaho senator 4 to 1; and in Massachusetts's write-in primary, almost 80 percent of those who bothered to go to the polls voted for the "Kansas Coolidge." These losses virtually eliminated Borah as a presidential candidate.[5]

Up to the California primary, Landon had gained by avoiding the battle; this one posed a complex political situation from which he could not emerge unscathed. Earl Warren, state chairman of the Republican party, headed a slate of delegates that was quite friendly toward former President Herbert Hoover. But William Randolph Hearst, whose chain of newspapers and magazines had contributed

1. See *Time*, March 30, 1936, pp. 21 and 23, for a contemporary comment on Borah's lack of active opponents in the primaries.
2. Ibid., April 27, 1936, p. 15.
3. Ibid.
4. *Newsweek*, May 16, 1936, pp. 12–13.
5. *Time*, June 1, 1936, p. 13.

much to Landon's prominence, headed along with Governor Frank Merriam a slate of delegates pledged to Landon. The Kansas governor was eager not to offend Hoover's supporters, but he did not wish to alienate the powerful press lord either. Landon resolved the problem by doing nothing—he neither endorsed nor repudiated the Hearst-Merriam slate.

The Warren slate won the California primary by a 57–43 margin and this was viewed as something of a loss for Landon. But such a contest was hardly a clear test of anything. And the defeat of the Hearst slate had the advantage, from Landon's point of view, of weakening his association with the unpopular Hearst.[6] Even after this "loss," Landon emerged from the presidential primaries in the same position he had achieved before New Hampshire: as the clear front-running candidate for the Republican nomination.

### ELIMINATION OF AN UNLIKELY NOMINEE: 1944

Thomas E. Dewey was the Republican party's leading candidate for the 1944 presidential nomination both as the primaries began and after they ended. The primaries served to eliminate his most dangerous challenger and to strengthen Dewey's lead. Having promised to serve his entire four-year term as governor of New York, Dewey could not actively campaign for the presidency or openly declare his candidacy. The only serious threat to his primacy was Wendell Willkie. Robert Taft had withdrawn from contention to seek reelection to the Senate, throwing his support to Governor John Bricker of Ohio, whose campaign seemed aimed at his becoming second choice to the New York governor. General Douglas MacArthur (backed by Senator Vandenberg) and Harold Stassen were on active military duty and therefore precluded from becoming active or acknowledged candidates.

Willkie's only chance to overtake the New York governor was by demonstrating overwhelming popular support in the primaries. The old guard party leadership thoroughly distrusted and disliked the maverick from Indiana, who would need some awesome display

6. For contemporary interpretations of the California results, see *Newsweek*, May 16, 1936, pp. 12–13; and *Time*, May 18, 1936, p. 18, and April 6, 1936, pp. 20–21.

of vote-getting prowess to convince them to choose him as their nominee.

Willkie won the New Hampshire primary, but the 1944 New Hampshire primary law did not provide for a preference poll between presidential candidates, and this early victory did not give him the momentum he needed. He chose next to run in strongly isolationist Wisconsin, where his chances were poorest. It was a bold tactic, calculated to provide proof of his effectiveness and popularity; ordinarily, presidential aspirants avoid primaries where they are likely to lose.

Slates of delegates pledged to MacArthur (a Wisconsin native), Stassen (from the neighboring state of Minnesota), and Dewey were entered as well as the Willkie slate. Only Willkie campaigned in person—indeed, Governor Dewey sought to dissuade delegate candidates from running pledged to support him at the convention. The result was a smashing victory for Dewey, who won seventeen of the twenty-four delegates without acknowledging or campaigning for them, and a crushing defeat for Willkie, who won no delegates at all. Willkie, shortly thereafter, withdrew from the race for the presidency. His challenge to Dewey had failed.[7]

RECOVERY FROM AN UPSET: 1956

Adlai Stevenson had been defeated in the 1952 election by an "unbeatable" opponent. In 1956 he was the popular leader if not "the man to beat" at the beginning of the primary season. Early primary defeats suffered at the hands of Estes Kefauver, a challenger without much chance of winning the nomination himself, staggered and seriously threatened him. But Stevenson redoubled his efforts, adjusted his campaigning strategy and style, and went on to score victories in the late primaries and then to win the presidential nomination.

Senator Kefauver had been decisively rejected by the Democrats at their 1952 convention despite an impressive string of primary victories and a commanding lead in the public opinion polls. The party professionals, labor leaders, and big-city machine politicians who had

7. See Ellsworth Barnard, *Wendell Willkie: Fighter for Freedom* (Northern Michigan University Press, 1966), chap. 21.

vetoed him in 1952 remained adamantly opposed to his nomination four years later. And in the meantime, most of his once massive popular following had drifted away—at the beginning of the primary season, Stevenson led Kefauver 3 to 1 as the first choice of ordinary Democrats in the polls. Kefauver's only chance was a string of primary victories which would destroy Stevenson as a front-runner and lead to a runaway Kefauver boom in the country. Even if this should happen, the same people who destroyed his candidacy at the 1952 convention would almost certainly do so again.

The most likely beneficiary of any Kefauver success was Governor Averell Harriman of New York.[8] But Harriman, while an able and experienced public official, was an elderly and not very popular first-term governor with only one winning electoral campaign under his belt. Any other alternatives were even less plausible, for the prospect of facing Eisenhower in the general election made few Democrats eager to seek nomination.

Stevenson's optimal strategy in the primaries was clear: he needed to score a few primary victories in order to stay in the news, maintain his lead among the party leaders and rank and file, and rekindle the enthusiasm of his amateur followers. He should enter only safe contests, avoiding states where Kefauver was believed to be strong. The senator from Tennessee could not start the kind of boom he needed by winning uncontested primaries. As the front-runner facing limited competition, Stevenson had everything to lose and nothing to gain from more than minimum involvement in the primaries.

Thus Stevenson avoided having his name entered in New Hampshire's preferential primary. Kefauver, of course, won the preferential poll unopposed. But the New Hampshire preference poll permits write-ins, and the number of New Hampshire Democrats who took advantage of this opportunity to vote for Stevenson was disappointingly small (Nixon received more write-in votes for vice president in the Republican primary). Moreover, a prestigious unpledged slate of delegates that was liberally sprinkled with Stevenson supporters was badly defeated by the Kefauver slate. Kefauver had scored a victory,

8. See Joseph B. Gorman, *Kefauver: A Political Biography* (Oxford University Press, 1971), pp. 232 and 247–48.

but Stevenson had not been clearly beaten. After all, Kefauver had stumped the state exhaustively in 1952 and 1956. New Hampshire was Kefauver country.

Minnesota held its primary a week later. Stevenson had entered this contest since he enjoyed the warm backing of Senator Hubert Humphrey, Governor Orville Freeman, and the powerful Democratic Farmer-Labor party organization. In addition an early private poll showed him well ahead of Kefauver.[9] A big victory over Kefauver here—for the senator from Tennessee had entered the Minnesota primary and was campaigning hard—would not only erase the mild embarrassment of New Hampshire but might well stop the Kefauver campaign in its tracks before it gained momentum. Such was not to be: Kefauver scored a resounding upset victory over Stevenson, polling over 55 percent of the vote.[10]

Stevenson's defeat in Minnesota drastically altered the strategic situation within the Democratic party. Stevenson's standing in the Gallup poll of rank-and-file Democrats dropped from 51 percent to 39 percent; Kefauver's soared from 18 percent to 33 percent (see Figure 5-1). The press and politicians began speculating about compromise candidates. While still maintaining a narrow lead in the polls, Stevenson was no longer the clear front-runner. His renomination was in serious jeopardy.

Stevenson's response to all this was a sharp increase in personal campaigning and a noticeable shift in style. The "new Stevenson" was given less to polished speeches and more to meeting the people and handshaking in the Kefauver manner.[11] And Stevenson moved toward a more offensive use of the primaries by entering Oregon as a write-in candidate (the filing deadline had already passed). Kefauver accepted the challenge and made plans for an active write-in campaign in Oregon as well.[12]

9. A second private poll, however, showed that Kefauver was gaining fast. Charles A. H. Thomson and Frances Shattuck, *The 1956 Presidential Campaign* (Brookings Institution, 1960), p. 39.

10. See ibid., p. 39; and Gorman, *Kefauver*, pp. 228–30, for interpretations of Stevenson's defeat.

11. Thomson and Shattuck, *1956 Presidential Campaign*, pp. 42–45.

12. Ibid., pp. 50–57.

FIGURE 5-1. *Preferences of Democratic Rank and File for 1956*
*Presidential Candidates*

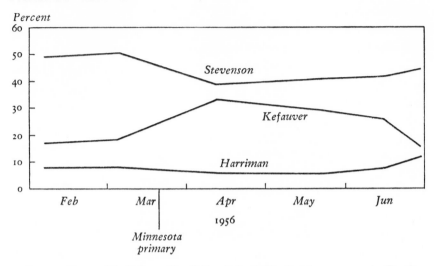

Source: George H. Gallup, *The Gallup Poll: Public Opinion 1935–1971* (Random House, 1972).

Before the Oregon primaries both candidates won several uncontested primaries, with Stevenson looking a little stronger than Kefauver.[13] But in Oregon the former governor won decisively, attracting more than 60 percent of the vote in a two-man race (Harriman, whose name was on the ballot, attracted less than 2,000 votes). Some of the press began referring to him as the Democrat's front-runner once again.[14]

Oregon turned the tide, and the Florida and California primaries destroyed Kefauver as a challenger. Stevenson won the Florida primary with 52 percent of the vote. In California, which had been counted as safe for Stevenson from the start, he decisively defeated Kefauver with over 60 percent of the vote. Stevenson was now

13. Kefauver won the Wisconsin, Maryland, and Indiana primaries, uncontested. He also won advisory primaries in Nebraska and New Jersey, but in both states a majority of the delegates chosen were anti-Kefauver. Stevenson won in Illinois and Pennsylvania, without challenge. A Stevenson slate of delegates defeated a Kefauver slate in the District of Columbia. The Alaska primary also resulted in a Stevenson victory over Kefauver. For details see ibid., pp. 48–50.

14. *Newsweek*, May 28, 1956, p. 25.

clearly back on top. Everyone, including Estes Kefauver, knew it;[15] two weeks before the convention was scheduled to meet, he withdrew.

## PROOF OF THE CANDIDATE'S STRENGTH: 1960

John F. Kennedy entered most of the Democratic primaries in 1960 and won them all. Numerous commentators have jumped from this demonstrable fact to the conclusion that he won the Democratic nomination because of this string of primary election victories. This overlooks the fact that Senator Kennedy entered the 1960 primary season as the leading Democratic candidate for the presidential nomination. In only the Wisconsin and West Virginia primaries was he opposed by a bona fide candidate for the presidency—Senator Humphrey, who was probably the weakest alternative to Kennedy of the Democrats' 1960 possibilities.

All of this is not to say that the primaries were insignificant, for John Kennedy faced two serious problems which his primary performance helped him to surmount. First, and foremost, was his Catholicism. He needed concrete evidence that the American electorate would not succumb, in the privacy of the polling booth, to religious bigotry. Public opinion polling data, no matter how favorable they were to Kennedy, were not enough to answer doubts on this score. His religion, and to a lesser degree his youth, placed an extra burden of proof on Kennedy; the primaries gave him an opportunity to provide that proof in a concrete and dramatic way. Kennedy's second problem was the unusually prominent and talented set of choices that the Democrats could fall back on if Kennedy should fail. Neither Adlai Stevenson, Stuart Symington, nor Lyndon Johnson was active in the primaries, but there was little doubt that each of them wanted the nomination and would make a creditable party standard bearer. Often the alternatives to early front-running candidates for presidential nominations are too little known, too unpopular, or of too little stature to be plausible candidates in November. "Go with me," the front-runner's argument becomes, "or agree on a compromise

15. See *Time*, June 18, 1956, p. 25.

candidate with no chance at all." This line of reasoning carried less weight than usual in 1960.

The stories of the Wisconsin and West Virginia primaries need no recounting.[16] Senator Kennedy was expected to win the Wisconsin primary and he did. But the margin of his victory over Hubert Humphrey—56 percent—was not as large as many expected, and his greatest support was concentrated in heavily Roman Catholic areas. In Wisconsin, Republicans can vote in the Democratic primary and vice versa; Kennedy was seen as benefiting not only from votes cast by Catholic Democrats, but from crossover votes by Republican Catholics as well. He won only six of the state's ten congressional districts; three of the four districts he lost were Protestant agricultural districts along the Minnesota border. Even though Kennedy won, he was not much better off than before: the primary had failed to refute the suspicion that his popularity was largely the result of his strength among fellow Catholics and that he had limited appeal among the Protestant majority of the country.[17]

While Kennedy was not helped by the Wisconsin outcome, Humphrey's always poor prospects were significantly damaged. A presidential aspirant with a 7 percent poll rating can ill afford to lose a primary in a neighboring state very similar to his own. Yet the primaries were Humphrey's only chance in 1960. He had narrowed Kennedy's initial Wisconsin lead through indefatigable campaigning, and West Virginia was a new and quite different contest. He continued in the race.

The West Virginia primary became significant in 1960 for basically one reason: only about 5 percent of the state's population was Roman Catholic. A Kennedy victory over a Protestant opponent in such an overwhelmingly Protestant state should demonstrate, once and for all, that religious prejudice in America was not what it had

16. They are well told in Theodore H. White, *The Making of the President, 1960* (Atheneum, 1961), chap. 4; Theodore C. Sorensen, *Kennedy* (Harper and Row, 1965), pt. 2, chap. 5; and Arthur M. Schlesinger, Jr., *A Thousand Days* (Houghton Mifflin, 1965), chap. 1.

17. For interpretations of the Wisconsin primary, see *U.S. News and World Report*, April 18, 1960, pp. 44–45; *Newsweek*, April 18, 1960, pp. 31–32; and *New York Times*, April 7, 1960, especially James Reston's column.

been in 1928. A Humphrey victory over Kennedy, on the other hand, would do nothing for Humphrey. If the senator from Minnesota won, it would be interpreted as a verdict against the Catholic Kennedy. Symington, Stevenson, and Johnson would be the big gainers, not Humphrey.[18]

After a long and expensive campaign, Kennedy won decisively in West Virginia. He had brought the religious issue out in the open, confronted it squarely, and collected 60 percent of the vote. He had demonstrated his ability to persuade Protestant voters to mark their secret ballots for him rather than a Protestant opponent. Kennedy emerged from West Virginia far stronger than he was before; the religious issue lost much of its significance thereafter.[19] Humphrey, deserted by his financial supporters, was forced to withdraw.

CONFIRMATION OF THE STATUS QUO: 1968

Like Kennedy in 1960, Richard Nixon in 1968 began the primaries as his party's front-runner, eager to prove that he was not a loser. At the last minute, after George Romney's abrupt withdrawal from the presidential race, there was no avowed opposition candidate to contest Nixon and the filing deadlines for many primaries had passed. Only Governor Rockefeller and Governor Reagan had enough prominence to consider a challenge starting at such a late date.

The collapse of George Romney's bid for the presidency placed Nelson Rockefeller in a particularly awkward position. The already strong pressures on Rockefeller to become a candidate—Governor Spiro Agnew of Maryland had organized a draft-Rockefeller campaign; self-starting groups in New Hampshire had begun to organize a write-in campaign; supporters in Oregon were laying the groundwork for a Rockefeller primary campaign there—were redoubled. Every Rockefeller press conference became a verbal sparring match with reporters, as he moved toward active candidacy. On March 21, however, he made the surprising announcement that he would not be

18. White, *Making of the President, 1960*, pp. 113–16, discusses the irony of this situation.

19. *New York Times*, May 12, 1960; *U.S. News*, May 23, 1960, p. 63; and *Time*, May 23, 1960, pp. 14–15.

an active candidate for the presidency in 1968. He would accept a draft, but he did not expect it and would do nothing "by word or by deed, to encourage such a call."[20] The press was quick to point out that his announcement was made the day before the deadline for withdrawal from the Oregon primary. Without such a statement he automatically would have been entered in Oregon (where he probably would have run well) and Nebraska (where a sound drubbing seemed inevitable). Since a race against Reagan in California was out of the question, the most that Rockefeller could hope for from running in the late primaries was an inconclusive stand-off.

Shortly after Rockefeller's withdrawal statement, President Lyndon Johnson shocked the political world by renouncing interest in another term in the White House. The character of the fall's presidential election had, quite unexpectedly, been drastically altered. The new unpredictability of the Democratic contest created uncertainty on the Republican side, too, uncertainties that were compounded by the polls showing Governor George Wallace's third-party bid building unexpected strength. And then, on April 4, the Reverend Martin Luther King, Jr., was assassinated and the nation's black ghettos erupted in a frightening outburst of destructive hatred and despair.

Forty days after Nelson Rockefeller's withdrawal statement, he reversed himself and announced his active candidacy, principally because he was "deeply disturbed" by the course of recent events and because of the "gravity of the crisis" confronting the United States.[21]

The late-starting Rockefeller campaign aimed squarely at Nixon's vulnerable point—the doubt about his ability to win the election in November. It took the form of an advertising blitz of the country calculated to cause such favorable comparisons against the possible Democratic candidates that convention delegates would be convinced they should back Rockefeller whether they liked him or not. This strategy, of course, assumed that the convention delegates wanted to win in November.[22] It further assumed that Rockefeller's

20. *New York Times,* March 22, 1968.
21. Ibid., May 1, 1968.
22. James P. Zais and John H. Kessel, "A Theory of Presidential Nominations, with a 1968 Illustration," in Donald R. Matthews, ed., *Perspectives on Presidential*

poll standings could be quickly and significantly improved through an expensive, hard-hitting mass media campaign.

The Rockefeller experiment in public relations politics failed to produce convincing results. In May, June, and early July, both the Gallup and Harris polls showed Rockefeller running a percentage point or two more strongly in a three-way presidential race than Nixon. But Gallup's final preconvention poll showed Nixon besting either Humphrey or McCarthy. The Harris poll, published a day later, showed Rockefeller the probable winner of the general election, with Nixon running behind the presumptive Democratic opponents. The differences were politically irrelevant:[23] Nelson Rockefeller had failed to prove his case beyond a reasonable doubt.

Unlike Nelson Rockefeller, Ronald Reagan persisted in his non-candidacy after George Romney's withdrawal and the disorienting rush of events. The governor moved about the country addressing Republican gatherings. Clifton White, a central figure in the Goldwater campaign of 1964, was hired as an adviser to the California delegation and proceeded to try to line up delegates for Reagan in other states. Reagan for President clubs were organized along with write-in campaigns in several states with primary elections. Reagan allowed his name to stay on the Wisconsin, Oregon, and Nebraska primary ballots, though he did not make any personal appearances to further his candidacy.[24] In Wisconsin, Nixon won with 80 percent of the vote, while Reagan got a little over 10 percent. In Nebraska, where the Reagan forces campaigned harder—and claimed, after the results were in, that their man was building momentum—Nixon won 70.5 percent of the vote, Reagan 22 percent, and Rockefeller 5 percent (write-ins). The Oregon primary proved to be the closest thing

---

*Selection* (Brookings Institution, 1973), pp. 128–29, present data suggesting that the candidates' relative chances of winning the presidential election did not loom large in the minds of most Republican delegates in 1968.

23. In a joint Gallup-Harris press conference, the pollsters explained that the Harris figures were based on interviews taken several days after Gallup's and that Rockefeller's greater strength in the large, metropolitan states probably made him a more likely electoral winner than Nixon. *New York Times*, Aug. 2, 1968.

24. The Reagan campaign is described in Lewis Chester, Godfrey Hodgson, and Bruce Page, *An American Melodrama: The Presidential Campaign of 1968* (Dell, 1969), pp. 209–22.

to a critical Republican primary in 1968—a two-man race between Nixon and Reagan. "Short of making Reagan an open candidate, everything that could be done was done,"[25] but Nixon still won easily with 73 percent of the Republican vote. Reagan's showing, at 23 percent, was well below expectations.

The net result of the primaries, then, was not large. Reagan's reputation as a vote-getter was blemished, but then he had not campaigned in person and was not an avowed candidate. Nixon had won by a large margin all the primaries in which he was entered, but the absence of strong opposition substantially reduced the significance of his victories. The former vice president's greatest problem at the end of the primaries remained the same as it was before New Hampshire —doubt about his ability to win the election in November. Rockefeller's failure to leap ahead in the polls meant that Nixon, by far the most popular of the three possibilities among rank-and-file Republicans and party leaders, was the heavy favorite for nomination when the convention opened.[26]

## Two Strong Contenders: 1948, 1952

Governor Dewey entered the 1948 Republican primaries leading the polls of the party rank and file with 33 percent. Five months later he emerged from these contests in the same position. In between he was almost destroyed. While the 1948 primaries did not change the competitive situation in the end, they did furnish much drama and excitement and a few new lessons on presidential nominating politics.

Dewey's foremost problem in the 1948 campaign was the fact that the Republicans had never renominated a defeated candidate for president. Moreover, Robert A. Taft, now leader of the Republican opposition to Truman in Congress, and still the favorite of the party professionals, was back in the running. Truman's apparent weakness

25. Ibid., p. 229.
26. The March Gallup poll standings were Nixon 60 percent, Rockefeller 25 percent, Reagan 6 percent. The final Gallup poll, conducted shortly before the Miami Beach convention in August, remained essentially unchanged, with Nixon 60 percent, Rockefeller 23 percent, Reagan 7 percent. *Gallup Opinion Index* (Princeton, N.J.), August 1968, p. 4.

as the Democrats' probable nominee strengthened Taft's claim to the Republican nomination: while the senator from Ohio was not one of the party's better vote-getters, it looked as if almost anyone could beat the unpopular President. Taft's presidential hopes did not, therefore, depend on a strong primary showing; he entered primaries only in his home state, and in Nebraska (where all candidates were entered, whether they wanted to be or not). His chances for the nomination seemed almost as good as Dewey's. Other strong contenders were the perennial but inactive Senator Vandenberg, General Douglas MacArthur, and the youthful maverick Harold Stassen.

The New Hampshire primary—never taken very seriously until a preferential poll was added for 1952—resulted in a modest win for Dewey. Six of New Hampshire's eight delegates favored the New Yorker.

The first important primary would be held in Wisconsin. Harold Stassen was conducting a very aggressive personal campaign there and a serious drive on behalf of General MacArthur was under way, headed by such local luminaries as former Governor Phillip La Follette. The general was expected to attract many favorite-son votes, and a MacArthur victory in Wisconsin might well lead to an explosive growth in his national popularity. Dewey belatedly decided that he had to campaign personally in Wisconsin.

The result was a whopping victory for Harold Stassen, who won nineteen delegates to eight for MacArthur and none for Dewey. The Wisconsin delegates, of course, were less important than the effects of the victory on the expectations and preferences of party members nationwide. Stassen's poll standings—not very impressive before Wisconsin—began to climb (see Figure 5-2). The press and party politicians had to consider him a serious candidate from then on. MacArthur, despite his charisma, had suffered a crippling blow at the hands of this lightweight candidate in his own backyard. And the Dewey push for the presidency could not withstand many more Wisconsins.

The free-for-all Nebraska primary followed. Dewey campaigned longer and harder than in Wisconsin, but he was still unable to catch up to Stassen, who won the preference poll with 43 percent of the

FIGURE 5-2. *Preferences of Republican Rank and File for 1948 Presidential Candidates*

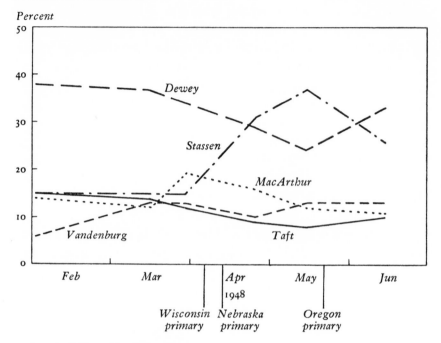

Source: Gallup, *The Gallup Poll.*

vote to Dewey's 35 percent and Taft's 10 percent. Stassen's stock continued to soar. After the Nebraska primary, Dewey dropped behind Stassen in the Gallup poll for the first time. A write-in victory in Pennsylvania added further to Stassen's momentum. Professional politicians in the party—who persisted in believing that they could win with anybody and therefore were reluctant to choose a relative newcomer like Stassen whom they did not entirely trust—began talking about dark-horse candidates. If Stassen destroyed Dewey's bid for a second chance at the White House, Taft would be the most likely beneficiary. But failing that, perhaps Arthur Vandenberg was the man. Or maybe even House Speaker Joe Martin.

The increasingly confident Stassen, perhaps in order to head off such a development, next embarked on a daring and unorthodox maneuver—a challenge to Taft in the senator's home state of Ohio.

Ohio's primary law, one of the most complex in the nation, ordinarily discourages out-of-state contestants, especially when the state has a candidate for president. But Stassen supporters succeeded in qualifying pro-Stassen candidates for twenty-three of the state's fifty-three delegate seats. The Minnesotan, predicting that he would win at least half these contests, stumped the big and diverse midwestern state on behalf of his delegates. The confident Taft, extraordinarily popular among Ohio Republicans and backed by the party organization, claimed that the entire delegation would be his. In the end, Taft won forty-four delegates and Stassen nine, each falling short of his proclaimed goal. Both claimed victory. Both lost.[27]

The Oregon primary, the final major test of the primary campaign, was crucial for both Stassen and Dewey. The one-time boy wonder of Minnesota politics had lost some momentum as a result of his abortive Ohio adventure. He had to keep on winning primaries and expanding his lead in the polls or the party professionals would turn to a more comfortable candidate at the convention. Fortunately for him, Oregon was not a state addicted to political orthodoxy. Stassen had invested much time and energy in his Oregon campaign. He was thought to be far ahead.

Governor Dewey, having lost two primaries and his poll lead to Stassen, was in trouble. While trusted more than Stassen by party leaders, he could not count on their goodwill alone to win the nomination. Taft seemed to be the first choice of the regulars. The only thing that gave Dewey an edge over the Ohio senator was his presumed greater popularity and ability as a campaigner. These claims on the nomination were now in serious jeopardy.

Knowing that he was behind, Dewey campaigned strenuously in Oregon, adopting a more aggressive and folksy campaigning style. The press now reported that Dewey was gaining. The capstone of the Dewey surge was a public debate, held on Stassen's initiative, on the question of whether or not to outlaw the Communist party. Stassen espoused the view that it should be outlawed. Dewey opposed the idea, making for one of the few clear-cut policy differences be-

27. See James Reston's comment, quoted in James T. Patterson, *Mr. Republican: A Biography of Robert A. Taft* (Houghton Mifflin, 1972), p. 407.

tween the two. In the debate Dewey seemed to get the better of the argument; Stassen was clearly on the defensive.

On election day, Dewey won by a narrow margin, 52 percent of the vote. While hardly an overwhelming victory, it was enough to demonstrate that Dewey could come from behind and win when he had to. The Stassen bandwagon, which had begun to slow down before the Oregon vote, had been stopped. His challenge to Dewey had failed.

Thus as the Republican convention began, the strategic situation was about the same as it was before the New Hampshire primary. Dewey's credentials as the party's strongest candidate, while tarnished, were still intact. In the wake of the Oregon primary, he had gotten back on top in the Gallup polls. Taft remained a strong possibility, despite having won only the Ohio primary and even that in an embarrassing way. The party was well endowed with compromise choices: Vandenberg, Martin, and Governor Earl Warren. Perhaps the most unlikely nominee of all was Harold Stassen, despite his superior campaign, primary victories, and strong poll standings. In 1948, one narrow, late defeat outweighed a string of early primary victories. Winning the primaries is more a matter of psychology and timing than arithmetic.

As the 1952 primary period began, General Eisenhower and Senator Taft had roughly equal chances for the Republican nomination. The general, while remaining on active duty in Paris, had acknowledged his availability for the nomination. His extraordinary popularity among independents and Democrats made him appear to be a nearly unbeatable candidate in November. But first he would have to win the Republican nomination, and here the prospects were cloudy. Senator Taft, for the first time in his career, had recently attracted a massive popular following among Republicans. Indeed, in the last poll of Republicans before the primaries began, Taft had edged the general by a single percentage point. Backed by a large, well-financed, and experienced organization, the senator from Ohio was committed to extensive personal campaigning in the primaries while Eisenhower would have to be represented by stand-ins. As in his earlier campaigns for the presidency, Taft would be greatly helped by his popularity among Republican party and public officials. Eisenhower's smaller band of experienced Republican politicians would benefit from the enthusiasm and energy of large numbers of political amateurs, who were beginning to organize themselves in the states.

Eisenhower got off to a good start in New Hampshire, where he had been expected to win. In fact, a narrow victory would have been quite damaging to his alleged superiority to Taft as a vote-getter. But his comfortable margin over Taft—50 percent to 39 percent—was interpreted as a victory.[28]

The general received an even bigger boost in Minnesota, which he lost to favorite-son Harold Stassen later in March. Eisenhower's name had been kept off the ballot by a technicality, but five days before the primary vote, Minnesota's attorney general ruled that write-in votes would be counted. After a five-day campaign, run by amateurs and costing an estimated $600, Eisenhower received more than 100,000 of some 300,000 votes cast. Indeed he came within 22,000 votes of beating Stassen. *Newsweek* called this outcome "the miracle of Minnesota" and proclaimed, after only modest hedging, that a "potentially runaway Eisenhower boom is on." *Time*, not to be outdone, announced that the New Hampshire and Minnesota primaries together were "a striking and momentous demonstration that an Eisenhower boom of tremendous proportions is sweeping across the land." Even the *New York Times* called the Minnesota results "fantastic," "astounding," "historic," "miraculous."[29] In retrospect it is clear that all these interpretations were overdrawn. The Eisenhower vote in Minnesota was certainly remarkable, given his absence and the limited campaign waged on his behalf. But Minnesota is not the United States. Eisenhower's national poll standings merely edged upwards after the first two primaries; they did not soar (see Figure 5-3). And by 1952, Harold Stassen's runs for the presidency were beginning to appear a little silly, even in Minnesota.

In the next two primaries, Senator Taft showed that he too could

28. *Time*, March 10, 1952, p. 23, and March 24, 1952, pp. 19–20.

29. *Newsweek*, March 31, 1952, pp. 19–20; *Time*, March 31, 1952, pp. 19–20; and *New York Times*, March 20, 1952.

FIGURE 5-3. *Preferences of Republican Rank and File for 1952 Presidential Candidates*

*Percent*

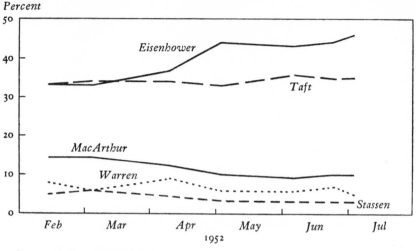

Source: Gallup, *The Gallup Poll*.

overwhelm Stassen, and even best Eisenhower when running in the Midwest. In Wisconsin the Ohio senator campaigned tirelessly against Stassen and Earl Warren—Eisenhower was not on the ballot. Taft won decisively.[30] In Nebraska, neither Eisenhower nor Taft was on the ballot and neither campaigned personally, though write-in campaigns were waged for both. Taft won 79,000 votes to Eisenhower's 66,000. "The GOP Presidential race is thus what it always has been," *Newsweek* retreated by saying afterwards "—a close contest between two evenly matched opponents."[31]

The Illinois primary was Taft all the way. The Ohio senator received over 900,000 of the 1.2 million votes cast. Stassen ran a poor second. Yet almost 150,000 Illinois Republicans went to the considerable trouble of writing in Eisenhower's name.

The New Jersey primary was only the second contest in which both Eisenhower and Taft were on the ballot. After the general's Minnesota victory, Senator Taft had tried to have his name removed from the New Jersey ballot, claiming a double cross when previously

30. For contemporary interpretation, see *Newsweek*, April 14, 1952, p. 27.
31. Ibid., April 14, 1952, pp. 27–28. See also *Time*, April 14, 1952, p. 23.

neutral Governor Driscoll declared for Eisenhower.[32] But these efforts were unsuccessful and Taft went down to defeat, attracting only 36 percent of the votes in an essentially two-man race.

The Pennsylvania nonbinding preference poll was a mirror-image of the Illinois primary: Eisenhower, whose name was on the ballot, won by a large margin but Taft attracted a surprising number of write-ins. The contest received rather little press attention and was not thought to be very significant. The Massachusetts primary was to be a fairer test. The state party was neutral and write-in campaigns were waged on behalf of both candidates. Eisenhower won by a better than 2 to 1 margin, sweeping twenty-seven of the twenty-nine district delegate contests decided at the same time.

A series of primaries then followed in which the two leaders did not meet. Taft bested Stassen by more than 3 to 1 in the senator's home state of Ohio, and by a comparable margin in West Virginia. Eisenhower won an overwhelming victory over Warren and several others in Oregon.

One final primary remained—South Dakota's. Both Eisenhower and Taft were on the ballot and the contest was expected to be close. It was—Taft won by less than 1,000 votes, but the nearly inconclusive result was forced onto the back pages by bigger news, Eisenhower's arrival in the United States to campaign for himself. When asked if he considered the South Dakota outcome a moral victory, the general replied: "I don't understand moral victories. When you go to war, it's win or lose."

Who won and who lost the 1952 Republican primaries? It is clear enough who the losers were: Stassen and Warren. Each had carried his home state, and lost everywhere else. Even Stassen's Minnesota victory was interpreted as a loss because of Eisenhower's remarkable write-ins.

But the long string of primaries had failed to have a decisive impact on either the Taft or the Eisenhower candidacy. At the end, as at the beginning, they were almost even. Nor did the pattern of primary returns provide any new information on the sources of strength of the two leaders. Taft was strongest in the Midwest, Eisenhower in

32. *Time*, April 28, 1952, p. 23.

the East. Eisenhower had shown a more geographically dispersed popularity than Taft, but he was expected to.

Finally, the public opinion polls, which sometimes gyrate wildly in response to primary victories and defeats, showed rather little change during the 1952 primaries. Taft began with a 34 percent rating and ended at 35 percent—his standings fluctuated within a range of 3 percentage points from March through June (see Figure 5-3). Eisenhower did gain 11 percentage points during the primaries, becoming the Republican rank and file's clear first choice after the New Hampshire and Minnesota contests. There is no way of knowing, of course, whether his gradual gain among ordinary Republicans resulted from the primaries or not. But certainly they did not hurt him. The Republican party emerged from the 1952 primaries in just about the same shape it was in before New Hampshire—with two strong, very closely matched contenders for the nomination. The convention itself would have to decide between them.

## No Clear Leader: *1940, 1964*

The Republican primaries of 1940 and 1964 began and ended with a group of comparably weak contenders for their party's nomination. Though Wendell Willkie arrived at the 1940 convention a formidable contestant, the primaries themselves did not make him so; indeed, the question of who would be nominated was as uncertain at the end of the primaries as it had been at the beginning. The 1964 primaries, equally indecisive in exposing a popular candidate, differed in one way: Barry Goldwater emerged from them with the committed votes of a large number of convention delegates.

In early 1940, although Thomas E. Dewey possessed an overwhelming lead in the polls of rank-and-file Republicans, most Republican party leaders and the national press were still not impressed. Dewey's popularity grew out of accomplishments that seemed less and less relevant as Norway, the low countries, and France successively fell to the Nazis. In such troubled times a thirty-eight-year-old district attorney without experience in high-level elective office or foreign affairs does not inspire much confidence. The party's most prestigious and experienced spokesman on foreign affairs, Senator Arthur Vandenberg, was not anxious enough to be president to campaign actively for the nomination. Senator Robert A. Taft of Ohio was eager but had served less than two years in the Senate. His popular following was limited, but his widespread popularity among Republican party leaders and professional politicians was enough to cause most neutral observers to rate a Dewey-Taft contest a toss-up. The disastrous electoral defeats of the 1930s had left the Republican party with a trio of leading presidential contenders who were either too young, too inexperienced, or too uninterested to have been considered very serious possibilities under more normal circumstances.

Dewey entered several primaries and won them all. The first and most important of these was in Wisconsin, where he faced Senator Vandenberg. Dewey campaigned hard, while Vandenberg remained in Washington relying on his prestige and the support of the party organization to bring him victory. Dewey surprised almost everyone by sweeping all twenty-four of the state's delegates. *Time* noted, perhaps prematurely, that Vandenberg's candidacy was "dead as a doornail."[33] Dewey and Vandenberg met again shortly thereafter in Nebraska. Again Vandenberg refused to campaign actively, and again Dewey won decisively. The New York prosecutor entered primaries in Illinois, Maryland, New Jersey, and Pennsylvania and won them unopposed. Maryland's was of most significance. Senator Taft, who had indicated that he would enter any primary within commuting distance of Washington, suddenly became much too busy on Capitol Hill even to campaign nearby. This retreat was interpreted as an admission of weakness.[34]

Thomas Dewey did everything he could during the 1940 primaries to increase his plausibility as a presidential candidate. His poll standings did improve after he officially declared his candidacy and again after he won the early primaries (see Figure 5-4). But given the absence of active opponents, the primary campaign received less and

33. Ibid., April 15, 1940, pp. 18–19. See also ibid., April 1, 1940, p. 18; and *Newsweek*, April 15, 1940, pp. 15–16.

34. *Newsweek*, April 29, 1940, pp. 31–32. See also Patterson, *Mr. Republican*, chap. 14.

FIGURE 5-4. *Preferences of Republican Rank and File for 1940 Presidential Candidates*

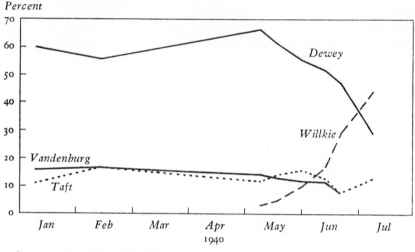

Source: Gallup, *The Gallup Poll.*

less attention from the press and the American people. World War II had finally begun in earnest and Wendell Willkie had launched a last-minute campaign for the Republican presidential nomination. These two developments soon overshadowed the primaries and rendered them nearly meaningless.

Wendell Willkie was one of the most colorful and personally appealing candidates for the American presidency in modern times. Rough-hewn, tousled, and warm, he evinced in appearance and manner his small town Indiana origins rather than his success as a Wall Street lawyer and public utilities executive. He was brash and self-confident, yet open and approachable. A dynamic and effective public speaker, he made Dewey, Taft, and Vandenberg—to say nothing of the lesser lights in the Republican party—seem cold and bland by comparison.[35]

Willkie's candidacy stimulated a new and previously inactive group of political amateurs to become involved in the Republican

35. See Donald B. Johnson, *The Republican Party and Wendell Willkie* (University of Illinois Press, 1960); Joseph Barnes, *Willkie* (Simon and Schuster, 1952); and Barnard, *Wendell Willkie.*

nominating politics of 1940. A twenty-nine-year-old lawyer who had never met Willkie, Oren Root, was so impressed by Willkie's speeches and writings that he sent out petitions to his friends and associates in order to measure their feelings about him as a candidate. He received such an overwhelmingly favorable response that he took a leave of absence from his law firm and began to create Willkie clubs nationwide. Within a matter of weeks, an untold number of amateur organizations were started, large sums of money raised, and more than three million signatures collected on petitions urging the Republican party to nominate Willkie.[36] Organizations of amateur candidate enthusiasts were to play an increasing role in presidential nominating politics thereafter—but the Willkie clubs were the first to harness the energy and drive of inexperienced enthusiasts and to convert them into a significant political resource.

The Willkie campaign did not rely on a relatively spontaneous swelling of grass-roots support alone. The movement—for it was as much that as a political campaign—was led by talented and highly experienced experts in the communications industry and public relations. The men who flocked to the Willkie banner and shaped his campaign were amateurs in party politics but professionals in public relations. The Willkie movement was a classic, highly professional public relations campaign.[37]

The Gallup poll first listed Wendell Willkie among the Republican presidential candidates on May 8. Willkie was the first choice of just 3 percent of the rank-and-file Republicans interviewed. Two months later, in Gallup's final poll, taken during the convention (but published subsequently), he was favored by 44 percent of all Republicans.[38] His closest competitor, Dewey, had fallen from 67 percent to 29 percent during the same period (see Figure 5-4). Without entering a single primary, a recently converted Democrat who had never held public office became the Republicans' most popular candidate

36. Johnson, *Republican Party and Willkie*, pp. 63–64; Barnes, *Willkie*, pp. 165–66; and Oren Root, *Persons and Persuasions* (Norton, 1974).

37. See Johnson, *Republican Party and Willkie*, pp. 64–68; and Barnes, *Willkie*, pp. 162–64, and the sources cited therein.

38. George H. Gallup, *The Gallup Poll: Public Opinion 1935–1971* (Random House, 1972), vol. 1, pp. 222 and 231.

for the 1940 presidential nomination in the short span of sixty days. His subsequent nomination is sometimes described as "the miracle at Philadelphia,"[39] but the miracle took place before the convention met.

The meteoric rise of Wendell Willkie, the darkest dark-horse candidate to win the presidential nomination in modern times, seems to have resulted from four factors, each essential to his success. First, and probably most important, was the dearth of experienced and prominent alternative candidates. If the Republicans had had a clear and qualified front-runner—like Landon in 1936 or Dewey in 1944—it would have been unlikely that Willkie's last-minute blitz would have succeeded. The Democratic sweeps of the 1930s, by destroying most established Republican leaders, contributed mightily to the Willkie miracle. Second, the ominous war in Western Europe made the youthful and inexperienced Dewey and the inexperienced and isolationist Taft seem even less plausible choices for the presidency than they already were. Only Vandenberg had the stature and expertise appropriate for the times. Defeated in two primaries and unwilling to campaign, he was rather easily brushed aside. Third, there were the qualifications and attractiveness of Willkie himself. Finally, without an extensive, costly, and professional public relations campaign, Willkie would probably have remained an obscure, barefoot boy from Wall Street.

Another kind of well-planned campaign attack was the key to success in 1964. The primary contest itself was confused from start to finish. All three of the party's most obvious presidential possibilities had seriously damaged their own prospects during the interelection years—Nixon by his reaction to his defeat in 1962 and his subsequent move to New York; Rockefeller by his remarriage; and Goldwater by his extreme positions. While Goldwater remained the overwhelming choice of the party workers—twice as many GOP county chairmen preferred him as preferred his nearest opponent in Gallup's March 1964 poll—his blunt right-wing rhetoric was proving less effective on the hustings than at Republican fund-raising affairs

39. Eugene H. Roseboom, *A History of Presidential Elections* (Macmillan, 1970), p. 460.

where the same words had evoked enthusiastic applause for years. As 1964 began, the competitive situation within the Republican party was murky. The primaries did little to clarify the situation.

For the New Hampshire primary, both Rockefeller and Goldwater were on the ballot and both waged exhaustive campaigns. Rockefeller could make little headway against the *Manchester Union Leader*'s attacks on him as a "wife swapper."[40] The senator from Arizona, meanwhile, alienated many New Hampshirites and made national headlines with casual remarks about making social security voluntary and unleashing attacks on Cuba.[41]

Two write-in campaigns were also waged. One was a lackluster effort on behalf of Richard Nixon, whose stepped-up travel schedule seemed to signal that he might become a candidate again.[42] But Nixon took no active part in the New Hampshire primary.

The write-in campaign on behalf of Ambassador Henry Cabot Lodge, on the other hand, was both more effective and more closely associated with the absent candidate. The campaign was organized by volunteers from neighboring Massachusetts, where they had been active in Lodge's son's unsuccessful campaign for the U.S. Senate. And while Lodge remained aloof in Saigon, he reportedly refused Governor Rockefeller's specific request that he withdraw.[43]

On March 10 the New Hampshire voters gave the absent Lodge a resounding victory with 35 percent of the vote to 22 percent for Goldwater, 21 percent for Rockefeller, and 17 percent for Nixon. Moreover, Lodge's entire slate of fourteen delegates was elected. The effect of this primary on the overall campaign was further to damage the prestige of Goldwater, Rockefeller, and Nixon (especially the first two, because they had campaigned actively), and to add one more candidate, Lodge, to the list of possible nominees. The Gallup poll published April 5 showed a striking leap in Lodge's nationwide popularity, from 16 percent in March to 42 percent. The former vice president had dropped to second place with 26 percent (see Figure

40. Robert D. Novak, *The Agony of the G.O.P. 1964* (Macmillan, 1965), p. 319.
41. See Harold Faber, ed., *The Road to the White House* (McGraw-Hill, 1965), chap. 3.
42. See, for example, *New York Times*, Feb. 5, 1964.
43. Ibid., Feb. 25 and 27, 1964.

FIGURE 5-5. *Preferences of Republican Rank and File for 1964 Presidential Candidates*

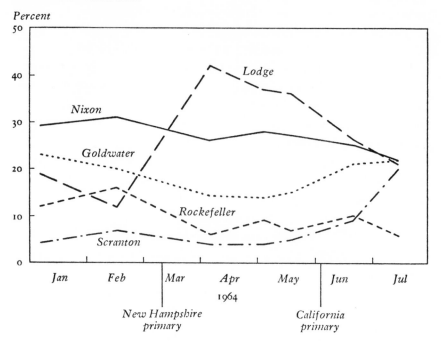

Source: Gallup, *The Gallup Poll.*

5-5), while the two declared candidates dropped to 14 percent (Goldwater) and 6 percent (Rockefeller).

While Lodge kept this poll lead throughout most of the primary season, he did nothing to exploit it. He remained silently in Saigon throughout the entire nominating period, never expressing interest in the nomination, let alone declaring his candidacy. Perhaps this was a sensible strategy. His imposing standing in the polls was less the result of positive appeal than of dislike of Goldwater and Rockefeller, the shopworn appearance of Richard Nixon, and the lack of any other well-known candidates.[44] Lodge at a distance was probably more popular with rank-and-file Republicans than he ever could be up close. And certainly the New Englander had no hope of eating into Goldwater's following among party workers—personal antipathy

44. Ibid., April 12, 1964.

to Lodge was almost an occupational disease among Republican workers, especially west of the Appalachians.[45] Yet the ambassador's aloof posture only compounded the uncertainty and ambiguity of the primaries.

The primaries between New Hampshire and Oregon on May 15th yielded inconclusive results. The Wisconsin primary was won unopposed by favorite-son John W. Byrnes. In Illinois Goldwater defeated Senator Margaret Chase Smith, but the fact that the lady from Maine received 25 percent of the vote and that another 13 percent went to the trouble of writing in other preferences made the victory pretty hollow. In Pennsylvania favorite-son Governor William Scranton, who was to become a candidate after the primaries, picked up a disappointing 58 percent of the write-in votes in the preference poll, to 21 percent for Lodge. In Texas the Goldwater-dominated state party held an advisory preference poll with only announced candidates' names listed on the ballot. Goldwater overwhelmed Rockefeller (74 percent to 5 percent), but with a lower total than expected due to a substantial write-in vote for Lodge (9 percent), Nixon (4 percent), and others. Ohio's Governor Rhodes won his state's delegation unopposed. In Indiana Goldwater was expected to win handsomely over Harold Stassen and two unknowns—he won, but with only 67 percent of the vote. Running in Nebraska unopposed, he managed only 49 percent of the vote, while an effective write-in campaign conducted on behalf of Nixon corralled 31 percent. Lodge got 16 percent with little effort. In West Virginia on the same day, Rockefeller won the preference vote unopposed. As the primary season wore on, it became increasingly apparent that none of the candidates was doing consistently well.

The Oregon primary offered the voters, for the first time, a choice between all the leading contenders—only Governor Romney was willing to sign the pledge of noncandidacy required to remove his name from the ballot. Rockefeller waged his usual strenuous cam-

45. Lodge's prominent role in the bruising Eisenhower-Taft battle of 1952, his languid vice presidential campaign in 1960, and his service as ambassador to South Vietnam under two Democratic presidents seem to have been the main reasons for his unpopularity among party regulars.

paign, and substantial efforts were made on behalf of the absent
Lodge and Nixon. Senator Goldwater's campaign was limited, perhaps because the early polls showed Lodge so far ahead that it seemed
unlikely that anyone could catch him.[46] Rockefeller, campaigning as
the candidate who "cared enough to come," won 33 percent of the
vote to Lodge's 27 percent. Goldwater ran a distant third (17 percent), edging out Richard Nixon by about 2,000 votes.

The victory did little for Rockefeller's hopeless candidacy; even
after Oregon he was unable to rise above fourth place and 10 percent
in the national polls of the Republican rank and file (see Figure 5-5).
Lodge's candidacy became less plausible as he slipped back to a virtual tie for first place with Nixon. By this time also it was clear that
Goldwater's campaign for pledged and favorable delegates to the
convention was so successful as to offset his indifferent performance
in the primaries.

The final primary, in California, was now the focus of attention
partly because it would determine whom the largest single bloc of
delegates to the national convention would vote for. No write-ins
were permitted and only Goldwater and Rockefeller were on the
ballot. While a Rockefeller win could not add much to the governor's negligible prospects of nomination, it might help the movement
to stop Goldwater in favor of a compromise candidate.

The chances for a Rockefeller victory in California seemed good.
Polls taken after the Oregon primary showed that the first-choice
preferences of the state's Republicans were almost evenly split between Rockefeller (26 percent), Lodge (24 percent), Goldwater
(21 percent), and Nixon (21 percent).[47] But given a forced choice
between Rockefeller and Goldwater, the New York governor came
out well ahead. Rockefeller was obviously a more popular second
choice of Lodge and Nixon supporters than was the senator from
Arizona; in order to win, he merely had to hold on to them and get
them to the polls. This Rockefeller failed to do. Second choices are
seldom as strongly held as first preferences. Those whose favorite
candidate is not on the ballot are less likely to vote than those whose

46. Novak, *Agony of the G.O.P.*, pp. 369 ff.
47. Ibid., p. 369.

champion is actively involved in the campaign. And mild preferences are more subject to change than intense ones. Without the psychological handle of party identification, voter preferences in primaries are far more volatile than in general elections.

None of the moderate-to-liberal candidates who might have benefited from a Goldwater defeat—Nixon, Lodge, Scranton, Romney —came out in support of Rockefeller (although the Lodge volunteer organization did work for the New York governor). So long as it looked as if Rockefeller would win in California, there was little for a potential compromise candidate to gain from endorsing Rockefeller, thereby running the risk of alienating those Goldwater delegates who would be at the convention in large numbers no matter what happened in California. Nor was former President Eisenhower willing to lead a movement to stop Goldwater. Finally the Rockefeller divorce and remarriage issue, which seemed to have faded from view, was rekindled by the birth of Nelson A. Rockefeller, Jr., in New York on May 30. Rockefeller dropped 7 points in the Harris poll from the day before the baby was born to the day after.[48]

The vote on June 2 was close. Barry Goldwater won with 51.6 percent of the vote. Except for the unofficial Texas contest, it was his first primary victory over a major opponent whose name was on the ballot. But he had beaten the only one of his opponents willing to run against him in the largest state in the land.

The annual Governors' Conference met in Cleveland the weekend following the California primary. The occasion provided one last opportunity for the anti-Goldwater forces to agree on a candidate and to organize a last-ditch attempt to stop the senator. A series of inept and ill-timed maneuvers resulted in no decision. Two days later, the reluctant William Scranton announced his candidacy and with Nelson Rockefeller's and Henry Cabot Lodge's endorsements in hand launched a whirlwind campaign to capture enough delegates before the convention to deny Goldwater the nomination.

As the Pennsylvania governor frantically barnstormed the country, the Gallup polls showed that President Johnson was ahead of

48. Theodore H. White, *The Making of the President, 1964* (Atheneum, 1965), p. 122.

Goldwater by a 78 percent to 14 percent margin. The first choice preferences of Republican voters for their party's nominee were a stand-off between Goldwater (22 percent), Nixon (22 percent), Scranton (20 percent), and Lodge (21 percent), though if the race were narrowed to a two-way choice between Goldwater and Scranton, the Pennsylvania governor came out comfortably ahead, 55 percent to 34 percent.

But the race was already over. By mid-June Goldwater had a majority of convention delegates publicly or legally pledged to vote for him on the first ballot.[49]

## *The Early Leader Fails: 1972*

The long series of Democratic primaries in 1972 had a larger impact on the party's choice of a presidential nominee than any other primary season in the years since 1936. They were the first to play a decisive role in denying a clear preprimary leader the nomination and in transforming a marginal candidate into the nominee. In early 1972 Senator Edmund Muskie—while losing some momentum and clearly headed for some trouble—was still the undisputed front-running candidate for the Democratic nomination and a heavy favorite to win. By the end of April, he had withdrawn from active competition, his candidacy in tatters. In early 1972, Senator George McGovern was seen as a lightweight, a single-issue candidate with little personal appeal and a small following largely confined to college campuses. By the end of the primary season, he was the most popular leader in the party and the Democrats' most likely nominee. Muskie's downfall and McGovern's rise occurred in two different periods, divided by the Massachusetts and Pennsylvania primaries on April 25.

Senator Muskie was expected to do very well in New Hampshire. It was a New England state—the senator's residence in Maine was only a few miles from the New Hampshire line—and he faced no stronger opponent in the primary than George McGovern. While Los Angeles Mayor Samuel Yorty, Indiana's Senator Vance Hartke, Arkansas's Congressman Wilbur Mills (a write-in candidate), and

49. *New York Times,* June 17, 1964.

Edward Coll, a 32-year-old community organizer from Hartford, Connecticut, were also in the race, they were even weaker candidates than the senator from South Dakota.

But as the primary day drew near, the Muskie forces began to show signs of anxiety. For one thing, the McGovern campaign was well designed for a small state like New Hampshire. The senator from South Dakota had spent far more time personally campaigning there than anyone else. Handshaking and face-to-face talks, speeches in school auditoriums, visits to factory gates can make a big dent on the small primary electorate of the minority party in a tiny state. McGovern's well-publicized opposition to the Vietnam war had given him a large following on college campuses. As Eugene McCarthy had done in 1968, the McGovern campaign had mobilized this student constituency into a sizable corps of door-to-door canvassers. Every weekend 400 to 500 students from northeastern colleges were bused into the state to join volunteers from Dartmouth, the University of New Hampshire, and elsewhere in the state. With only 60,000 to 80,000 Democrats expected to vote, such a grass-roots campaign can make a lot more difference than in California or Ohio.[50]

Then too, the Yorty, Hartke, and Mills campaigns were chipping away at Muskie's support among the old-line ward heelers and ethnic voters in New Hampshire's cities. Mills had given a widely publicized address to the state legislature and had launched a slick television advertising campaign. Mayor Yorty was backed by the shrill *Manchester Union Leader*, the only daily newspaper in the state.

Things started going wrong within the Muskie campaign. Some of those problems (Muskie's alleged slur on persons of French-Canadian descent, for example) resulted from systematic efforts to sabotage the Democratic front-runner by agents working on behalf of President Nixon.[51] But more of them seemed to flow from unrealistic, early ambitions of the Muskie organization. Muskie had committed himself to enter all twenty-three primaries. Since New Hampshire seemed safely in the Muskie column, relatively few days of campaigning there had been sandwiched into his schedule between visits

50. See David Broder, *Washington Post*, Feb. 14, 1972.
51. See *Washington Post*, Sept. 23 and Nov. 1, 1973.

to Florida, Wisconsin, and the West Coast where more important primaries would be held soon. As the New Hampshire campaign seemed to take a turn for the worse, it proved difficult to find time for the senator from Maine to get back there. And the overscheduled Muskie was very tired. On February 22 he became so angered by a *Union Leader* editorial attack on his wife that, speaking in front of the newspaper's offices in Manchester, he attacked the paper and its publisher, breaking into tears before he could complete his talk. Broadcast on national television, Muskie's loss of self-control was damaging to his reputation as a calm and stable leader able to withstand the pressures of the White House.[52]

The "numbers game" was still another cause for concern.[53] No one doubted that Muskie would win the primary, but by how much? Ultimately, the communications media decided what proportion of the vote Muskie needed in order to be called a winner. But Muskie's workers, in attempting to persuade the press to set the winning margin at a figure their candidate could surpass, were in an awkward position. "I spend half my time," one of them said, "telling people that we are so far ahead that they might as well join up; the other half of my time I spend telling the press we are not as strong as they say we are." Finally, the figure stabilized at 50 percent—Muskie needed to poll at least half the votes cast in the preference primary in order to win.

On March 7 the New Hampshire Democrats went to the polls, and Muskie received 48 percent of their vote. While not a serious loss, the New Hampshire results scarcely made the Maine senator's nomination look inevitable.[54] Yet the big news to come out of New Hampshire was not Muskie's lackluster performance, but the sur-

52. That seems to have been the evaluation in the long haul. The immediate, local reaction to Muskie's outburst was more favorable. *Washington Star*, Feb. 29, 1972.

53. See the thoughtful analysis of the phenomenon by R. W. Apple, Jr., "New Hampshire Primary Fades into Numbers Game," *New York Times*, Feb. 14, 1972. For Muskie's reaction, see Don Oberdorfer, *Washington Post*, Feb. 3, 1972.

54. Assuming that most of the votes cast for minor candidates would have gone to Muskie rather than McGovern, their 15 percent of the primary vote was an important factor in Muskie's relatively poor showing. A large number of challengers (even relatively weak ones) can make a front-runner's total look bad in comparison with the accustomed majorities of two-party politics.

prisingly strong second-place showing of George McGovern. Not only did his 37 percent of the vote considerably surpass expectations; he had also demonstrated his appeal to voters in blue-collar areas as well as on college campuses. In New Hampshire, at least, he had shown that he was more than an antiwar candidate with a limited, and highly ideological, appeal. He would have to be taken more seriously in the future.

The next primary, held in Florida, sent the Muskie candidacy reeling. From the day George Wallace entered the Florida primary, he was conceded victory there—no conventional northern Democrat could match the Alabaman's appeal in a southern state embroiled in controversy over school desegregation and busing. Yet Wallace was so unacceptable to the party outside the South that he was given no chance for the nomination. As a result, the real contest in Florida was for second place: the race included eleven candidates, seven of whom campaigned actively.

The Florida outcome was a severe blow to Muskie, not so much because of Wallace's remarkable winning of 42 percent of the vote, but because the Maine senator came in a distant fourth. He was beaten 4 to 1 by Wallace and 2 to 1 by Hubert Humphrey, and he trailed Senator Henry Jackson by 4 percentage points. While Muskie had much second-choice support,[55] he was the first choice of only 9 percent of the Democratic voters. This was scarcely the kind of performance expected of a front-running candidate.

The results of the Florida primary threw the Democratic race wide open. Since Wallace was not seen as a potential nominee, the second-place finisher Hubert Humphrey gained the most from the Florida verdict. Senator Jackson had also shown surprising strength. The big losers were Senator Muskie and Mayor John Lindsay of New York, whose expensive campaign had won him only a fifth-place finish, 1 percentage point ahead of George McGovern. No one had expected the South Dakota senator to do well in Florida and he had invested little time or effort there. Thus, his sixth-place finish did McGovern little harm, while Lindsay's fifth-place showing was more damaging.

55. See *New York Times*, March 17, 1972.

A week later, Senator Muskie did much better, leading to some talk about a comeback: he defeated Senator Eugene McCarthy in the preference vote and McGovern in the delegate contest in Illinois. But while this victory kept Muskie's candidacy alive, press and public attention were already beginning to focus on the April 14 primary in Wisconsin, where all the major active candidates were involved.

Wisconsin was another Florida for Muskie. Again he finished a poor fourth, this time with 10 percent of the votes. Once again he failed to carry a single congressional district, even losing a district with a heavy concentration of Polish voters. Even more notable than Muskie's defeat was George McGovern's victory. Relying heavily on a grass-roots organization manned by amateurs, the South Dakotan won his first primary with 30 percent of the votes, running against eleven other candidates. He carried seven of the state's nine congressional districts, again showing surprising strength in working-class areas. The senator's unswerving liberalism and opposition to the Vietnam war may have attracted the middle-class volunteer workers who manned the McGovern organization, but his appeal was obviously broadening to include new groups as well. For the first time, McGovern's national poll standings began to improve in the wake of his Wisconsin victory. Now, he was tied for third place with Muskie, whose poll ratings had been dropping since before New Hampshire (see Figure 5-6).

The only other beneficiary of Wisconsin was George Wallace, whose 22 percent of the vote earned him a surprise second-place finish. Wallace had campaigned only briefly in the state, and Wisconsin had no active school busing controversy as Florida (and later Michigan) did. Obviously, his appeal outside the South had been underestimated—and yet his nomination still seemed inconceivable. Humphrey, who finished third, and Jackson, who came in fifth, both looked unimpressive. Mayor Lindsay's sixth-place finish indicated, once and for all, that he had lost the battle to become the leader and spokesman of the Democrats' left wing; he withdrew from the race, leaving the Democratic left wide open for McGovern. But, increasingly, McGovern appeared to have the potential to appeal rather broadly to the whole party.

FIGURE 5-6. *Preferences of Democratic Rank and File for 1972 Presidential Candidates*

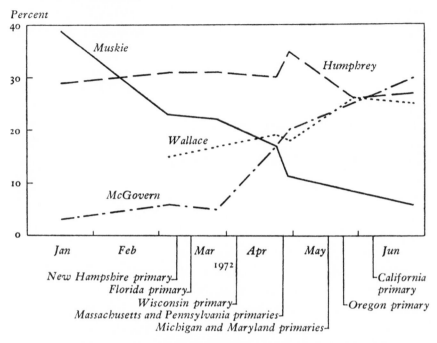

Source: American Institute of Public Opinion, Gallup releases, various dates.

The next two primaries were to take place, after a three-week gap, on the same day in Pennsylvania and Massachusetts. Humphrey focused his attention and energies on Pennsylvania, McGovern on Massachusetts. Muskie, once again plagued by his commitment to run in all the primaries, tried to campaign in both states. In Massachusetts, McGovern overwhelmed Muskie 2 to 1, while in Pennsylvania Hubert Humphrey won his first major presidential primary ever with 35 percent of the vote. Wallace, Muskie, and McGovern trailed the Minnesotan with about 20 percent of the vote apiece. Since neither Wallace nor McGovern had campaigned extensively in Pennsylvania, their performances were considered laudable. But Muskie, who had campaigned more, and who was backed by the governor and much of the state party organization, was defeated once again while attracting about the same number of votes as Wallace and

McGovern. Within days of the Massachusetts and Pennsylvania primaries, Senator Muskie withdrew from active competition in the remaining primaries—although he stayed in the race as a potential compromise candidate in the event of a convention deadlock. "I have no choice," Muskie told a news conference. "I do not have the money to continue."[56]

Viewed in absolute terms, Muskie's performance in the first six primaries was not a disaster: he had won two primaries, as had George McGovern; Humphrey and Wallace had each won a single contest. But when his primary record was compared to initial expectations and the investment of effort and other resources on his behalf, the results were deeply disappointing. The early front-runner—the man considered most likely to win—has to do better than two wins, a weak second, a third, and two fourth-place finishes in order to remain viable.

Muskie's withdrawal left Hubert Humphrey and George McGovern as the leading candidates for the nomination, with George Wallace playing a spoiler's role. Humphrey led in the polls of rank-and-file Democrats[57] and was even more clearly the choice of the party leaders and professional politicians.[58] His second to Wallace in Florida and decisive victory in Pennsylvania had placed him squarely back in the running. Even his disappointing showing in Wisconsin was, at least in part, a result of Republican cross-over voting.[59] George McGovern, while still well behind in the polls, had achieved much momentum since the early days in New Hampshire. He had either won (Wisconsin, Massachusetts) or done surprisingly well (New Hampshire) in the primaries he had contested strenuously. His poorer showings in Florida, Illinois, and Pennsylvania had not hurt him—little was expected of him in these states and he had avoided extensive personal campaigning in them. And while Humphrey was the favorite of the politicians, they had not proven as

56. *Congressional Quarterly Weekly Report*, April 29, 1972, p. 928.

57. Indeed, while it was not public knowledge until after the New Hampshire primary, Humphrey had moved ahead of Muskie in the last poll of Democrats before New Hampshire. See *Gallup Opinion Index*, April 1972, p. 3.

58. Ibid., May 1972, pp. 11–20.

59. See the Yankelovich survey reported in *New York Times*, April 6, 1972.

effective at getting supporters to the polls as McGovern's organization of political amateurs. George Wallace's performance in the early primaries was as surprising as McGovern's and yet his potential popularity outside the South was still grossly underestimated and he was not viewed as a conceivable nominee.

The second—post-Muskie—stage of the 1972 Democratic primaries was dominated, at first, by George Wallace. On May 2 the Alabama governor won his own state, while losing to Humphrey in Indiana. Wallace received more than 40 percent of the vote in Indiana, yet he was still perceived as predominantly a southern candidate. Victories in Tennessee on May 4 and North Carolina on May 6, and a loss to Humphrey in West Virginia on May 9 did nothing to change this view. However, the Alabama governor's decisive defeat of both Humphrey and McGovern in Maryland and Michigan on May 16 changed all that. The busing issue was particularly intense in Michigan; Wallace attracted a remarkable 51 percent of the vote there. The Alabama governor was clearly on the popular side of the most volatile issue of the day. He represented a national force of imposing dimensions.

He was also in a hospital struggling for his life. The day before the Michigan and Maryland primaries, Wallace was shot down while speaking at a shopping center in Maryland.[60] For the second time in four years, one of the Democrats' leading presidential contenders had been the target of an assassination attempt. Unlike Robert Kennedy, Wallace survived, partially paralyzed and apparently crippled for life. But he was obviously eliminated as an active contender for the nomination.

It is impossible to know how much George Wallace's shooting affected the course of subsequent events. The Wallace campaign had proven curiously unprepared and inept at electing pledged delegates outside the former Confederate states. The dramatic indications of voter support for him in the northern and border states were not accompanied by sufficient first-choice delegate strength to put him

60. Wallace's strong showing was based primarily on the appeal of his position on issues, and not on voters' sympathy, according to surveys conducted by *New York Times*, May 17, 1972, and *Washington Post*, May 17, 1972.

even close to winning the nomination. Wallace was almost no one's second choice. This would still have been the case if he had been able to remain actively in the race until the end. If Wallace had been prepared to translate his surprising popularity into Wallace delegates at Miami Beach, the Democrats' 1972 story could have been very different. But he was not and thus never had any real chance of winning the nomination.

The race for the Democratic nomination next became a head-to-head contest between Hubert Humphrey and George McGovern. The relative strength of these two had not been clarified much by the primaries that occurred between Muskie's withdrawal and Wallace's shooting.[61] The two Senate colleagues had split the two contests that were most like a confrontation between them. Humphrey won the Ohio primary, 41.5 percent to McGovern's 39 percent, while McGovern won Nebraska, 41 percent to 35 percent. But when both primaries were examined for indications of the contestants' strengths and weaknesses as candidates, McGovern came out ahead. Humphrey claimed that the Ohio results showed that he was the leader of the "progressive vital center" of the Democratic party. But reading of the returns from Ohio shows the voters were delivering a different kind of message.

Humphrey's center turns out to be composed of the black, the elderly, the poor, and the residents of the central cities.

Without the overwhelming support of the black vote, Humphrey clearly would have finished well behind George McGovern.

It was McGovern who was putting together a new kind of political coalition.

McGovern, facing Humphrey head-to-head in their first true test of strength here, did so well in Ohio for several important reasons. He not only held the same groups of voters who supported him in other primaries—the young, the upper income, the liberal, and the suburban dweller—but he substantially improved his position among other key segments of the electorate.

61. Neither Humphrey nor McGovern was significantly involved in the Alabama, North Carolina, Tennessee, or District of Columbia primaries (the last won by Delegate Walter Fauntroy as a favorite son, the others won by Wallace). Humphrey had beaten Wallace in Indiana and West Virginia. McGovern came in second to Wallace in Michigan and third in Maryland; Humphrey was third in Michigan and second in Maryland.

He cut into the blue-collar vote, the labor union vote, the potential George Wallace vote, and the small town and rural vote. And perhaps most important of all, McGovern captured half of all voters who said they were planning to vote for Muskie earlier this year.[62]

Senator McGovern was to win every one of the primaries remaining after the Wallace shooting: Oregon, Rhode Island, New Mexico, New Jersey, South Dakota, California, and New York. Yet the California primary received far more press attention and cost more time, effort, and money than all the others put together. And it was to have far more impact on electoral politics in 1972.

Senator McGovern's prospects in California rose in step with his gains elsewhere in the nation. The Field poll showed him to be first choice of 7 percent of California Democrats in February, 31 percent in May, and 46 percent in the final poll conducted a few days before the June 6 primary—a 20-percentage-point margin over Senator Humphrey.[63] McGovern's California campaign was perhaps the largest and most ambitious in the history of the state. His volunteer organization—much of it young people who poured into the state from thousands of miles away after working for the senator in earlier primaries—put on a massive door-to-door canvassing campaign in a state where face-to-face contact with voters is generally considered to be impossible. The McGovern forces vastly outspent the Humphrey campaign, and paid advertisements for their candidate dominated the airwaves and newspapers. The press corps covering McGovern's activities had swollen from a small handful in New Hampshire to hundreds of reporters, photographers, and television camera crews from all over the nation and much of the free world; McGovern dominated the news as well. His string of primary victories—arithmetic and otherwise—had resulted in seemingly irresistible momentum.[64]

But Hubert Humphrey, underfinanced and understaffed, would not be counted out. His private polls showed that numerous McGov-

---

62. *Washington Post*, May 4, 1972. See also R. W. Apple, Jr., *New York Times*, May 5, 1972, and the Hart survey published in the *Washington Post*, May 7, 1972.

63. *Washington Post*, May 12, 1972; and *New York Times*, June 2, 1972. In the same three Field polls, Humphrey's ratings had gone from 23 percent to 35 percent to 26 percent.

64. On the California campaign, see *Washington Post*, May 28, 1972; *New York Times*, June 6, 1972; and Andrew Glass, *National Journal*, June 10, 1972.

ern supporters were unaware of their candidate's position on key issues and that they disagreed with many of them—a not surprising result of McGovern's meteoric rise from obscurity. Early in the campaign, when most persons weren't paying much attention to McGovern, the senator from South Dakota had endorsed or personally advocated some controversial if not dubious policy positions—especially on the defense budget and income maintenance programs. Several televised debates, held at the close of the California campaign, gave Senator Humphrey an opportunity vigorously to attack McGovern on these and other positions before a nationwide audience. Humphrey's tactic seems to have worked.[65] McGovern's lead in California shrank during the last few days of the campaign. Instead of a 20-point landslide, McGovern had to settle for a 44 percent to 39 percent victory over Humphrey.

While McGovern was never to regain the steamroller-like momentum he had before the California debates, he still won the most important and critical primary of the season by a comfortable margin. With his victory went 271 delegate votes at the convention, the largest single bloc of delegates at Miami Beach. And subsequent polls showed that McGovern's base of support in California was far broader than Humphrey's. Not only had he held on to his original constituency of youth, liberals, and affluent suburbanites; he also led Humphrey among blacks, urban residents, and blue-collar workers, and tied him among low-income voters.[66] The costs of McGovern's California victory were high (as was to become increasingly apparent later on), but it was a solid win over his most dangerous opponent.

The New York primary, held two weeks later, was an anticlimax. Senator Humphrey was not prepared to compete in the hundreds of loosely related congressional district contests that New York law requires. The McGovern forces swept the state's primary, picking up more than 250 delegate votes.

The final preconvention Gallup poll showed Senator McGovern in the lead, the first choice of 30 percent of the nation's Democrats, to

65. See *Washington Star*, June 8, 1972; Glass, *National Journal*, June 10, 1972; and Yankelovich survey, *New York Times*, June 6, 1972.

66. See Hart survey, *Washington Post*, June 8, 1972.

27 percent for Humphrey, and 25 percent for Wallace.[67] Senator McGovern, in less than four months, had transformed himself from a very long shot to the most likely winner of the 1972 Democratic nomination. For the first time in the 1936–72 period an outside candidate for the presidency had been able to translate success in the primaries into widespread if not overwhelming national appeal.

The reasons for McGovern's primary successes and for the remarkable growth of his popular following are numerous. One of the most prominent factors was the senator's ability to motivate a large corps of volunteer workers and to raise substantial sums of money in small contributions. This ability was immensely aided by his long and vociferous opposition to the war in Vietnam, and probably also by his credentials as a liberal spokesman.

But Barry Goldwater had had a comparable cadre of volunteer supporters and ability to raise money, derived from comparable kinds of issue stances in the other party. And Goldwater's performance in the primaries in 1964 was lackluster in spite of these resources and the poverty of his opposition.

McGovern had used resources like Goldwater's to develop an impressive string of primary victories against the most numerous and active field of contestants in the last ten elections. At least for a time, McGovern said some things that were persuasive to people, that they wanted to hear. And he got his message across despite a cacophony of other, contrasting voices. In retrospect, it appears that much of McGovern's strength with primary voters was based on misperceptions, but his ability to appeal to voters at that time must not be ignored.[68]

But the McGovern campaign could not have taken off if Muskie's drive for the nomination had not collapsed first. The reasons for this unusual development are also complex, but again one factor stands out. Usually, primary competition against a front-runner is sparse:

67. Irving Crespi, "The American Voter—1972" (Princeton, N.J.: The Gallup Organization; processed).

68. For an account of television coverage of McGovern's campaign, see Marc F. Plattner and James R. Ferguson, *Report on Network News Treatment of the 1972 Democratic Presidential Candidates* (Bloomington, Ind.: Alternative Educational Foundation, Inc., 1972).

Nixon sailed through in 1968 with negligible primary opposition. Kennedy's active primary opponent in 1960 was Senator Humphrey —hardly the most likely candidate to deny Kennedy the nomination. Stevenson's 1956 campaign was temporarily derailed by a single opponent—Estes Kefauver, a most unlikely nominee whether he beat Stevenson in the primaries or not. Dewey in 1948 was challenged by Harold Stassen, not Robert A. Taft, the most likely nominee if Dewey failed.

Yet no less than ten people actively campaigned against Senator Muskie in one or more of the first six primaries. This group of challengers contained marginal candidates, like Mayor Yorty and Senator Hartke, but also Senators Humphrey and McGovern and Governor Wallace. Only the addition of Senator Edward Kennedy to the list of active opponents could have made it more difficult for Muskie. Could the other front-runners have survived the competition Muskie faced?

The Muskie failure to establish a clear identity on the issues was probably the most commonly mentioned difficulty of his campaign. And yet his "fuzzy" and "murky" stance on issues probably would have helped him in a two-man race. Certainly in other opposition-party contests, front-runners who managed to win—Landon, Dewey, Stevenson, Kennedy, Nixon—were not notable for the clarity and precision of their policy positions. But because of the large number of active candidates within the Democratic party representing a very wide array of policy positions in early 1972, there was likely to be at least one who appealed more strongly to almost any voter than a vague, bland centrist who avoided specific commitments. Muskie sought to aggregate broad-ranging, partywide support in a balkanized contest. He ended up the second-choice candidate of a great many voters. Unfortunately for Senator Muskie, only first choices are counted in presidential primaries.

☆

*Chapter Six*

☆

# THE CONVENTION'S DECISION

TELEVISION has brought the sights and sounds of the national party convention into the American home. Most of the audience for these quadrennial political spectacles apparently has not been reassured: public opinion polls regularly show that a large majority of the electorate would prefer to nominate presidential candidates some other way.[1] Nonetheless, the national party conventions remain, as they have since Andrew Jackson's time, the bodies that officially make presidential nominations on behalf of the Democratic and Republican parties.

Convention nominations are the aggregate result of individual decisions made by thousands of men and women who have served as convention delegates.[2] Most of their votes, however, are responses to

---

1. A Gallup poll, taken in May 1972, showed 72 percent of the American electorate in favor of a national primary. *Congressional Quarterly Weekly Report*, July 8, 1972, p. 165.

2. The role of convention delegates is discussed in Paul T. David, Ralph M. Goldman, and Richard C. Bain, *The Politics of National Party Conventions* (Brookings Institution, 1960); William A. Gamson, "Coalition Formation at Presidential Nominating Conventions," *American Journal of Sociology*, vol. 68 (September 1962), pp. 157–71; Steven J. Brams and G. William Sensiba, "The Win/Share Principle in National Party Conventions" (Department of Political Science, New York University, 1971; processed); James P. Zais and John H. Kessel, "A Theory of Presidential Nominations, with a 1968 Illustration," in Donald R. Matthews, ed., *Perspectives on Presidential Selection* (Brookings Institution, 1973), pp. 120–42; Loch K. Johnson and Harlan Hahn, "Delegate Turnover at National Party Conventions, 1944–1968," in Matthews, *Perspectives*, pp. 143–71; John W. Soule and James W. Clarke, "Amateurs and Professionals: A Study of Delegates to the 1968 Democratic National Convention," *American Political Science Review*, vol. 64 (September 1970), pp. 888–

situational factors that are experienced by most of the delegates in much the same way. Indeed, presidential nominations are often predictable, on the basis of the competitive situation within the party, before the delegates are even chosen. The individual attributes and decision processes of delegates are in these cases not very important in explaining convention outcomes.[3] No matter who attends these conventions and how they go about making up their minds, the results would be very much the same.

But this is not invariably the case. The outcomes of some nominating contests hinge on who the delegates are and how they decide.

The nominating decisions of American party conventions are made by absolute majority rule—50 percent plus one of the delegates must vote for a person before he becomes the party's presidential nominee. This is a high standard; it requires the winner to enlist more delegate votes than all his opponents combined. It provides a powerful incentive for the parties to find a candidate on whom they can agree. The search for a consensus candidate, which begins long before the formal process gets under way, often produces an unofficial and provisional nominee—a front-runner—before the first primaries. Usually, these front-runners survive the primaries with their advantages intact.

Yet the drive for agreement is in tension with several potential or actual sources of conflict within the party. One of these is factionalism, relatively stable cleavages based on regional and ideological dif-

---

98, and "Issue Conflict and Consensus: A Comparative Study of Democratic and Republican Delegates to the 1968 National Conventions," *Journal of Politics*, vol. 33 (February 1971), pp. 72–91; Eugene B. McGregor, Jr., "Rationality and Uncertainty at National Nominating Conventions," *Journal of Politics*, vol. 35 (May 1973), pp. 459–78; Frank Munger and James Blackhurst, "Factionalism in the National Conventions, 1940–1964: An Analysis of Ideological Consistency in State Delegation Voting," *Journal of Politics*, vol. 27 (May 1965), pp. 375–94; Gerald M. Pomper, "Factionalism in the 1968 National Conventions: An Extension of Research Findings," *Journal of Politics*, vol. 33 (August 1971), pp. 826–30; and Anne Nicholas Costain, "A Coalition Study of Candidate Competition in National Party Conventions, 1940–1972" (Ph.D. dissertation, Johns Hopkins University, 1973).

3. Johnson and Hahn, "Delegate Turnover," p. 147, report that over 50,000 delegates and alternates served at national party conventions from 1944 through 1968; about 65 percent of them attended only one convention during the period.

ferences.[4] Another is stratification—party leaders and the party rank and file tend to have somewhat different values and orientations.[5] Recently, important conflicts in political style between party regulars and intermittently active political amateurs also have been manifest in both major parties.[6]

Whether such conflicts seriously hamper agreement on a presidential candidate depends as much on whether the leading contenders aggravate them as on how numerous and large the raw conflicts are. A deeply divided political party can quickly arrive at agreement on a presidential nominee or find it nearly impossible, depending on such factors as the number and relative strength of the available alternatives, the strategies candidates pursue, and the nature of their support.

And the achievement of consensus can be obstructed by sharp or frequent change in the group of potential nominees. Choosing a presidential candidate is very much a relative matter; whom the delegates favor depends a great deal on the alternatives. When these options change drastically—when, for example, an early front-running candidate withdraws or a new and popular leader emerges in the midst of the formal process of choice—the movement toward agreement can be so disordered that only the convention itself can disentangle the situation.

Each of the twenty major party nominations between 1936 and 1972 can be classified according to the ease with which the party achieved agreement on its candidate. The most common type of

4. See especially Munger and Blackhurst, "Factionalism in National Conventions"; Pomper, "Factionalism in the 1968 Conventions"; and Costain, "Coalition Study of Candidate Competition."

5. See especially Herbert McCloskey, Paul J. Hoffman, and Rosemary O'Hara, "Issue Conflict and Consensus Among Party Leaders and Followers," *American Political Science Review*, vol. 54 (June 1960), pp. 406–27; Sidney Verba and Norman H. Nie, *Participation in America: Political Democracy and Social Equality* (Harper and Row, 1972); and David Nexon, "Asymmetry in the Political System: Occasional Activists in the Republican and Democratic Parties, 1956–1964," *American Political Science Review*, vol. 65 (September 1971), pp. 716–30.

6. See especially Soule and Clarke, "Amateurs and Professionals"; Denis G. Sullivan and others, *The Politics of Representation; the Democratic Convention 1972* (St. Martin's, 1974), chap. 5; and James Q. Wilson, *The Amateur Democrat* (University of Chicago Press, 1966), and *Political Organizations* (Basic Books, 1973).

presidential nomination—the consensual nomination—was the most easily achieved: a single provisional leader appeared before the formal process of choice began and held on to this lead, advantages intact, until he was officially chosen by the convention. The list of potential nominees remained stable; no important disagreement between party leaders and followers developed. The leading candidate's support was so broad that most or all party factions favored him, and most opposing candidates withdrew. Eight nominations share the consensual characteristics.

Five additional nominations have those same characteristics except for having been marked by factional cleavage within the party during the process of choice. Thus while there was a single early leader who survived to the convention with enough support to win, he was opposed by one or more candidates with substantial strength in one or more of the party's factions. While all five of the initial front-runners in these semiconsensual nominations won on the first ballot, the absolute majority requirement for nomination made their victory somewhat problematic: though no single challenger was nearly as strong as the front-runner, a coalition between several weak candidates and their supporters might have denied victory to the strongest.

In the remaining seven contests there was not a single provisional leader who remained ahead throughout the entire nominating period. Factional competition was intense and often complicated by sharp differences in candidate preferences between party leaders and the party rank and file and by the emergence of an active and enthusiastic movement of political amateurs in support of one of the contenders. These nonconsensual nominations are less clearly patterned than the others and less predictable.

## Consensual Nominations

In the consensual nominations there was one obvious choice as the party's presidential candidate who was acceptable, if not always preferred, in all strata and factions of the party. Several of these nominees faced no active opposition at all, and what little opposition the others encountered had dissipated by convention time.

The percentage of delegate votes reflects the consensus in favor of these nominees:

| | |
|---|---|
| Roosevelt (1936) | 100.0 |
| Landon (1936) | 98.1 |
| Roosevelt (1944) | 92.3 |
| Dewey (1944) | 99.7 |
| Eisenhower (1956) | 100.0 |
| Nixon (1960) | 99.2 |
| Johnson (1964) | 100.0 |
| Nixon (1972) | 99.9 |

Only two of these consensual nominations—Landon and Dewey—were made by the party out of power. The only departure from virtual unanimity came from the South in 1944; all but 2½ of the 90 votes withheld from Roosevelt came from that region. This foreshadowed the almost unanimous opposition of the South to Truman four years later, but in 1944 more than two-thirds of the southern delegates still supported the President.

Of course, not all delegates voting for these nominees were equally enthusiastic. Nixon, for example, faced a possible revolt in 1960 after his preconvention compact with Nelson Rockefeller, and at still other times the virtual unanimity of delegate votes disguised discontent or preferences for other candidates. Nevertheless, each of these nominees had clearly emerged before the first primaries as the strongest candidate and the most likely choice; the nomination itself was a pro-forma ratification of a decision that had already been made informally.[7] Who the delegates were and how they were selected were quite unimportant. Virtually all potential delegates from any part of the country would have supported the obvious nominee. These nominees won because virtually everyone within the party agreed on them.

7. Not all decisions at these conventions were pro forma. In 1936, for example, the Democrats abandoned their ancient rule that two-thirds of the delegates must agree on a nominee. The selection of Senator Harry Truman as vice presidential nominee was in reality the selection of the next president. Senator Hubert Humphrey's vice presidential nomination would help him become the presidential nominee next time. The 1964 Democratic compromise over seating of the Mississippi delegation foreshadowed more extensive and divisive credentials contests in 1968 and 1972.

## Semiconsensual Nominations

In each of the five semiconsensual nominations a provisional nominee existed before the primaries who was popular with the rank and
file, supported by party leaders,[8] and acknowledged by the press as
the candidate to beat. Each of these five survived the primaries, entered the convention as the front-runner, and won on the first ballot
with the following vote percentages:

|                    |      |
|--------------------|------|
| Roosevelt (1940)   | 86.0 |
| Truman (1948)      | 75.0 |
| Stevenson (1956)   | 66.0 |
| Kennedy (1960)     | 53.0 |
| Nixon (1968)       | 51.9 |

Roosevelt and Truman were nominees for reelection; the others represented the party out of power.

Each of these candidates was stronger than any of his opponents
in virtually every respect, yet all of them were more vulnerable than
the consensual nominees. Roosevelt, while still very popular, faced
the third-term issue. Truman seemed sure to lead his party to defeat.
Stevenson and Nixon had run before and lost, and Kennedy's religion
and youth were potentially damaging arguments against him.

Such vulnerability may or may not bring a candidate close to defeat. Whether it does or not depends on the nature and strength of his
opposition, on the degree to which the leading candidate is able to
mobilize his own support, and on the availability of compromise candidates in case of deadlock.

Discontent with Roosevelt in 1940 was poorly reflected by active
opposition. Vice President Garner was the most threatening opponent, but his candidacy had fizzled in the primaries and nobody else
had mobilized a substantial bloc of anti-Roosevelt delegates. Truman's 1948 victory was assured when Eisenhower irrevocably refused any prospective Democratic draft. Yet southerners were so
adamantly opposed to Truman that all but thirteen of the delegate

---

8. As far as we know. Usually the best evidence of support is the Gallup county
chairman poll, a measure with severe limitations; before 1952, not even this exists.

votes from the Confederate states were withheld from him, and not one southern delegate moved to his support in the ritualistic vote-switching that followed his first-ballot victory. When Kefauver withdrew in favor of Stevenson in 1956, Harriman was the Illinoisian's only major opponent, and he had gathered only 120 votes outside his home-state delegation.

Kennedy's 1960 and Nixon's 1968 opposition was much more active and potent. Johnson, Stevenson, Symington, and some favorite sons were able to keep Kennedy's vote close to 50 percent, while Rockefeller, Reagan, and some favorite sons were able to do the same for Nixon.

Just as discontent with a front-running candidate is not automatically or precisely reflected in delegate votes, there is no fixed amount of effort that front-runners must expend to secure the support of the required majority of delegates. For example, in 1940 and 1948, respectively, Roosevelt and Truman did not develop personal campaign organizations to insure the selection of a majority of delegates loyal to them. The existing leadership of the Democratic party could be counted on to be loyal to the president. Delegates chosen through the usual channels of state and local party control for the most part favored the incumbent, whether out of enthusiasm or grudging loyalty to their party's president. Had Garner been more potent in 1940, or had Eisenhower challenged Truman in 1948, things would have been different, but with the limited strength of the challenge, delegate votes more or less automatically reflected the incumbents' dominance.

At the other extreme was the 1960 Democratic nomination. Senator Kennedy was acknowledged as the man to beat, clearly favored by the party rank and file, and with strong support among party leaders. Yet Kennedy was vulnerable enough and faced so much competition that he needed what was probably the most potent campaign organization developed in nominating politics up to that time in order to win.

With the aid of this organization he was able to win some delegations by convincing the existing state party leadership that he deserved their support. In Michigan, Illinois, and Pennsylvania, for example, the Kennedy forces cultivated a handful of top party leaders, and with their endorsement the bulk of all three states' convention votes was assured.[9] In others, where his prospects of winning the support of existing leaders were dimmer, he undercut them by challenging their control of their own states. In factionalized New York, for instance, several distinguished Kennedy partisans enlisted the loyalties of much of the middle and lower levels of state party leadership before leaders at the top realized what had happened.[10] In Ohio, favorite-son Governor DiSalle's leaning toward Kennedy was strongly reinforced by the threat that a Kennedy slate would oppose him in the primary if he were not openly pledged to the Massachusetts senator.[11] Other delegations were won directly by victories in primaries, as in Wisconsin, Maryland, and Oregon. Delegates who remained uncommitted until convention time were monitored continuously by the Kennedy organization.[12] No other candidate had an organization approaching Kennedy's in effectiveness, yet his opponents and favorite-son candidates together held him to 53 percent of the delegate votes.

Stevenson in 1956 and Nixon in 1968 led campaigns that depended less on the loyalty of those regularly in control of their parties than did Roosevelt and Truman, but theirs were less highly organized than Kennedy's. All five of these nominees had sufficiently widespread followings that they could depend on considerable delegate support generated automatically through the usual channels of state and local party control. But neither Kennedy in 1960 nor Nixon in 1968, given the competition they faced, could have won first-ballot victories that way.

Because absolute majority rule makes it possible to stop a front-runner without a single, stronger candidate, some of these nominations were closer than the distance between the leader and his nearest

9. See Theodore H. White, *The Making of the President, 1960* (Pocket Books, 1961), pp. 165–67 and 191–93; and Paul Tillett, ed., *Inside Politics: The National Conventions, 1960* (Oceana, 1962), chaps. 16, 17, and 21.

10. See White, *Making of the President, 1960*, pp. 167–70; and Tillett, *Inside Politics*, chap. 18.

11. See Tillett, *Inside Politics*, chap. 10.

12. See ibid., chaps. 2 and 4.

competitor would indicate.[13] Only Kennedy with 53 percent of the convention delegate votes and Nixon with 52 percent came close to being stopped. Just how close depends on such variables as the relative firmness of the various candidates' support and the second-choice preferences of the delegates. But the factional-ideological structure of the contests suggests that even though their winning percentages were almost identical, Kennedy came closer to losing in 1960 than Nixon did in 1968. Nixon's leading opponents were Governor Rockefeller, with a sizable following in the party's left wing and declining support to the center and right, and Governor Reagan with the opposite pattern. Kennedy, in contrast, was challenged by Adlai Stevenson and Stuart Symington, both with centrist appeals at least as broad as Kennedy's, and by Lyndon Johnson, the strongest southern candidate in more than three decades.[14] If Kennedy had been stopped, it is easier to imagine the 1960 convention turning to Stevenson or Symington, if not Johnson, than to imagine the Republicans turning to Rockefeller or Reagan in 1968.[15]

All five semiconsensual nominees won because each was the most popular aspirant in all strata of the party. While not sufficiently popular to forestall the appearance of serious opponents and factional strife within the party, they were so much stronger than any single alternative that their victories, while not inevitable, were hardly surprising.[16] All efforts by alternative candidates and disgruntled fac-

13. The only one of these semiconsensual nominations in which the second strongest candidate had as much as half as many votes as the leader was 1960, when Lyndon Johnson had 409 to John Kennedy's 806.

14. Though Kefauver was from a southern state, he was never seen as a southern candidate. In fact, he was weaker in the South than anywhere else both in 1952 and in 1956.

15. See Lewis Chester, Godfrey Hodgson, and Bruce Page, *An American Melodrama: The Presidential Campaign of 1968* (Dell, 1969), pp. 484–539; Theodore H. White, *The Making of the President, 1968* (Atheneum, 1969), chap. 8; and Jules Witcover, *The Resurrection of Richard Nixon* (Putnam, 1970), chaps. 13–14.

16. Of these five contests the one whose outcome was in doubt the longest was the renomination of Roosevelt in 1940. This was not because of any lack of delegate support, but rather because the President never indicated his willingness to accept renomination until after not only he, but also Henry Wallace, his choice for vice president, had been nominated. This 1940 convention was thus one of the strangest political events in American history. See Bernard F. Donahoe, *Private Plans and Public Dangers: The Story of FDR's Third Nomination* (University of Notre Dame

tional leaders to block their drive for the nomination short of an absolute majority of delegate votes failed—although sometimes by a narrow margin.

## Nonconsensual Nominations

The nonconsensual nominations were characterized by even more factional conflict than the semiconsensual ones. But still other factors complicated these nominations. Rather often, the candidate preferences of the party leaders and party rank and file diverged.[17] Political amateurs, not routinely active in presidential nominating politics, were active on behalf of one of the contenders in most of the nonconsensual races.[18] On top of this, no single front-running candidate emerged early and remained the leading contender until the end; rather, different individuals seemed to be strongest at different times during the period when convention delegates were being selected.

Whatever the reason, agreement on a presidential candidate was difficult to achieve. Having failed to arrive at consensus on a candidate early and informally, the convention had to reach agreement "artificially," by majority vote. The percentages gained by the nominees were as follows:

| | |
|---|---|
| Willkie (1940), sixth ballot | 65.5 |
| Dewey (1948), third ballot | 100.0 |
| Eisenhower (1952), first ballot after shift | 70.1 |
| Stevenson (1952), third ballot | 50.2 |
| Goldwater (1964), first ballot | 67.5 |
| Humphrey (1968), first ballot | 67.1 |
| McGovern (1972), first ballot | 56.8 |

Press, 1965). The President's silence may have been designed to weaken the arguments of those who suspected him of too great a lust for power while making it difficult for an alternative candidate to mobilize support. For an account of the way Calvin Coolidge may have mishandled a similar situation, see William Allen White, *Puritan in Babylon* (Capricorn, 1965), chaps. 32, 34, and 37.

17. For example, the Gallup reports on preferences of county chairmen indicate that, in all of the nonconsensual nominations since 1952 with the exception of the Democrats' in 1968, the chairmen's preferences have diverged from those of the rank and file. This appears also to have been the case for the Republican nominations of 1940 and 1948.

18. Specifically, in the Democratic nominations of 1952, 1968, and 1972 and the Republican nominations of 1940, 1952, and 1964.

Stevenson in 1952 and Humphrey in 1968 were nominated by the party in power, the other five nominees by the opposition party. These nonconsensual nominations illustrate the variety of ways in which a party can reach a decision on a presidential candidate in the absence of a natural consensus choice.

## REPUBLICAN NOMINATION, 1940

As the Republicans convened in 1940 to nominate their party's candidate for president, the world was on the brink of war. Nazi armies had recently plunged through the low countries; France had collapsed. The British had retreated across the English Channel where they were bracing themselves for aerial bombardment and invasion.

The Republicans had no single, consensus candidate to lead them in this time of international crisis. The party's most prestigious foreign affairs spokesman was Senator Arthur Vandenberg, an outspoken isolationist who did not want the nomination enough to campaign for it and who had been soundly beaten in the primaries. The favorite of the party professionals seemed to be Senator Robert Taft, son of a president. But Taft had been elected to the Senate only two years before, and he had rather little support from the party's rank and file. Thomas Dewey, the crime-busting New York district attorney, had led the polls since 1939 and seemed sure to lead on the first ballot in delegate votes. But his popularity had been declining steadily; he was not yet forty years of age; and he had lost his only attempt at statewide political office.

And there was Wendell Willkie. Until recently a Democrat, Willkie had never run for elective office; even Dewey and Taft looked experienced by comparison. His internationalism and his partial support of some New Deal programs made his party credentials all the more suspect, yet the ground swell of his popularity was without precedent. In about two months his support among the Republican rank and file had risen from 3 percent to 29 percent, and during the convention it rose to 44 percent.[19]

19. George H. Gallup, *The Gallup Poll: Public Opinion 1935–1971* (Random House, 1972), vol. 1, pp. 222 and 231.

If this ground swell had not been apparent to delegates back home, it was obvious in and around the convention at Philadelphia. Telegrams from home, the people on the street, and the convention galleries themselves documented it; many seemed convinced that Willkie would be the party's strongest candidate against Roosevelt.[20]

The first ballot showed that no candidate was close to commanding an absolute majority of delegate votes. Dewey was closest with 36 percent, trailed by Taft with 18.9 percent and Willkie with 10.5 percent. This nomination would not be a simple ratification of a decision that had been made beforehand. The convention itself would have to make the decision.

Delegate preferences were unusually fractionalized and fluid. Partly as a result of New Deal elections, leadership of the Republican party at the state level had been weakened. Only nine governors and six U.S. senators were delegates to the 1940 convention.[21] Without such prominent elective officials at their head, an unusual number of state delegations were cast adrift without experienced and authoritative leadership.

This lack of direction is reflected in the pattern of first-ballot voting. Aside from 187 votes from his home state and 5 states where he had won primaries, Dewey won only 173 votes from 31 states and territories, an average of less than 6 votes per unit. Without his home state (52 votes), Taft had only 137 first-ballot votes from 31 states and territories for an average of less than 5. Willkie's 105 first-ballot votes were distributed over 25 states and territories for an average of less than 5 per delegation.

Figure 6-1 shows that Willkie made substantial gains on each succeeding ballot, moving into second place on the third ballot, first place on the fourth, and winning position on the sixth. His gains were almost all piecemeal, in keeping with the generally decentralized character of the convention. Table 6-1 shows that his movement

20. See Ellsworth Barnard, *Wendell Willkie: Fighter for Freedom* (Northern Michigan University Press, 1966), chap. 9; Donald B. Johnson, *The Republican Party and Wendell Willkie* (University of Illinois Press, 1960), pp. 107–08; and Joseph Barnes, *Willkie* (Simon and Schuster, 1952), chap. 11.

21. David, Goldman, and Bain, *Politics of National Party Conventions*, pp. 96, 98, and 345.

FIGURE 6-1. *Votes for Presidential Candidates on Six Ballots at the Republican Convention, 1940*

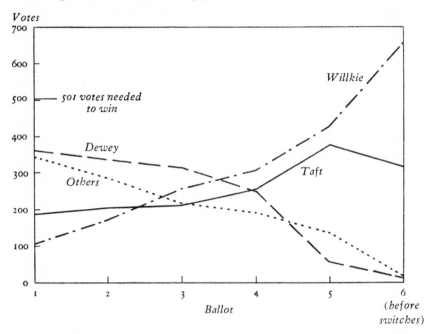

Source: Richard C. Bain and Judith H. Parris, *Convention Decisions and Voting Records* (2d ed., Brookings Institution, 1973).

TABLE 6-1. *Strength of Willkie Gains on Each Ballot at the 1940 Republican Convention*

| Ballot | Gain in votes | Delegations shifting votes to Willkie | Average gain per delegation | Loss of votes | Net gain in votes |
|---|---|---|---|---|---|
| Second | 67 | 21 | 3.2 | 1 | 66 |
| Third | 92 | 25 | 3.7 | 4 | 88 |
| Fourth | 47 | 20 | 2.4 | 0 | 47 |
| Fifth | 126 | 25 | 5.0 | 3 | 123 |
| Sixth | 226 | 37 | 6.1 | 0 | 226 |

Source: Computed from Richard C. Bain and Judith H. Parris, *Convention Decisions and Voting Records* (2d ed., Brookings Institution, 1973).

from 105 votes on the first ballot to 655 on the decisive sixth was built on average gains of between 2 and 7 votes per delegation. Only four states shifted 20 or more votes to him on any single ballot: Massachusetts (20 on the third), New York (40 on the fifth), Michigan (35 on the sixth), and Pennsylvania (51 on the sixth). These last two came after the fifth ballot had put him only 72 votes away from the 501 needed to win the nomination. Nobody played the role of kingmaker at the 1940 Republican convention.

The reasons for the nomination of Wendell Willkie are not so evident as are those of nominees at other conventions. He was, however, the emerging popular leader. While no published national poll had shown Willkie in the lead at convention time, he was clearly on the way up just as Dewey was clearly on the way down. In fact, the pattern of delegate votes in Figure 6-1 bears a striking similarity to the preferences of rank-and-file Republicans in Figure 5-4. It is almost as if the first ballots reflected the distribution of rank-and-file support before Willkie gained momentum, with subsequent ballots reflecting Dewey's decline, Willkie's rise, and Taft's relatively stable base of support. This makes some sense, since delegates began to be selected while Dewey was still fairly strong, and a substantial part of his early delegate support came from states in which he had won primaries. Figure 6-2 shows that Willkie was the chief beneficiary of the shifts away from Dewey in the states where the latter was strongest.

In fact, on the fifth ballot, after Taft had reached his peak and much of the Dewey support had coalesced behind Willkie, the pattern of division in the party began to look like that which would reappear in 1948, 1952, and 1964.[22] In Willkie, the so-called eastern internationalist wing of the party had found a champion who would lead them in the first of three victories over the Taft-led conservative wing, before the conservatives prevailed in 1964.

The Northeast was the most apparent base for that liberal wing of the party, giving Willkie 91.4 percent of their sixth-ballot votes. But his appeal extended into all sections; the South, Far West, and Midwest each gave him more than half of their sixth-ballot votes, even

22. See Munger and Blackhurst, "Factionalism in National Conventions."

FIGURE 6-2. *Voting on Successive Ballots of Twelve State Delegations Carried on the First Ballot by Dewey at the 1940 Republican Convention*

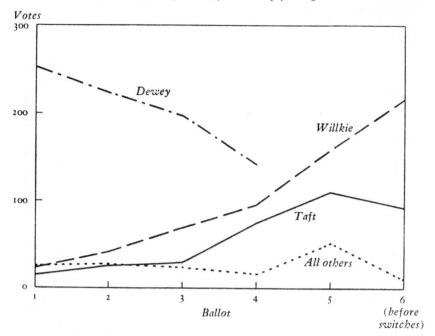

Source: Computed from Bain and Parris, *Convention Decisions.*

before the switches that made him the virtually unanimous choice. He was also the most-favored candidate in the states that had on the first ballot supported minor candidates and favorite sons (see Figure 6-3).

Willkie's nomination is consistent with another common feature of multiballot conventions: the winner is usually the candidate who gains the most from the first ballot to the second. McGregor suggests that this is consistent with delegate uncertainty and desire to maximize influence by supporting a winner.[23]

Surging fast from far behind, Wendell Willkie had more of the look of a winner than the declining Dewey, the plodding Taft, or the diffident Vandenberg. He took this convention by storm in a way that no other candidate in the 1936–72 period did.

23. McGregor, "Rationality and Uncertainty."

FIGURE 6-3. *Voting on Successive Ballots of Eleven State Delegations Carried by Minor Candidates on the First Ballot at the 1940 Republican Convention*

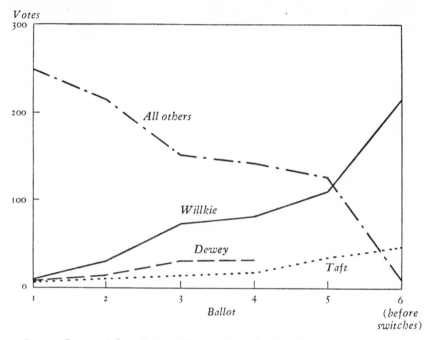

Source: Computed from Bain and Parris, *Convention Decisions*.

## REPUBLICAN NOMINATION, 1948

In 1948 the Republicans did not have one single, dominant candidate, as Dewey had been in 1944, but the candidate options were clearer than in 1940. Dewey and Taft seemed to have equally good chances for the nomination both before the 1948 primaries and after. Dewey's advantage in rank-and-file support, which he recovered from Stassen after the Oregon primary, seemed to many observers to be offset by Taft's advantage with party regulars and leaders. Vandenberg, Warren, and Stassen were available as compromise choices in case Taft and Dewey should deadlock.[24]

On the surface, the early stages of the Republicans' 1948 conven-

24. There are no Associated Press delegate polls before 1952 to trace how candidates translate their resources into delegate votes through the preconvention period.

tion were routine. The usual oratorical excesses were committed from the podium; the reports of the committees on permanent organization, credentials, and the platform were approved without debate and by voice vote. Behind this calm exterior, however, Governor Dewey and his operatives were strenuously at work, seeking to blitz the convention on the first ballot. The other candidates, while conceding that the New York governor was ahead, frantically sought to stop Dewey and to find an alternative compromise candidate.[25]

It was easier to agree on the first objective than the second. The reluctant Senator Vandenberg was often mentioned as a compromise candidate by the anti-Dewey faction. If Stassen were unable to win the nomination himself—a contingency he was unwilling to admit—he was believed to favor the senator from Michigan. Moreover, his mostly young, liberal, and internationalist followers would probably accompany him in any move toward the prestigious foreign affairs spokesman. Vandenberg, however, was anathema to Senator Taft and his conservative constituency. Even if Taft put aside his personal reservations and sought to swing his support to Vandenberg, most of his delegates from the South and the Midwest would end up voting for Dewey. Much the same result might occur if Taft backed Governor Warren, although the fact that Warren was little known outside of California and had not accumulated as many enemies as Dewey, Taft, Vandenberg, or Stassen made him a more plausible compromise.[26] For a few days, talk of a Taft-Stassen ticket—sparked by the editorial endorsement of the *Chicago Tribune*—circulated among the delegates and in the press. But efforts to build such a coalition collapsed.[27] Given a choice between Taft and Dewey, Stassen's followers would reluctantly take Dewey.

Thus the balloting began without agreement among those opposed to Governor Dewey except that he should be denied renomination.

25. See Jules Abels, *Out of the Jaws of Victory* (Holt, 1959), chap. 3; Irwin Ross, *The Loneliest Campaign: The Truman Victory of 1948* (New American Library, 1968), chap. 5; and James T. Patterson, *Mr. Republican: A Biography of Robert A. Taft* (Houghton Mifflin, 1972), chap. 27.

26. See James Reston, "Compromise Talk Turns to Warren," *New York Times*, June 24, 1948.

27. *New York Times*, June 17, 19, 20, and 23, 1948.

Perhaps if they could stop him on the first few ballots, agreement would come more easily. But even this chance failed to materialize (see Figure 6-4).

The beginning of the end was signaled by the last-minute withdrawal of two favorite-son candidates, Senator Edward Martin of Pennsylvania and Congressman Charles Halleck of Indiana. The large blocs of delegates they led into the Dewey camp gave the governor a better lead than expected on the first ballot, with 434 of the 548 votes needed to win. Taft with 224 and Stassen with 157 followed far behind. While no other candidate came close to pulling 100 votes, the favorite sons and minor candidates received almost 300 votes between them. A stop-Dewey blocking coalition had held together at least for the first ballot.

FIGURE 6-4. *Vote for Presidential Candidates on Three Ballots at the 1948 Republican Convention*

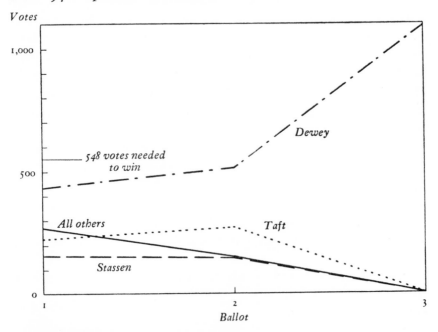

Source: Bain and Parris, *Convention Decisions.*

The second ballot was nearly disastrous for the stop-Dewey forces, despite the fact that the net shift between the candidates was only 131 (out of 1,094) delegate votes. Dewey crept up by 81 votes to 515, Taft gained 50 votes for a total of 274. Governor Stassen's support, as expected, proved to be the softest of the major candidates'; his total dropped by 8 to 149. But the biggest losers of all were the favorite-son and minor candidates, who suffered a net loss of 123 votes. At this point, with the acquiescence of the Dewey leadership, the convention adjourned for the night. After surveying the situation, the leading Dewey opponents—Taft, Warren, Stassen, Vandenberg, Governor Raymond Baldwin of Connecticut, General MacArthur—all withdrew. Governor Dewey was unanimously nominated on the third ballot held the next day.

Several factors led the other contestants to conclude that Dewey could not be beaten. While the New York governor had registered only modest gains on the second ballot, he had come within 33 votes of a majority. Once a candidate is so close to winning, the bandwagon becomes nearly irresistible.[28] Moreover, detailed examination of the voting shifts between the first and second ballots made Dewey's gains look impressive (see Table 6-2): he had picked up 21 votes from Stassen, 16 from Taft, and 45 elsewhere, and lost only 1 vote. The net shifts toward Dewey were not large in any state save New Jersey— where 24 delegates followed Governor Alfred Driscoll's endorsement of Dewey—but they were widespread and consistently in his favor and against his leading opponents. The delegations pledged to favorite sons that held firm on the second ballot—especially California's 53 votes for Warren, Connecticut's 19 for Baldwin, Michigan's 41 for Vandenberg—would overwhelmingly opt for Dewey over Taft if confronted with a two-way choice.

The convention voting alignment in Dewey's successful bid for renomination in 1948 was similar to that first manifested in the ideological fissures within the Republican party in 1940 (see Table 6-3). Senator Taft was by far strongest in 1948 in the conservative states

28. No candidate has ever lost an absolute-majority-rule convention after leading with as much as 47 percent of the delegate votes.

TABLE 6-2. *Net Shifts in Delegate Voting between the First and Second Ballots at the 1948 Republican Convention*

| Votes shifted from | Votes shifted to | | | | |
|---|---|---|---|---|---|
| | Dewey | Stassen | Taft | Others | All candidates |
| Dewey | ... | 0 | 1 | 0 | 1 |
| Stassen | 21 | ... | 0 | 0 | 21 |
| Taft | 16 | 5 | ... | 0 | 21 |
| Others | 45 | 8 | 70 | ... | 123 |
| All candidates | 82 | 13 | 71 | 0 | ... |
| Net change | 81 | −8 | 50 | −123 | ... |

Source: Computed from Bain and Parris, *Convention Decisions*.
... = not applicable.

which he had carried on the fifth ballot in 1940 and Dewey's areas of greatest strength in 1948 were the predominantly eastern and liberal states which had been strongly opposed to Taft eight years before.

Yet Dewey's support was notably broader than Taft's. Taft received just over half the votes in the states that had been strongly for

TABLE 6-3. *Second-Ballot Votes for Presidential Candidates at the 1948 Republican Convention, by Ideological Alignment*[a]

| Alignment[b] | Percent of votes for | | | | | Percent of all votes in group |
|---|---|---|---|---|---|---|
| | Dewey | Stassen | Taft | Others | Total | |
| Conservative | 36 | 10 | 53 | 1 | 100 (N = 207) | 19 |
| Moderately conservative | 31 | 30 | 38 | 1 | 100 (N = 149) | 14 |
| Moderate | 48 | 22 | 23 | 7 | 100 (N = 77) | 7 |
| Moderately liberal | 49 | 10 | 21 | 20 | 100 (N = 311) | 29 |
| Liberal | 58 | 11 | 6 | 25 | 100 (N = 337) | 31 |
| Total | 47 | 14 | 25 | 14 | 100 (N = 1,081) | 100 (N = 1,081) |

Sources: Computed from Frank Munger and James Blackhurst, "Factionalism in the National Conventions, 1940–1964: An Analysis of Ideological Consistency in State Delegation Voting," *Journal of Politics*, vol. 27 (May 1965), pp. 375–94; and Bain and Parris, *Convention Decisions*.

N = total number of votes.

a. Votes of territorial delegations omitted.

b. Alignment determined by state delegations' vote for Taft on the fifth ballot at the 1940 Republican convention. Those designated conservative gave 80 percent or more of their vote to Taft, moderately conservative 51–79 percent, moderate 50 percent, moderately liberal 20–49 percent, and liberal under 20 percent.

him in 1940, but his support dropped sharply in the other states. Dewey, on the other hand, received about half of the second-ballot votes of the states that Taft had lost in 1940, and he also did well in the pro-Taft states, attracting about a third of the votes there. He seems to have appealed to all ideological elements of the party, while Taft's strength was concentrated in the party's conservative states.

Dewey had also, after the Oregon primary, once again become the most popular candidate with the party rank and file. Taft was not only weaker with GOP voters, he also ran more poorly than any other major Republican in trial-heat polls against President Truman. Dewey's assets in 1948 were not so overwhelming that he was unbeatable, yet his victory fits the general patterns of presidential nominations over the last forty years better than anyone else's would have.

REPUBLICAN NOMINATION, 1952

After the primaries, as well as before them, Taft and Eisenhower seemed to have relatively even chances for the 1952 nomination. Eisenhower had moved into a clear lead in the polls of the party rank and file and had the support of 13 of the 25 Republican governors, while Taft had a considerable popular following in some sections of the country and was the favorite of lower-level party leaders such as the county chairmen.[29]

This was very similar to the competitive situation between Taft and Dewey in 1948, but there was one important difference. On the first ballot in the 1948 convention, Taft and Dewey between them mustered only 60 percent of the total delegate vote, and they would have had even less but for some late switches to Dewey just before the first ballot. On the first ballot Taft and Eisenhower had well over 90 percent of the delegate votes committed in 1952. Many delegates in 1948 (and 1940) came to the convention without their minds made up, and the convention's decision came only after delegates chose a candidate or shifted their preferences over successive ballots. The

29. The Gallup poll of Republican party county chairmen had pointed out some shrinkage in the lead—from 3 to 1 in December 1951, to 2 to 1 in June 1952—but the senator's lead among the party wheelhorses was still very large.

effective decision point for most delegates in 1952 took place earlier; they either became committed to Eisenhower or Taft in the process of being chosen or lined up behind one of them shortly thereafter. Uncommitted delegates and favorite-son supporters were relatively scarce in 1952. Thus, more than any of the other nomination contests, the 1952 Republican contest was like a war whose outcome grew out of the results of a series of battles taking place over a period of months. Neither Taft nor Eisenhower had the necessary absolute majority as the convention met, but it would take a shift or crystallization of few delegate votes to determine the outcome.

Because Ike was more popular with rank-and-file Republicans than Taft (except in the Ohio senator's backyard), it is easy to assume that his victory was based on a strong showing in the primary states, where rank-and-file GOP members directly chose national convention delegates. Taft, on the other hand, could be expected to have won the lion's share of delegates from states selecting delegates at local caucuses and state conventions, where the preferences of state and local party leaders ordinarily prevail.

Curiously, that was not the case. While 275 of the delegates chosen in the primary states voted for Ike on the first ballot (before switches), 216 cast their first-ballot votes for Taft (see Table 6-4). Only 59 of Eisenhower's 95-vote margin over Taft came as a result of the primaries. Indeed, if the New York outcome is ignored—the presidential preferences of delegate candidates were not listed on the

TABLE 6-4. *First-Ballot Vote for Eisenhower and Taft at the 1952 Republican Convention, by Delegation Selection Procedure*

| Selection procedure and candidate | Number of votes | Percent of total possible votes | Percent of candidate's first-ballot votes |
|---|---|---|---|
| Primary states | 590 | . . . | . . . |
| Eisenhower | 275 | 47 | 46 |
| Taft | 216 | 37 | 43 |
| Caucus and convention states | 616 | . . . | . . . |
| Eisenhower | 320 | 52 | 54 |
| Taft | 284 | 46 | 57 |

Source: Computed from Bain and Parris, *Convention Decisions*.
. . . = not applicable.

ballot and Taft did not contest the state in the face of strong opposition from Governor Dewey—the Ohio senator won the contest for delegates' votes in the primary states!

Thus Eisenhower's mass popularity was not enough to permit him to win via the primaries alone. But, again contrary to expectation, the general beat Taft in the caucus and convention states.

How could Taft have been bested in the search for delegates in the states with selection procedures that seem to favor the candidate backed by the bulk of the party professionals? The politics of national delegate selection varies widely from one nonprimary state to the next, and from election year to election year within the same state.[30] Many of these delegates are selected on the basis of criteria unrelated to their presidential preferences—personal popularity, local factional affiliations, service to the party, previous financial contributions, geographical considerations, and the like. Others are chosen by procedures that largely insulate their selection from presidential politics. In 1952, some delegates to the Republican convention were picked in head-on confrontations between Eisenhower and Taft forces that converted local caucuses and conventions into popularity contests between the presidential candidates. But in this vast and confusing mosaic, two factors stand out as keys to Eisenhower's performance.

First of all, Eisenhower was supported by the majority of the Republican governors.[31] Of the 25 Republican governors in 1952 only the governors of Idaho, Utah, and North Dakota were supporters of the senator from Ohio. A grand total of 64 convention delegates were selected in these three states. Eisenhower, on the other hand, was actively supported by the Republican governors of Colorado, Connecticut, Iowa, Kansas, Maine, Minnesota, Nebraska, New Hampshire, New Jersey, New York, Oregon, Washington, and Wisconsin. These 13 states sent a total of 370 delegates to the 1952 Republican convention. Taft may have been the hero of the party wheelhorses

---

30. See Paul T. David, Malcolm Moos, and Ralph M. Goldman, eds., *Presidential Nominating Politics in 1952* (Johns Hopkins Press, 1954), vols. 2–5, for a state-by-state description of delegate selection in 1952.

31. *Time*, June 30, 1952, p. 15.

in the counties and precincts, but Ike was the favorite of Republicans in the governor's mansions. State politics tend to revolve around governors; they usually have much influence over the selection of their states' delegates to the national convention and often dominate the behavior of the delegations once formed. Governors are especially significant in the party out of power, nationally, for they distribute most of the party's favors. Governor Dewey, for example, reminded his colleagues upon his election as chairman of the New York delegation that he would be governor for another two years; the message was clear.

In Eisenhower's successful bid for the presidential nomination he received 74 percent of the convention votes cast by states with pro-Ike Republican governors while Taft got exactly 19 percent (see Table 6-5)! Taft did even better than Eisenhower in the states where

TABLE 6-5. *First-Ballot Vote for Presidential Candidates at the 1952 Republican Convention, by Governor's Commitment and Delegate Selection Procedure*

| Governor's commitment and selection procedure | Percent of votes for candidate[a] | | | |
|---|---|---|---|---|
| | Eisen-hower | Taft | Others | Total |
| Republican governor for Eisenhower (13 states) | 74 | 19 | 7 | 100 (N = 370) |
| Primary | 70 | 19 | 11 | 100 (N = 242) |
| Caucus and convention | 81 | 19 | 1 | 100 (N = 128) |
| Republican governor for Taft (3 states) | 10 | 86 | 4 | 100 (N = 42) |
| Primary | 0 | 0 | 0 | 0 |
| Caucus and convention | 10 | 86 | 4 | 100 (N = 42) |
| Republican governor uncommitted or for minor candidate (9 states) | 42 | 28 | 30 | 100 (N = 242) |
| Primary | 39 | 21 | 40 | 100 (N = 178) |
| Caucus and convention | 52 | 48 | 0 | 100 (N = 64) |
| Democratic governor (23 states) | 40 | 58 | 2 | 100 (N = 531) |
| Primary | 21 | 78 | 1 | 100 (N = 170) |
| Caucus and convention | 52 | 47 | 1 | 100 (N = 363) |

Sources: Presidential preferences of governors from *Time*, June 30, 1952, p. 15. Voting figures computed from Bain and Parris, *Convention Decisions*.

N = number of votes.

a. Before switches. Votes of territories omitted.

his supporters were governors—86 percent for Taft to 10 percent for Eisenhower—but of course there were very few states and delegates involved. All told, Eisenhower edged Taft by 203 votes in the states with pro-Ike governors, losing by 32 votes in states with pro-Taft chief executives. And Eisenhower did best of all in caucus and convention states headed by a friendly Republican governor. Apparently, the pro-Ike governors mostly won the struggle with pro-Taft party officials over which of the two leading contenders their state should support.

A second cause of Eisenhower's strong showing in the nonprimary states was the large number of enthusiastic amateurs his candidacy mobilized into political action. Precinct caucuses and county and state conventions are routinely dominated by the party regulars by default; they are the only ones who bother to attend them. But Ike appealed to many people who felt strongly that he should be the next president of the United States and were willing to work and attend meetings and caucuses in an attempt to bring this about. In suddenly swollen precinct caucuses, Eisenhower people were elected to state conventions and then voted for pro-Ike national delegates. This situation was particularly common in the South where large numbers of disaffected Democrats were attracted to the Eisenhower campaign. The old-guard southern Republican leaders, heavily pro-Taft, were often overwhelmed by newcomers. Sometimes the Taft supporters, facing certain defeat, walked out of the caucuses and conventions to hold rump meetings of their own. Incidents of this sort in Georgia, Louisiana, and Texas resulted in extraordinarily important seating contests at the convention.[32]

Outside of the three small states with pro-Taft governors, Taft received less than 45 percent of the votes in all but the convention and caucus states with uncommitted Republican governors or Democratic governors and in primary states with Democratic governors. Most of this latter set of votes was from Illinois and his home state of Ohio, two of the few large states in the union where Taft could win a popularity contest with General Eisenhower. Ike stayed out of both (though he obtained an impressive number of write-in votes in Illi-

32. See ibid., June 9, 1952, pp. 25–26.

nois), and Taft earned 115 votes to Eisenhower's one on the first ballot from these two states.

As the convention had gotten under way, it was apparent that the two leading candidates were exceedingly close in pledged delegate support. The Associated Press and most other neutral observers believed Taft to be somewhat ahead—the AP estimated Taft at 530 delegates to Eisenhower's 427—but the difference consisted largely of the contested delegates from Georgia, Louisiana, and Texas.[33] In making up the temporary role of the convention, the pro-Taft Republican National Committee[34] had provisionally seated the pro-Taft delegate slates over their pro-Eisenhower challengers. If the convention's committee on credentials recognized the insurgent delegate slates in their stead, then the nomination outcome would be a toss-up.

Two things happened before the credentials committee was able to make its report.[35] First, 23 of the 25 Republican governors, attending the Governors' Conference in Houston, issued a manifesto urging that contested delegates not be allowed to vote in the national convention until after the contests had been settled (under long-standing rules of the party, delegates on the temporary roll, contested or otherwise, could vote on any question except their own contest). This idea was presented to the convention on its first day as a substitute for the report of the committee on rules. Following long and heated debate on this so-called fair play amendment, an amendment was proposed that would have exempted convention delegates selected from congressional districts from its provisions. The vote on that amendment—the Brown amendment—was perhaps the most critical of the convention. It failed 658 to 548 and immediately thereafter the fair play amendment was adopted unanimously

33. The Associated Press has since 1952 kept an account of delegates pledged to the various candidates throughout the formal nominating campaign. Being based on public commitments, they tend to be conservative. They are usually published as aggregate totals for candidates; the unpublished state breakdowns are on file in the offices of the Associated Press.

34. All states had the same number of representatives both on the National Committee and the credentials committee of the convention. Taft had support in more states than Eisenhower and thus had an advantage at the committee stage of decision.

35. For a more detailed description of these events see David, Moos, and Goldman, *Presidential Nominating Politics*, vol. 1, pp. 72 ff.

without a roll call. This was an important victory for the Eisenhower forces but it exaggerated his strength since Warren and Stassen delegates had voted for the Eisenhower position.

The Taft forces, in control of the credentials committee, sought to entice the Eisenhower followers with a compromise proposal that would have yielded the entire contested portion of the Louisiana delegation to Ike. But the Eisenhower managers would have none of this deal and a minority report of the committee was prepared insisting that all the seats "stolen" in Georgia, Louisiana, and Texas be granted to the pro-Eisenhower slates. A roll call vote was held after extensive and highly emotional debate. The Eisenhower forces once again prevailed—the minority report was approved 607 to 531. Soon thereafter, the Taft leaders conceded the other contests without demanding a vote. They had lost the battle and the war. Taft had fallen just short of gaining a majority of the delegates. The subsequent roll call on the nomination itself was anticlimactic. Taft's support had shrunk from its high point of 548 to an even 500; Eisenhower strength, swollen by the contested southern delegates plus the subsequent swings of delegates from Maryland, Michigan, and a few other scattered states, had grown to 595, just short of the necessary 604.

Before the first ballot was officially concluded, the shift of 19 Minnesota delegates from Stassen to Eisenhower put the general over the top. Subsequent shifts on the same ballot left Eisenhower with 845 votes to 280 for Taft. The Ohio senator had lost his party's nomination for the third time in the closest two-man race of the twenty nominations in the 1936–72 period.

Looking back on the decision, it is clear that Eisenhower may not have had much more support at the 1952 Republican convention than Senator Taft, but the support he had was more broadly based. If the states are ordered according to the liberal-conservative alignment exemplified in Senator Taft's 1940 battle with Wendell Willkie, it is clear that Eisenhower appealed more to conservative state delegations than Taft did to liberal ones (see Table 6-6). But Ike's ability to attract support from Republicans of a wide variety of ideological and factional persuasions was not manifest in the primary states. Taft

TABLE 6-6. *First-Ballot Vote for Presidential Candidates at the 1952 Republican Convention, by Delegate Selection Procedure and Ideological Alignment*[a]

| Selection procedure and ideological alignment[b] | Percent of votes for | | | |
|---|---|---|---|---|
| | Eisenhower | Taft | Others | Total |
| *Primary states* | | | | |
| Conservative | 0 | 100 | 0 | 100 (N = 70) |
| Moderately conservative | 12 | 71 | 17 | 100 (N = 122) |
| Moderate | 0 | 0 | 0 | 0 |
| Moderately liberal | 100 | 0 | 0 | 100 (N = 14) |
| Liberal | 79 | 18 | 3 | 100 (N = 290) |
| *Caucus and convention states* | | | | |
| Conservative | 53 | 43 | 4 | 100 (N = 143) |
| Moderately conservative | 53 | 47 | 0 | 100 (N = 40) |
| Moderate | 39 | 56 | 5 | 100 (N = 79) |
| Moderately liberal | 37 | 36 | 27 | 100 (N = 266) |
| Liberal | 72 | 28 | 0 | 100 (N = 162) |
| *All states* | | | | |
| Conservative | 35 | 62 | 3 | 100 (N = 213) |
| Moderately conservative | 22 | 65 | 13 | 100 (N = 162) |
| Moderate | 39 | 56 | 5 | 100 (N = 79) |
| Moderately liberal | 41 | 34 | 25 | 100 (N = 280) |
| Liberal | 77 | 22 | 1 | 100 (N = 452) |

Sources: Computed from Munger and Blackhurst, "Factionalism in National Conventions"; and Bain and Parris, *Convention Decisions*.

N = total number of votes.

a. Votes of territorial delegations omitted.

b. Alignment determined by state delegations' vote for Taft on the fifth ballot at the 1940 Republican convention. Those designated conservative gave 80 percent or more of their vote to Taft, moderately conservative 51–79 percent, moderate 50 percent, moderately liberal 20–49 percent, and liberal under 20 percent.

beat Eisenhower overwhelmingly in historically pro-Taft primary states while Eisenhower swept the primary states that had supported Willkie just as emphatically. But in the nonprimary states, once the contested delegates from Texas, Louisiana, and Georgia were won, the general actually carried the pro-Taft strongholds by a narrow margin while holding a safe lead in the vote-rich liberal Republican states of the Northeast.

While Eisenhower's popular following did not translate very directly into delegate votes, Taft's advantage among county chairmen was vitiated by the general's superior support from candidate enthusiasts and governors. The governors may have been more influenced than the lower levels of party leadership by the argument—strongly reinforced by trial-heat polls—that Eisenhower was far more likely than Taft to end twenty years of Democratic control of the White House.[36]

### DEMOCRATIC NOMINATION, 1952

After President Truman's withdrawal from the 1952 contest, the Democrats no longer had a consensual candidate. Kefauver was clearly the first choice of the party rank and file from then until convention time, but Stevenson was the choice of party leaders from president to county chairmen. Stevenson, however, would not agree to accept the nomination until after the convention met.

For a candidate with strong popular support but opposition from party leaders, the primaries seem to be the route to success. Kefauver entered 13 of the 17 state primaries, winning 12 of them, mostly unopposed. These victories both reflected and reinforced the Tennessean's strength with the rank and file, but for several reasons they did not translate into a winning number of delegate votes.

In the first place, the 17 primary states had only 592 votes at the convention—616 votes were needed to win the nomination. Thus if Kefauver had won all the primary state delegates, he still would have fallen slightly short of victory. In fact, he decided against running in New York and Minnesota (where favorite sons Averell Harriman and Hubert Humphrey might well have beaten him), and in Alabama and West Virginia (where he was also relatively unpopular). This reduced the maximum number of delegate votes he could obtain directly through the primaries to 430. In fact, he obtained only 208 of these votes on the second ballot, his peak. Even in the states where he won primaries, Kefauver obtained only 50 percent of the delegate votes as a result (see Table 6-7).

In some states, primary victories automatically result in convention votes. In California, South Dakota, and Wisconsin, slates of pledged delegates ran against each other; in Maryland and Oregon, delegates were bound by the results of the preference poll. Kefauver obtained all but 2 ½ of the votes cast by these states on the second ballot. But in the other states holding primaries, there was no automatic connection between winning the primary and garnering votes at the convention. For example, Kefauver won nonbinding preference primaries in Illinois, Massachusetts, Nebraska, New Jersey, and Pennsylvania but he received only 17 percent of the first-ballot votes cast by these states!

The main reason for this massive slippage was Kefauver's failure to contest delegate races. He had run in the primaries for their publicity value but failed to exploit their potential for seating pro-Kefauver delegates at the convention. Apparently he had hoped, by demonstrating his popularity in the primaries and the polls, to force established party leaders to accept him as their candidate. This was a crucial miscalculation.

The failure of the Kefauver campaign to elect a large number of pro-Kefauver delegates resulted from other factors as well. Not many Kefauver supporters were willing to campaign for a seat at the national convention. Mostly politicians went to this convention, and most of them were anti-Kefauver. And while the senator from Tennessee was very popular among nonpoliticians, his supporters for the most part were not highly dedicated and eager to enter politics in order to further the cause of their presidential candidate. Kefauver

TABLE 6-7. *Second-Ballot Vote for Kefauver at the 1952 Democratic Convention, by His Standings in Primaries*

| Kefauver's preconvention standing | Vote for Kefauver | Total vote from these states | Percent for Kefauver |
|---|---|---|---|
| Primary states won | 203 | 406 | 50.0 |
| Primary states entered but not won | 5 | 24 | 20.8 |
| Primary states not entered | 33 | 162 | 20.4 |
| Nonprimary states | 113 ½ | 610 | 18.6 |
| Territories | 8 | 28 | 28.6 |
| Total | 362 ½ | 1,230 | 29.5 |

Source: Computed from Bain and Parris, *Convention Decisions*.

had no large, enthusiastic corps of amateur politicians to draw upon as delegate candidates, as later challengers like Senators Goldwater, McCarthy, and McGovern would.

Also, some primary laws made it difficult for insurgent candidates for convention delegate to get on the ballot, even if they wanted to. For example, the filing date for candidacy to a seat at the convention was February 16 in Pennsylvania—the Kefauver campaign was barely started by then. In New York the presidential candidates favored by delegate candidates were not identified on the ballot. Without Kefauver's name on the ballot, a little-known enthusiast for the Tennessee senator would have been at a distinct disadvantage running against an established politician. Kefauver thus let many convention votes go to the opposition by default, even as he swept the preferential portion of state primaries.[37]

Kefauver proved no more successful in translating his rank-and-file support into delegate votes in the nonprimary states. The indirect selection of delegates in these states usually begins at precinct caucuses and proceeds through one or more intermediate party conventions to a state convention, each conclave choosing representatives to the next higher meeting. These caucuses and conventions are routinely controlled by party politicians, for they are usually the only ones who take the time and trouble to attend them. A presidential candidate who lacks support among the existing party organization, like Senator Kefauver, has little chance of gaining many national convention delegates in these states unless he can mobilize enough highly enthusiastic followers to pack the local meetings and to defeat the party professionals at their own game. Senator Goldwater succeeded in doing this when necessary in 1964, as did Senator McGovern in 1972. But while Kefauver had a larger popular following within the party than either Goldwater or McGovern, he had far fewer supporters who were strongly enough motivated or well enough organized to capture control of local caucuses and state con-

---

37. When Kefauver's slates did contest against unpledged organization slates, they did remarkably well. In New Hampshire, Kefauver not only won the preference poll but also all 8 delegates. In Ohio, he won all 8 at-large delegates and 23 of the 27 district races contested by pro-Kefauver people.

ventions. In 1952 many of the state laws and party rules regulating the selection of delegates in nonprimary states discriminated against insurgents.[38] But just as notably, Kefauver's supporters in nonprimary states made no great effort.[39]

In the 31 nonprimary states, Kefauver won the majority of the delegates in only three: Michigan, Washington, and his own home state of Tennessee. All told, he received support on the first ballot from only 19 percent of the delegates from nonprimary states (Table 6-7). Where the rules of the delegate selection game favored the party professionals, Kefauver was nearly wiped out. His only chance remained to convince a convention made up of largely hostile delegates that he was the Democrats' only viable candidate.

He failed miserably. On June 8, immediately after the California primary, Kefauver was credited with 246 delegate votes. While these Associated Press estimates are usually conservative, the senator was less than half way to the 616 votes needed to win. After weeks of lobbying and cajoling delegates he reached 260 on the eve of the convention in late July. While far ahead of all his opponents, Kefauver still had less than half the strength needed to win. The party leaders and professionals—still without a candidate of their own—had stopped him.

Another major question about the Democrats' 1952 convention— why the Democrats nominated reluctant Adlai Stevenson—can be answered more simply. All the Democratic presidential possibilities save Stevenson had serious liabilities either as candidates or as potential presidents.

Kefauver was unacceptable to the party leadership and professional politicians, nor did he have much popular support in the South. Vice President Alben Barkley—much beloved in North and South, by leaders and rank and file, by New Deal–Fair Deal Democrats and the party conservatives—was seventy-four years old. Senator Richard Russell of Georgia was certainly of presidential caliber, but his

38. See, for example, the description of delegate selection procedures in Georgia, Arkansas, Rhode Island, Idaho, and Michigan in David, Moos, and Goldman, *Presidential Nominating Politics*, vol. 2, pp. 113–14; vol. 3, pp. 109 and 255–56; vol. 4, p. 57; and vol. 5, p. 34.

39. See ibid., vols. 2–5.

years of leadership against civil rights proposals made him unacceptable outside the South. Another possibility was Mutual Security Administrator Averell Harriman. Harriman, an extremely wealthy New Yorker, had had a distinguished career in the public service, but he had never held elective office. His popular following was scarcely visible, and his austere manner suggested that he could not be sold to the voters quickly. An outspoken liberal, Harriman was not acceptable to the South. Senator Robert Kerr of Oklahoma had been discredited in the primaries. Below this set of seriously flawed leaders were a few other possibilities—freshman Senator Humphrey of Minnesota, Senator Brien McMahon of Connecticut, Governor Paul Dever of Massachusetts, and others—who were either too young or too little known to be seriously considered in 1952.

Especially by comparison, Governor Stevenson had no serious liabilities (though his divorce was a minor problem) and numerous strengths. He was a successful chief executive of the nation's fourth largest state who was experienced in national and international affairs as well. He had won election to the governorship by a large margin in a difficult year (1948). A moderate man, Stevenson was the only possibility (save the aged Barkley) with a chance of carrying both the North and the South. The conclusion was inescapable: Stevenson was the only potentially strong candidate the Democrats had, aside from the unacceptable Kefauver.

There was only one problem. Stevenson did not want the nomination and had rejected several attempts by President Truman to make him his political heir. But Stevenson could not avoid speculation about his nomination no matter how hard he tried. A draft-Stevenson organization, manned largely by amateurs, was begun in February in Chicago. They received no encouragement from Stevenson but helped to keep his name alive as a potential candidate.[40] As the liabilities of all the other contenders sunk in after Truman's abrupt withdrawal, the pressures on the governor of Illinois to declare himself a candidate increased. He refused to do so, although never going so far as to say that he would reject the nomination if it were offered to

40. See Johnson, *How We Drafted Adlai Stevenson* (Knopf, 1955).

him.[41] Stevensonians took heart at this: perhaps the governor merely wanted to avoid being President Truman's chosen successor. Truman's support would be a mixed blessing at best; Stevenson would be in a more independent and powerful position if drafted by the convention. Be that as it may, Stevenson continued to reaffirm his reluctance to be a candidate for anything but governor of Illinois.

In May, Vice President Barkley announced that he was available for the presidential nomination. President Truman had privately indicated to Barkley that he would support him if Stevenson were not available. But Barkley's move toward candidacy was stopped short by organized labor. Barkley was a fine man with an excellent record on labor issues, they told him, but he was just too old. He therefore could not win, nor could they support his nomination. The day before the convention opened, Vice President Barkley withdrew from the race.[42]

Barkley's withdrawal virtually assured the nomination of Stevenson, if he would take it. As governor of the host state of Illinois, Stevenson, still disclaiming candidacy, gave a short welcoming speech to the convention. Its eloquence and wit, along with the enthusiasm of his reception, contributed to the foreordained outcome. At the same time that the Illinois governor was pleading with his own delegation not to support him, and as the Associated Press credited Stevenson with a grand total of 64 convention votes, the press reported that his nomination was virtually certain.[43]

One potentially explosive issue remained to be resolved before balloting could begin. Early in the convention a resolution proposed by Senator Blair Moody of Michigan had been adopted that required the delegates to "exert every honorable means" to see that the convention's nominee appear on their state's ballot under the Democratic label. In 1948 the Dixiecrat rebellion had resulted in President Truman's name not appearing on the ballot in several deep southern

---

41. See Jacob M. Arvey, "The Reluctant Candidate—An Inside Story," *Reporter*, Nov. 24, 1953, pp. 19–26.
42. See David, Moos, and Goldman, *Presidential Nominating Politics*, vol. 1, p. 117; and Harry S. Truman, *Memoirs*, vol. 2, *Years of Trial and Hope* (Doubleday, 1956), p. 495.
43. *New York Times*, July 22–25, 1952.

states; this resolution required that all delegates affirm their loyalty to the party as a condition for being seated at the Chicago convention. During the call of the states to make nominations, chairman Rayburn ruled that the delegations from Virginia, Louisiana, and South Carolina had failed to comply with this new rule. A motion was made to seat the delegations in question anyway—since the statements they had filed with the convention were in "substantial compliance" with the spirit of the Moody resolution. The roll call on this amendment was quite disorderly. In the midst of much parliamentary confusion, the Illinois delegation, which was known to be controlled by Stevenson supporters, switched their vote from 15 for and 45 against to 52 for and 8 against, accompanying the announcement with a statement of confidence in the Virginia governor. The motion seating the Virginia delegation passed. (The two other challenged delegations from the South were seated later.) This interlude was universally interpreted as meaning that, unlike the Kefauver forces and some northern liberals, Stevenson supporters did not wish to drive the South from the party. Indeed, they were willing to bend over backwards to lure the wayward southerners back home.[44]

A potentially damaging party split having been avoided, the balloting could proceed. On the first ballot, Kefauver led with 340 but Stevenson was a close second with 273 votes. The senator from Tennessee continued to hold the lead on the second ballot, although Stevenson recorded a bigger gain. At this point Harriman and Massachusetts's favorite son, Governor Dever, withdrew in favor of the governor of Illinois. On the third ballot, Stevenson won by the narrow margin of 5 votes.[45]

The 1952 Democratic nomination illustrates how a candidate with an overwhelming advantage in popular support can fail to win nomination. With the McGovern-Fraser commission reforms imple-

44. See David, Moos, and Goldman, *Presidential Nominating Politics*, vol. 1, pp. 119–47.

45. The closeness of Stevenson's margin of victory underestimates the breadth of his appeal. Kefauver had sought, without success, to throw his votes to the governor during the third ballot. Senator Russell pledged himself to support Stevenson and most southern delegates were less unhappy than they had been for years. The urban-northern-liberal forces behind Averell Harriman were also quite satisfied by the choice of Stevenson.

mented in 1972,[46] Kefauver's position would have been stronger, and his opponent's weaker, because there were more primaries, and because more delegate votes were tied directly to the expressed preferences of primary voters.

Still, without more of an effort directly to control the delegate selection process, there may have been enough delegates selected "through the usual channels" to deny Kefauver the nomination. Kefauver's experience shows that in a nonconsensual nomination, unless those who are normally active in delegate selection are sympathetic, a candidate must work aggressively to substitute his own delegates.

### REPUBLICAN NOMINATION, 1964

The nomination of Barry Goldwater by the Republicans in 1964 is often considered an anomaly. How could the nation's minority party choose a conservative ideologue who was not clearly the most popular candidate among the party's rank-and-file membership and whose chances for electoral victory in November were almost nonexistent?

It is tempting to try to answer this question in terms of the unique events of the 1964 Republican nominating contest. If Nixon had not been defeated in the 1962 California gubernatorial election, if President Kennedy had not been assassinated, if Rockefeller had not been divorced and remarried (or if the Rockefeller baby had not been born two days before the California primary), if Lodge had not won the New Hampshire primary—if one or more of these events had not occurred—then Barry Goldwater might not have been the Republicans' candidate in 1964. But—aside from standing as a reminder of the soberingly large element of chance in determining convention outcomes—such an approach does not contribute to an understanding of presidential nominations in general. And Goldwater's victory is quite easily explained in other, more general terms.

True, Goldwater was not clearly the most popular man in the party. But no one else was very popular with the party rank and file, either. Those Republicans who opposed the Arizonan did not

46. Commission on Party Structure and Delegate Selection, *Mandate for Reform*, Report to the Democratic National Committee (April 1970).

have a single strong, willing, and untarnished champion—the anti-Goldwater majority was divided and disorganized. It is also true that only four Republican governors were openly in the Goldwater campaign. But there were only sixteen Republican governors in 1964, leaving the rest of the state parties without the "coherent leadership embodied by a man in the Governor's chair. . . . Decentralized state parties . . . become happy hunting grounds for early starters in the presidential sweepstakes. They can move into a vacuum . . . and build delegate strength from the ground up."[47] Goldwater did just that.

Goldwater's drive for delegate votes was immeasurably aided by his extraordinary popularity among two groups within the party. Almost half of the county chairmen responding to Gallup's polls preferred Goldwater (with 48 percent) while his nearest competitor was the first choice of only 21 percent. (This in spite of the fact that many county chairmen did not think Goldwater would be the party's strongest candidate.)[48] And Goldwater was popular among party activists as well. In Wisconsin, dues-paying Republicans or those who worked in or contributed money to the party's campaigns were the state's strongest Goldwater supporters.[49] And nationwide, essentially the same thing was true: the more active the Republican, the more likely he was to be a conservative for Goldwater.[50]

Moreover, Goldwater's messianic appeal created new activists. His following was dedicated, enthusiastic, committed—the republic was going to hell in a handbasket; only Barry Goldwater could save it.[51] Theodore White has provided a classic example of how this enthusiasm was translated into convention votes. It is the story of one Luke Williams, a successful businessman who had never been active in

47. Nelson Polsby, "Strategic Considerations," in Milton C. Cummings, Jr., ed., *The National Election of 1964* (Brookings Institution, 1966), p. 95.

48. American Institute of Public Opinion, Gallup releases, March 29 and April 3, 1964.

49. Leon D. Epstein and Austin Ranney, "Who Voted for Goldwater: The Wisconsin Case," *Political Science Quarterly*, vol. 81 (March 1966), pp. 82–94.

50. Philip E. Converse, Aage R. Clausen, and Warren E. Miller, "Electoral Myth and Reality: The 1964 Election," *American Political Science Review*, vol. 59 (June 1965), pp. 321–36.

51. See, for example, Aaron Wildavsky, "The Goldwater Phenomenon: Purists, Politicians and the Two-Party System," *Review of Politics*, vol. 27 (July 1965), pp. 386–413.

politics before 1960, and the Republican party of the State of Washington. An old-fashioned conservative, Williams had admired Goldwater for years.

So when Clifton White came into Seattle in June of 1963 to talk about drafting Goldwater for President, Luke Williams was ready to listen—and then to work. . . . Seattle, which dominates King County, has 1,800 precincts; but the Republican Party had precinct leaders in only 300 or 400 of these precincts. If you went down into the streets; if you gave the conservatives you found there a vent for their emotions; if you registered them on rolls as you found them, the vacant precincts would have Republican precinct chairmen. The Republican organization in Seattle, headed by Mort Frayn, who was deputy national chairman of Rockefeller's national campaign, was glad to have precinct captains in blank areas; but "once we got a precinct captain named," said Luke, "we knew where he'd be when it came to voting." Only 2,500 precincts in the State of Washington (out of 5,500) had Republican precinct organization when Luke began his work—of which perhaps 50 percent were led by Republican moderates and 30 percent by natural conservatives. But when all 5,500 precincts in Washington were filled with Republican activists by the end of 1963, 65 percent were people controlled by Williams—and by Clif White. The people whom Williams organized were people who felt, as he did, that the Republic was in danger—people willing to go up and down the street ringing doorbells to find their kin-in-spirit, and register and motivate kinsmen when they found them.[52]

When the State of Washington cast its ballots at convention time, Goldwater received all but two of its twenty-four votes.

Goldwater was not the first candidate to inspire a cadre of amateurs who were prepared to volunteer extraordinary amounts of time and energy on his behalf. Willkie, Stevenson, and Eisenhower had all done this in varying degrees before, but Goldwater, drawing on the organizational talents of F. Clifton White, was able to harness this energy into the most effective and elaborate candidate organization seen in presidential nominating politics up to that time.

Since Goldwater's support was weakest among the rank and file, he might be expected to have performed most poorly in primary states, where the rank and file have the most direct hand in influenc-

52. Theodore H. White, *The Making of the President, 1964* (Atheneum, 1965), pp. 133–34.

ing delegate choice. Table 6-8 shows that he did do less well in primary than in nonprimary states, but the difference was not great, and he received 63 percent of the votes even in the primary states. While his performance in the primaries was hardly inspiring, it was no worse than any of his opponents'. When a victory in a preference primary did not automatically bring delegate votes, as it did in California, Goldwater's support among leaders and activists made him all the stronger relative to his opponents. The only primary states in which he was denied more than twenty delegate votes were Lodge's Massachusetts, Rockefeller's New York, and Scranton's Pennsylvania.

Given his resources, Goldwater could be expected to have been strongest in nonprimary states, where the delegate selection process normally favors candidates who have the support of either the established party leaders or highly active amateurs. With the support of both groups, Goldwater was able to win three-fourths of the votes from all the nonprimary states (Table 6-8). But a different attribute of states' politics seems to have had an even greater impact on Goldwater's success.

The Arizonan did best in the four states controlled by Republican governors who were among his supporters—in fact, every single delegate sent to the convention from these states voted for him! He ran next best in states with Democratic governors: whether the state selected convention delegates in primaries or in caucuses and conven-

TABLE 6-8. *Vote for Goldwater at the 1964 Republican Convention, by Control of State Governorship and Delegate Selection Procedure*

| | Percent of votes for Goldwater | | |
|---|---|---|---|
| Control of governorship | Primary states | Caucus and convention states | All states |
| Republican, for Goldwater | 0 | 100 (N = 64) | 100 (N = 64) |
| Democratic | 77 (N = 387) | 82 (N = 461) | 80 (N = 848) |
| Republican, not for Goldwater | 32 (N = 246) | 51 (N = 142) | 39 (N = 388) |
| Total | 59 (N = 633) | 78 (N = 667) | 100 (N = 1,300) |

Source: Computed from Bain and Parris, *Convention Decisions*. Territorial delegates excluded, District of Columbia included.

N = total number of delegates.

tions mattered not at all. About 80 percent of the votes cast by these 35 states were for Goldwater. States with Republican governors not for Goldwater were another matter: Goldwater did poorly in almost all of them, especially those with primaries. Both formal delegate selection procedures and gubernatorial influence (or lack thereof) seems to have affected Goldwater's ability to obtain national delegates in 1964.

The Arizonan's support was strongest in the states that had supported Taft in 1940, 1948, or 1952. In them he received well over 90 percent of the delegates. He failed to sweep only 13 traditionally liberal states, largely in the Northeast, where he received only 16 percent of the delegate votes, as the percentages of votes he received in states grouped by their ideological alignment shows: [53]

| | |
|---|---|
| Conservative | 99 |
| Moderately conservative | 91 |
| Moderate | 96 |
| Moderately liberal | 90 |
| Liberal | 16 |

Goldwater's overwhelming first-ballot victory is thus not hard to explain. Though he had little support from the rank and file, he had strong support from all party strata in between the rank and file and the party's governors. Since there were only sixteen Republican governors, the fact that only a fourth supported him did not hurt much. And since his opponents were all wounded or unwilling to campaign, the consequences of his weakness with the rank and file were minimized. Capitalizing on the disarray of his opponents and on his superior organization, Goldwater easily translated his resources into a decisive victory.

### DEMOCRATIC NOMINATION, 1968

By May of 1968, Vice President Humphrey had taken the lead in the preferences of the Democratic rank and file, of party leaders, and of delegates to the national convention. He did not lose any of these advantages and was nominated in August with 67 percent of the dele-

---

53. The classification of states is from Munger and Blackhurst, "Factionalism in National Conventions," pp. 375–95.

gate votes. But the similarity between the Democrats' 1968 contest and the consensual or semiconsensual nominations stops right there.

Throughout the contest there was great confusion. Candidate options changed from month to month; only McCarthy was a candidate from start to finish. Kennedy entered and Johnson withdrew in March. Humphrey did not declare until April. Kennedy was killed in June and McGovern declared in the same month. The instability of the candidate options was most apparent in the primaries. Humphrey was on the ballot in none, apparently delaying his declaration until the filing dates were past. McCarthy faced Johnson in two and Kennedy in five, but neither of the latter was still in the race by convention time. In fact, only McCarthy of all the candidates who lasted to the convention had been in the primaries at all.

Yet this confusion did not stand in the way of a convention decision that reflected both rank-and-file and leader preferences. Ironically, the dizzying changes in the list of candidates during the period that convention delegates were being selected probably contributed to this result. By the end of the delegate selection process, so few delegates were committed to viable candidates that the late-starting Humphrey experienced little difficulty in attracting a majority of their votes.

While Humphrey was the most popular candidate among rank-and-file Democrats, his margin over McCarthy was scarcely the 3 to 1 edge he achieved on the first and only ballot. Under 1968 procedures, like those of 1952, established party leaders tended to have disproportionate influence over the selection and mandating of convention delegates.[54] In primary states, of course, an insurgent candidate has a chance to capture convention delegations despite opposition from the local party establishment, as McCarthy did in New Hampshire. In states where convention delegates are selected in a series of party meetings beginning with precinct caucuses and ending in state conventions, insurgency is more difficult and leadership control of the make-up of the national delegation is the norm. An effective challenge to the party powers-that-be requires the capturing of hun-

---

54. See *Mandate for Reform*, pp. 17–32; Chester, Hodgson, and Page, *American Melodrama*, acts 4, 8, and 10; White, *Making of the President, 1968*, chaps. 3, 6, and 8.

dreds of precinct caucuses and prolonged parliamentary maneuvering at subsequent county, congressional district, and state conventions before delegates to the national convention pledged to an insurgent candidate can be won.

Eugene McCarthy's followers—intensely committed to the candidate and his cause, heavily middle-class suburbanites with the verbal and parliamentary skills, free time, or flexible work schedules typical of such status—were the sort of people most likely to be effective challengers to established leadership in nonprimary states.[55] They launched campaigns for McCarthy in a number of nonprimary states,[56] but their efforts were too little or too late and resulted in very few votes for McCarthy at the convention (see Table 6-9). Only 16 percent of the delegate votes from nonprimary states were for McCarthy, while 76 percent went for Hubert Humphrey. McCarthy was most successful in garnering delegates in primary states in which he campaigned (and, of course, especially in those he won). But those primary states that he did not enter gave him a niggardly 12 percent of their votes; over half their votes went to Humphrey. Thus while McCarthy was less popular than Humphrey, the 1968 delegate selection procedures combined with the preferences of party leaders for Humphrey made it more difficult for him than for Humphrey to translate the rank-and-file popularity he had into delegate votes.

But this was not the only reason for McCarthy's poor showing at the convention. Another was the ideological structure of the contest, which again favored the vice president. McCarthy, Kennedy, and McGovern all challenged the Democratic establishment from a position to the left of the party's center of gravity. With George Wallace abandoning the party for a third-party candidacy, Humphrey faced no challenger from the party's right wing. When confronted with this choice, Democratic conservatives from the South and West could only turn to Humphrey (see Table 6-10). If the McCarthy,

55. See Aaron Wildavsky, *Revolt Against the Masses* (Basic Books, 1971), chap. 13; Soule and Clarke, "Amateurs and Professionals," pp. 888–95; and John M. Orbell, Robyn M. Dawes, and Nancy J. Collins, "Grass Roots Enthusiasm and the Primary Vote," *Western Political Quarterly*, vol. 25 (June 1972), pp. 249–59.

56. See David Lebedoff, *Ward Number Six* (Scribner, 1972); and Eugene J. McCarthy, *The Year of the People* (Doubleday, 1969), chap. 11.

*The Convention's Decision* 199

TABLE 6-9. *First-Ballot Vote for Humphrey, McCarthy, and McGovern at the 1968 Democratic Convention, by Each Candidate's Standings in Primaries*

|  | Percent of votes for | | |
|---|---|---|---|
| Candidate's preconvention standing | Humphrey | McCarthy | McGovern |
| Primary states won | ... | 59 | ... |
| Primary states entered but not won | ... | 35 | ... |
| Primary states not entered | 53 | 12 | 9 |
| Nonprimary states | 76 | 16 | 3 |
| All states | 67 | 23 | 6 |

Source: Computed from Bain and Parris, *Convention Decisions.*
... = not applicable.

Kennedy, and McGovern supporters had been able to get together, they would have defeated the vice president in the most liberal Democratic states. But in the middle-of-the-road states, Humphrey bested his challengers handily and completely overwhelmed them among the party's right wing.

The combined effects of all these factors can be seen in Figure 6-5 which shows the growth of pledged delegate support for the various Democratic candidates in 1968. Until the end of the primary season

TABLE 6-10. *First-Ballot Vote for Presidential Candidates at the 1968 Democratic Convention, by Ideological Alignment*

| Ideological groupings of states[a] | Percent of votes for | | | | |
|---|---|---|---|---|---|
| | Humphrey | McCarthy | McGovern | Others or no one | Total |
| Very liberal | 43.0 | 36.0 | 15.0 | 6.0 | 100 (N = 604) |
| Liberal | 73.0 | 19.0 | 5.0 | 3.0 | 100 (N = 338) |
| Left-center | 73.0 | 22.0 | 5.0 | * | 100 (N = 286) |
| Right-center | 61.0 | 35.0 | 2.0 | 2.0 | 100 (N = 522) |
| Conservative | 87.0 | 12.0 | 0.5 | 0.5 | 100 (N = 251) |
| Very conservative | 83.0 | 7.0 | 1.0 | 9.0 | 100 (N = 527) |

Sources: Computed from Munger and Blackhurst, "Factionalism in National Conventions"; and Bain and Parris, *Convention Decisions.*
N = number of delegates.
* = less than 0.5 percent.
a. Alignments determined by frequency of state delegations' votes for or against most liberal candidate in 1944–60 nominating conventions.

FIGURE 6-5. *Shifts in Delegates' Support for 1968 Democratic Presidential Candidates*

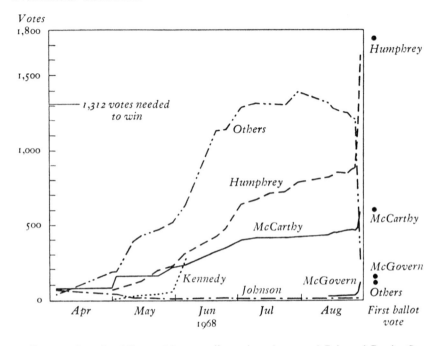

Sources: Associated Press, delegate polls, various dates; and Bain and Parris, *Convention Decisions*.

in mid-June, McCarthy was able to stay only a few delegate votes behind the vice president, according to the Associated Press. Then the McCarthy delegate hunt stalled at about 400 for two months, while Humphrey's delegate count doubled as he swept through the nonprimary states.

As the convention approached, the major threat to Humphrey's nomination no longer came from McCarthy but from the majority of the delegates who were either uncommitted or pledged to one of the twelve favorite-son candidates who had emerged during the spring. Eight of these favorite-son delegations were from southern states; Hubert Humphrey gained 381 of their 427 votes (89 percent), while McCarthy picked up 15½ and McGovern half a vote. It would be a mistake to conclude from this that Humphrey was nominated by southern conservatives—he was, after all, the most popular candidate in all ideological factions within the party. But if a candidate more acceptable to conservative southerners than Humphrey had been available, they might have been able to block his nomination. The two men who might have played this role—Lyndon Johnson and George Wallace—had other plans.

Had Robert Kennedy lived, he would have attracted some votes that ultimately went to Humphrey, but it is unlikely that he could have won the nomination. Even though he had the best record in the primaries, he was trailing Humphrey in the last poll of the Democratic rank and file before his death (Humphrey 40 percent, Kennedy 31 percent, McCarthy 19 percent). In the Gallup poll of county chairmen, Humphrey led with 67 percent to Kennedy's 19 percent and McCarthy's 6 percent, and there is no evidence that Kennedy was the most-preferred candidate of any other leadership stratum.[57] At no point had Kennedy more pledged delegate votes than Humphrey, and he had trailed McCarthy as well in that crucial commodity except for the day of his death, when he won the California primary.

There are many similarities between this 1968 contest and the Democratic race of 1952. Both were thrown into confusion by the withdrawal of the president soon after he was embarrassed in the first primary. As in 1952, the challenger who had brought on this embarrassment failed to translate his resources into the delegate votes needed to win the nomination.[58] As in 1952, the candidate who was most preferred by the president and his supporters was nominated, not so much through his own organizational efforts as through the support of the party regulars who normally control party machinery and who were not effectively challenged in either year. Humphrey was of course a much more eager candidate than Stevenson, and he campaigned extensively on his own behalf after his belated announce-

57. Gallup, *The Gallup Poll*, vol. 3, pp. 2127 and 2129.
58. Kefauver's greatest strength was rank-and-file support, but he was lacking in even the rudimentary kind of organization of activists that McCarthy had. McCarthy had less rank-and-file support (in part because of more competition), but he had at least the beginnings of the kind of organizational apparatus that did so much for McGovern in 1972.

ment of candidacy. Still, he won not so much because he was able to control the delegate selection process as because he was the overwhelming choice of those who controlled this process independently of his candidacy.

### DEMOCRATIC NOMINATION, 1972

As the Democrats prepared to convene in Miami Beach for their thirty-sixth national convention, Senator George McGovern was the favorite to win the presidential nomination. His surge ahead in the crowded field of active Democratic contenders during the primaries had been extraordinary—no one since Wendell Willkie in 1940 had risen so far in so little time.

Yet McGovern was neither an overwhelming popular choice nor a compromise candidate acceptable to all strata and wings of the party: The final preconvention Gallup poll showed him the first choice of 30 percent of rank-and-file Democrats to 27 percent for Senator Humphrey and 25 percent for Governor Wallace.[59] In the Gallup poll of Democratic county chairmen, Humphrey was well ahead (with 27 percent of the first preferences), trailed by Muskie, Jackson, and Kennedy; McGovern was fifth choice (with 11 percent), only 2 points above Wallace. He had no doubt improved on this dismal showing by convention time,[60] but certainly he was far from being the party organizational leaders' choice even then. McGovern's support had been built on his opposition to the Vietnam War and his advocacy of liberal causes, which had made him suspect at the center and on the right wing of the party. Though he had demonstrated an ability to broaden his appeal during the primaries, his advocacy of sharp cuts in the defense budget and an ill-conceived income maintenance scheme, plus the prominence of youthful longhairs in his campaign, had served to intensify rather than moderate these suspicions as the long campaign came to a close.

These weaknesses of the party's apparent front-runner plus an unusually large number of alternative candidates in 1972 would seem

59. Irving Crespi, "The American Voter—1972" (Princeton, N.J.: Gallup Organization; processed).

60. The Gallup poll of county chairmen was taken before McGovern's late primary victories. Questionnaires were sent out a week after the Wisconsin primary and were still coming in as the poll was published on May 7.

to be a sure formula for a multiballot convention and the ultimate emergence of a compromise candidate. In fact, George McGovern won a majority on the first ballot with over 200 votes to spare.[61] This outcome was the result of Senator McGovern's extraordinary effectiveness in translating his popular support into delegate votes.

By mid-May, after the Wallace victories in Michigan and Maryland, McGovern had won only three primaries to Humphrey's four and Wallace's six. Yet McGovern led in total delegate votes from the primary states (see Table 6-11). Wallace led with Humphrey second

TABLE 6-11. *Total of Delegate Votes Won by McGovern, Humphrey, and Wallace in Primary States, May 22, 1972*

| Primary delegations | Delegates won by McGovern | | Delegates won by Humphrey | | Delegates won by Wallace | |
|---|---|---|---|---|---|---|
| | Number | Percent of all possible delegates | Number | Percent of all possible delegates | Number | Percent of all possible delegates |
| Won by candidate | 172.0 | 89 | 204 | 46 | 296 | 71 |
| Not won by candidate | 173.5 | 17 | 53 | 6 | 23 | 3 |
| Total, to May 22 | 345.5 | 28 | 257 | 21 | 319 | 26 |

Source: Associated Press, poll of delegates.

and McGovern third when only those delegates from the primaries each candidate won are counted. But the reverse is true for each candidate in the primaries he failed to win; here McGovern led. At this point in May, he had slightly more delegate votes from primaries he had lost than from the primaries he had won!

McGovern picked up 17.5 votes in his losses to Muskie in New Hampshire and Illinois. (On the first ballot, McGovern received 129.8 votes from these two states.) In Pennsylvania, where he came in third in the preference vote, close behind Wallace, McGovern won 39 votes to 2 for the Alabaman. (On the first ballot it would be 81 to 2.) In Ohio, where McGovern narrowly trailed Humphrey, the South Dakotan won 66 delegate votes to the Minnesotan's 74. In West Virginia, where he left the preference contest to Humphrey

61. The vote was 1,715.35 for McGovern, 534 for Jackson, 385.7 for Wallace, and a few scattered for other candidates for a total of 3,016; 1,509 votes were required for nomination.

and Wallace, McGovern won 7 votes to Humphrey's 20 and none for Wallace. McGovern and Humphrey both lost to Wallace in Michigan and Maryland, but the former won 44 votes from the two states, while the latter won 28. The point is clear; even where he was not able to win the primaries, McGovern was almost always able to compete effectively for at least some of the delegate votes. They added up.

McGovern won every one of the seven remaining primaries, including vote-rich California and New York. From these seven, Humphrey won 13 votes in New Jersey and Wallace won 8 votes in New Mexico. McGovern won 649 pledged delegate votes immediately, which became 706 on the first ballot.

Out of 3,016 total delegate votes (1,509 needed to nominate), 2,007 were from primary states. McGovern ultimately received 1,301.8 of these votes to 312 for Wallace. At his peak before withdrawing, Humphrey had 413 of them (including the 106 from California which were returned to McGovern). Senator McGovern not only used the primaries to transform himself from a long shot into a serious candidate with a large popular following; he used them directly and indirectly to win more than 85 percent of the votes needed to be nominated.

Although the bulk of McGovern's votes came from primaries, his superiority over his opponents was comparable in the nonprimary states. By the time all the delegates were selected in late June, the South Dakotan had (according to the AP delegate poll) 281.15 votes from 24 nonprimary states, while Humphrey had 85.3 votes from 14 nonprimary states and Wallace had 55 from 3 such states. By the final vote, McGovern's total outside the primary states had risen to 413.55, while Wallace's was only 69.7. Humphrey had been credited with 98.8 such votes in the last AP poll before his withdrawal. The only nonprimary state in which McGovern was shut out of any delegate support was Senator Jackson's home state of Washington.

As a result of his extraordinarily successful delegate hunt, McGovern leapt ahead of all the other candidates in delegate support on April 25th (with his gains from the Massachusetts and Pennsylvania primaries) and never again lost the lead (see Figure 6-6). At the same time that he was trailing Humphrey and Wallace in the public opin-

FIGURE 6-6. *Growth of Delegate Support for 1972 Democratic Presidential Candidates*

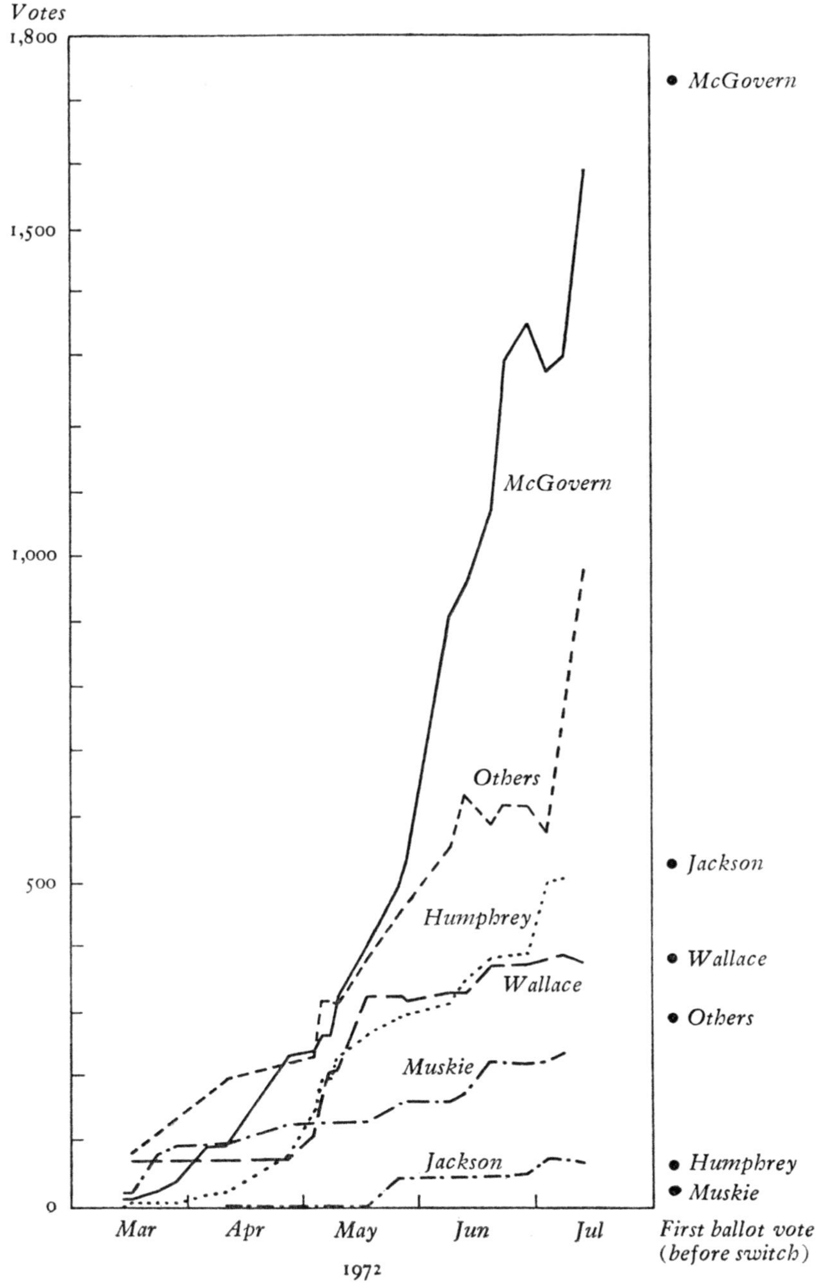

Sources: Associated Press, delegate polls, various dates; and Bain and Parris, *Convention Decisions.*

ion polls, he was broadening the chasm between himself and all the other candidates in delegates committed to support him at the convention.

Senator McGovern was able to translate his modest popularity into a majority of the convention delegates because of his nationwide campaign organization, manned mostly by young, unpaid volunteers. The only other 1972 Democratic candidate with a comparably strong organization had been Senator Muskie—his organization, however, had consisted of professional party politicians. Muskie's withdrawal in the midst of the primaries left an organizational vacuum in the states yet to be contested. McGovern was the only one of the three leading survivors prepared to fill that vacuum.

The Humphrey and Wallace campaigns concentrated their resources on a limited number of primaries they hoped to win. A series of primary victories, they assumed, would lead to favorable publicity, soaring poll standings, and delegate votes more or less automatically.

The Wallace campaign, in particular, aimed almost exclusively at generating publicity. Little was done to canvass the candidate's potential supporters, to make sure that they voted, or to see that there were pro-Wallace delegates on the ballot for them to vote for once at the polls. But Wallace's popular appeal was so great that he could do very well in popularity contests without campaigning at all— witness his second-place finishes in Oregon and New Mexico while he lay seriously wounded in a Maryland hospital. And Wallace was almost totally unprepared to translate his surprising popular support into delegate votes. In fact, were it not for the primary laws in Maryland, Michigan, North Carolina, and Tennessee which automatically turned his victories into pledged delegate votes, Wallace would have received many fewer delegate votes than he did. Not all primary state delegates are chosen through preference votes. Senator McGovern was eminently prepared to capitalize on that fact. Governor Wallace seemed scarcely aware of the problem—or of his own potential.[62]

Senator Humphrey's organizational effort was superior to Wallace's but still a pale shadow of McGovern's. After more than a de-

62. See Jim Clark, "Could Wallace Have Won?" *Washington Post*, July 9, 1973.

cade of striving for the presidency, Humphrey just did not "turn on" volunteers and amateurs anymore. But he was popular with the party professionals and the leaders of the labor movement. Neither, in 1972, proved as useful as bases for a candidate organization as in the past. Many of the party professionals had been lined up by Muskie or one of the other candidates before Humphrey entered the race. While Muskie had dropped out as an active campaigner, he was still a possible compromise candidate whom many of these leaders did not believe they should abandon. George Wallace had much strength among rank-and-file union members, and support from union leaders was of limited value if they could not keep their own members in line. Nonetheless, the Humphrey organization was most successful where he received active labor support, as in Pennsylvania, and least successful where he received limited organizational help from labor, as in Wisconsin.

Humphrey's most consequential organizational failure was in New York, where 278 delegates were at stake. Most of them were to be selected in district primaries. Senator McGovern had filed slates in 37 of 39 districts, but Senator Humphrey had filed none.[63] While McGovern may well have been more popular than Humphrey in New York statewide, the Minnesotan undoubtedly could have picked up a significant minority of the New York delegation if pro-Humphrey delegate candidates had filed (as McGovern supporters had done in Pennsylvania and Ohio). The Minnesotan essentially conceded 263 first-ballot votes to McGovern.

Senator McGovern began building his campaign organization years before the convention. The small group of enthusiastic followers that his strong antiwar position had given him provided the hard core of his volunteer workers. During the 1970 election the senator had raised money for other liberal Democratic senators through the mails, and with this large mailing list of known financial contributors to liberal causes he began his presidential fund-raising campaign. Even when the candidate was scarcely surfacing in the

63. See *Washington Post*, June 18, 1972. Humphrey "had anticipated a Muskie-McGovern donnybrook . . . and couldn't move fast enough to file after Muskie's New York office closed."

polls, McGovern's campaign was well financed by mostly small contributions. As the campaign picked up momentum after McGovern's wins in Wisconsin and Massachusetts, the money flowed in, in ever-increasing amounts. By the time of the California primary, McGovern was able to launch one of the most expensive campaigns in the state's history, outspending Humphrey 2 to 1. And McGovern organizers were out working in the states before either Humphrey or Wallace had even decided to run. Gene Pokorny, who organized the McGovern campaign in Wisconsin, began work in that state in November of 1970. Starting with the 50 Wisconsin delegates who had voted for McCarthy or McGovern in 1968, Pokorny developed a list of supporters that eventually became a cadre of 3,000 volunteer workers canvassing voters from 35 field offices by primary day. The same story was repeated in state after state from New Hampshire to California. Even in the states that McGovern lost, such as Pennsylvania and Ohio, his grass-roots organization, by concentrating their canvassing efforts in areas of greatest McGovern strength, could win some delegate contests merely by turning out a far larger proportion of McGovern's potential supporters than the other candidates were able to do among their following.

Yet McGovern's delegate strength in the primary states was not enough; he needed his somewhat more modest superiority in the convention states in order to win. Here, too, he began early:

In the fall of 1970 Senator George S. McGovern resolved to commit substantial resources during his presidential campaign to the pursuit of delegates in the non-primary states. On May 10, 1972, Senator Hubert H. Humphrey . . . his principal rival for the nomination, decided to do the same thing.[64]

The successful McGovern delegate selection effort in the nonprimary states was led by Richard G. Stearns, a former staff member of the Democratic party's commission on party structure and delegate selection. Stearns estimated that the average participation in delegate selection in convention states was about 5 percent of the registered Democrats; an insurgent would only have to stimulate a turnout of

64. Jonathan Cottin, "McGovern Swept Convention States on Work of Silent Majorities," *National Journal*, July 1, 1972, p.1084.

5–6 percent in order to control the outcomes. This the McGovern campaign set out to do. Starting early and using such sources as McGovern's own fund-raising lists and mailing lists of organizations such as the American Civil Liberties Union, they laid the groundwork for control of the precinct caucuses and subsequent delegate-selecting bodies in these states. They even contested the home states of their opponents, such as Maine, Minnesota, and Washington.

No other candidate put nearly as much effort into the nonprimary states. The Muskie campaign had banked heavily on the influence of party leaders who were themselves often displaced by McGovern supporters. The Humphrey campaign virtually ignored the convention states until the middle of the campaign, banking almost exclusively on the primaries. The Wallace campaign outside the primary states was even more vestigial than Humphrey's. The only such state in which the Alabaman invested a noticeable campaign effort was Texas, where he received 52 of his nonprimary votes. Even so, McGovern won more delegate votes out of the seven southern nonprimary states than did Wallace, 118.25 to 73.[65]

Surely, if Humphrey and Wallace had expended the effort in the delegate selection contests in both primary and nonprimary states that they put into the preference primaries, they would have done better than they did in winning delegate votes. But could they have beaten McGovern?

One reason for McGovern's organizational success was the fact that he had something to organize—plentiful volunteers and superior financial resources. Without a highly emotional issue like the Vietnam War to serve as a catalyst, it is not likely that McGovern would have been able to attract these resources so effectively. Governor Wallace was also campaigning on an emotional issue in 1972—antibusing. But his predominantly working-class following was less easily organized than McGovern's and his initial supporters were a less certain source of funds. In 1968, as governor, Wallace had utilized the state government of Alabama as an organizational resource in his drive to get on the ballot as a third-party candidate. This had resulted in much criticism, a Justice Department investigation, and several in-

65. Most of this account relies on ibid., pp. 1084–92.

dictments. In 1972, when he could not exploit this resource in the same way, the Wallace campaign was short of both money and staff.[66] Hubert Humphrey's organizational base was twofold—the party professionals and organized labor, both of whom were rather badly divided in 1972. Thus neither Humphrey nor Wallace had as favorable organizational potential as McGovern in 1972. But, then, neither of them seems to have tried very hard to exploit the potential he had.

But could McGovern's army of volunteers have won him so many delegate votes in the absence of the reforms that opened up the selection process? McGovern's coordinator for the convention states argues that "under the 1968 rules McGovern could at best have counted on the votes of 1,195 delegates, or 239 short of the 1,434 he needed to win the critical California challenge." The crucial votes came principally from the convention states which, prior to the reforms, were a reservoir of potential votes for the party regulars. "By opening up the process in the convention states, the reforms stripped McGovern's opposition of the power to take the nomination away."[67]

Another unique factor in the 1972 campaign was McGovern's well-coordinated and potent organization for selecting delegates from nonprimary states. The only comparable candidate organization was that of Barry Goldwater in 1964, but Goldwater was also the overwhelming choice of grass-roots Republican leaders in 1964.

McGovern was able to mobilize the manpower to go into caucuses and conventions usually controlled by unfriendly regulars and often to out-vote them. True, in 1968 many delegates were selected through processes that were not this open and public, and the reforms helped insure that they would be open and public in 1972. But Senator McCarthy's 1968 effort in the nonprimary states scarcely deserves to be compared with McGovern's. A challenge of the potency of McGovern's would surely have shaken up the process even in the absence of the reforms, especially when no other candidate sought out delegates in the nonprimary states in the same systematic way.[68]

66. James R. Polk, "Wallace Money," *New Republic*, June 10, 1972, pp. 17–19.
67. Richard Stearns, "Reforming the Democrats' Reforms," *Washington Post*, Dec. 3, 1972.
68. Austin Ranney, "The Line of the Peas: The Impact of the McGovern-Fraser Commission's Reform" (paper presented at the 1972 annual meeting of the American

Thus the story of the Democrats' 1972 presidential nomination was almost entirely written before the convention met in Miami Beach. And yet one final hurdle remained for the senator from South Dakota and his followers. The delegate selection guidelines drafted by the McGovern-Fraser commission and promulgated by the Democratic National Committee had resulted in an extraordinary number of credentials disputes—twenty-three from fifteen different states. The most critical of these controversies was over the seating of 151 California delegates pledged to Senator McGovern—for without these votes McGovern's claim to a majority of the convention delegates was problematical at best. The dispute was, in substance, over California's primary provision that the entire delegation (271 votes in 1972) goes to the primary winner. Supporters of Senator Humphrey argued that this was not only unfair but contrary to the McGovern-Fraser commission guidelines which outlawed the application of a unit rule at any stage of the delegate selection process. The California delegates should be prorated among the candidates in the primary according to their popularity at the polls. To do so would require McGovern to surrender 151 California votes, giving 106 to Humphrey and dividing the remainder among seven other candidates. The convention's credentials committee ruled in favor of this position.

This situation was distinctly embarrassing to McGovern and his supporters—he had chaired, for a time, the commission that recommended that the unit rule be abolished! His campaign had benefited in other states from the proportional distribution of delegate seats. And yet the California primary had been conducted with the full understanding that it would be a winner-take-all affair. To follow the decision of the credentials committee would be to change the rules of the election after it was over. On the critical convention roll call to overturn the committee report and to reseat the 151 McGovern delegates from California, the McGovern forces—joined by some Humphrey and Muskie supporters—carried the day. Senators

Political Science Association; processed), argues persuasively that the McGovern-Fraser commission guidelines contributed to the increase in state presidential primaries from 1968 to 1972. If this is true, it also helped the McGovern candidacy.

Humphrey and Muskie withdrew from the race shortly thereafter. McGovern had won a small but solid majority of the delegates. With that went the Democratic presidential nomination.

In retrospect, the McGovern nomination—and his choice of Senator Thomas Eagleton of Missouri as his running mate—was unfortunate. But several things are worth remembering about it. As of the final preconvention poll, McGovern was the candidate with the most support of the Democratic rank and file (by a small margin). He was at that time also the Democratic candidate who ran strongest in trial heats against President Nixon (also by a small margin). Furthermore, he had earned his delegate votes by starting early, organizing well, and fighting hard. The fact that his opponents failed to do the same thing can hardly be held against him.

## Influencing the Decision

"Great leaders of parties are not elected," the Right Honorable Ernest Pretyman, Member of Parliament, observed some years ago; "they are evolved . . . the leader is there, and we all know it when he is there."[69] Like most British Tories of his generation, Pretyman felt it undesirable to cast ballots for a leader; a leader should "emerge" in mystical ways until everybody who matters accepts his authority. The formal procedures by which the major American parties pick their leaders—public, governed by the calendar, rule-bound, and mechanical—are about as far from this traditional Tory ideal as it is possible to get.

Yet in numerous cases an American party leader emerges and wins the presidential nomination in a way that makes the elaborate mechanics of delegate selection and convention decision making superfluous. The eight consensual nominations since 1936 were like that; Mr. Pretyman would have approved. In the five semiconsensual nominations a single leader of the party also emerged during the interelection period. But his dominance was not so overwhelming that he could squelch the ambitions of all other presidential con-

69. Quoted in Robert T. McKenzie, *British Political Parties* (Praeger, 1964), p. 34.

tenders or attract the support of all party factions. The formal, complex, and mechanical way the front-runner's unofficial leadership is made authoritative by party convention vote gave his opponents one last chance to stop him. In each of these cases the leader of the party who emerged informally won the battle for the formal nomination, too—although in two cases by narrow margins. In the semiconsensual nominations the elaborate machinery of presidential nominations served as a check on the results of the informal processes of leadership selection.

Finally, in seven of the last twenty presidential nominations, the major parties failed to evolve a leader of sufficient strength to last all the way. Lacking a stable consensus on who the leader was, or ought to be, the parties divided along lines of cleavage which, for the most part, were already there but usually muted by loyalty to and respect for a common champion. Factional competition, apparent in varying degrees in semiconsensual nominations, was often complicated by different candidate preferences of party leadership groups and the rank and file, between party regulars and political amateurs. Under such circumstances the formal machinery of party choice can become a significant factor in determining the ultimate winner. Formal rules and procedures are never neutral; depending on the situation, they tend to favor some groups within the party, and hence some candidates, more than others. The translation of the presidential aspirant's resources—publicity, popularity, money, and the like— into convention votes is by no means an automatic process when a party is divided along several dimensions simultaneously. The seven nonconsensual nominations between 1936 and 1972 make clear that a wide variety of outcomes is possible.

☆

*Chapter Seven*

☆

# THE BEST POSSIBLE CANDIDATE

CHOOSING POLITICAL leaders is a problem as old as society. Human fallibility and mortality insure that the problem will never go away. The United States is committed to choosing its presidents through popular election.[1] For these elections to have meaning, the number of possible candidates for the presidency must be narrowed to a manageable few—the voters cannot be expected to make a reasoned choice among the millions of Americans who have the legal qualifications for the nation's premier public office. The major American political parties perform this screening function by making nominations, thereby usually reducing the task of the electorate to making a choice between one Republican and one Democrat.[2] Obviously, most of the narrowing of the alternatives takes place at the nominating stage.

Presidential nominations can be evaluated by measuring how good the process is and also by evaluating how good the candidates are who are selected. While the quality of the process undoubtedly affects the quality of results, each standard needs to be separately employed. At least in presidential nominating politics, a single set of institutional arrangements and procedures can lead to widely different outcomes, depending on the situation. Good procedures can sometimes have bad results, and vice versa. One of the more sobering consequences of this fact is that there can be no perfect method of choosing presidential

---

1. The electoral college, however, introduces complications.
2. But see Daniel A. Mazmanian, *Third Parties in Presidential Elections* (Brookings Institution, 1974).

nominees. It is nevertheless important to try to maximize the chances of desirable outcomes.

## The Characteristics of Presidential Nominees

The outcomes of presidential nominating processes are assessed in this study of the last twenty nominations of the major parties in terms of who won the nomination and why rather than the characteristics of presidential nominees as a group. Yet an informed assessment of the value of the presidential nominating system depends, in good part, on judgments about the quality of presidential candidates in general.

Good presidential candidates must be able both to win presidential elections and to serve successfully as president of the United States. Thus, in a two-party system only one of the nominees can pass the first test in each election. A brief look at the more superficial traits of the presidential nominees since 1936 may help in evaluating the outcomes of the presidential nominating process.

### PARTY POPULARITY

The presidential nominees over the past forty years have been with remarkable regularity the leaders of the final preconvention poll of their party's rank and file. The only clear exception to this pattern is Stevenson in 1952, who trailed far behind Kefauver. Three other cases are close or ambiguous. In 1940 Dewey led the last poll before the convention, but he was clearly slipping fast; Willkie led in the final poll, taken during the convention. In 1964, Goldwater was tied for first at 22 percent in the final poll; all told, four candidates had between 20 percent and 22 percent support from the GOP rank and file. McGovern's lead in the final 1972 poll was narrow. If second and third choices had been taken into account, some other candidate might well have stood higher on the average in these last two cases (and perhaps a few others as well). Nevertheless, even though the party rank and file does not directly make the nominating decision, the results have been remarkably congruent with their preferences.

STRENGTH AS A CANDIDATE

Most of the time, the nominee is also the party's strongest potential vote-getter in the November elections. There was little doubt that each of the renominated incumbents was his party's strongest candidate, though in 1948 this was more a testament to the lack of Democratic presidential timber than to Truman's popularity. Nor was there much doubt that Landon, Dewey (in 1944), Eisenhower (in 1952), Stevenson (in 1956), and Kennedy were likely to run better than alternative nominees. In 1940, 1948, and 1960, the polls were too sketchy to be of much help, but it seems likely that the GOP picked its strongest vote-getter in all three years.

In the other five contests, however, the parties may not have picked the most likely November winner. In 1952, Stevenson did not run as well as Kefauver against either Eisenhower or Taft in the trial-heat polls, though this is partly a function of Stevenson's inactivity before the convention. In 1964, no Republican came within hailing distance of President Johnson in the polls, but Goldwater was the weakest of all the possible candidates.

Four years later, the trial-heat polls were confusing; most of them showed Rockefeller running stronger against likely Democratic opponents than Nixon, but the last Gallup poll narrowly reversed this finding, while a still later Harris poll showed Rockefeller again stronger.[3] The same year some polls showed Humphrey running a stronger race than McCarthy, but the final Gallup trial heat before the Democratic convention showed McCarthy trailing Nixon by 5 percentage points while Humphrey trailed by 16 percentage points. McGovern had a modest edge over Humphrey and Muskie when paired against Nixon in 1972, but in retrospect he was clearly not the strongest candidate the Democrats had.

Trial-heat polls are often ambiguous, and even when they are clear they are hardly infallible estimates of campaign performance. The parties do not seem to take them too seriously. Usually the same person seems to be the most popular person in the party and the party's

3. See Jules Witcover, *The Resurrection of Richard Nixon* (Putnam, 1970), pp. 327–37, for an analysis of this situation and its effect on the nomination.

strongest vote-getter. But when this is not true, the convention usually picks the more popular person in the party. This should be somewhat reassuring to those who are concerned that the parties retain an identity and provide a choice, rather than routinely picking the candidate who seems most likely to win.

## SOCIAL BACKGROUND

Presidential candidates are far from a sample of ordinary Americans. Since 1936, they have all been white males, and most have been Protestant, well-to-do if not rich, and considerably older than the thirty-five years required by the Constitution. In this sense the outcomes of presidential nominations are quite unrepresentative of the nation.[4]

The presidency is no place for an average man. One of the most complex, demanding, and powerful offices in any country, the modern presidency demands extraordinary talent from anyone who seeks to fill it. It seems altogether appropriate, therefore, that the Democratic and Republican parties ordinarily choose presidential candidates from among those who have already demonstrated a capacity to fill high public office and to win the popular elections that lead to them.

But the opportunities to achieve these positions of political prominence are grossly unequal in the United States. Since the positions from which presidential possibilities emerge are overwhelmingly held by well-to-do, middle-aged, white, Anglo-Saxon males, then presidential candidates overwhelmingly fit that description. The solution to this bias in the recruitment of presidential candidates requires basic change in American values and social structure more than tinkering with presidential nominating procedures.[5]

4. For a discussion of various views on this subject, see Donald R. Matthews, *The Social Background of Political Decision-Makers* (Doubleday, 1954).

5. Some interpret this class bias as an indication that American public life is dominated by a power elite, an establishment, or a ruling class which manipulates the system to perpetuate its own power and privilege. See C. Wright Mills, *The Power Elite* (Oxford, 1956); G. William Domhoff, *Who Rules America?* (Prentice-Hall, 1967), and *Fat Cats and Democrats* (Prentice-Hall, 1972). Whatever the validity of such interpretations of American politics, the composite of the social backgrounds of presidential nominees is one of the least conclusive pieces of evidence in support of the thesis.

But the similarity in personal backgrounds of major-party presidential nominees and its consequences can be exaggerated. While Franklin Roosevelt and Adlai Stevenson, if not John Kennedy, were born into the closest thing the United States has to an aristocracy, most nominees were raised in more modest circumstances. Moreover, it is far from clear that wealthy presidents do more to protect the economic interests of the rich than do presidents of more modest background. One of the wealthiest American presidents, Franklin Roosevelt, is considered by some to have been the most radical in recent times.[6] More conservative presidents like Eisenhower and Nixon had more modest backgrounds. In 1964, two rich men from the Southwest ran against one another for the presidency. One was a conservative, the other a liberal who, on his election, proceeded to ram through Congress the most sweeping package of domestic reforms since the New Deal. Thus there are discernible differences in political attitude and opinion within the group of nominees despite their social and economic similarities (which can also be overdrawn). And these political viewpoints seem to have rather little to do with their personal background.

### QUALIFICATIONS

The presidency is a quantum leap in power and responsibility for any man, no matter how experienced he may be in high affairs of state. It demands a level and variety of skill far beyond that required by any other office in the land. Thus there is no entirely adequate training and testing ground for the presidency. Vice presidents gain much experience at handling ceremonial and partisan chores but ordinarily are kept at a safe distance from the important responsibilities of the White House. Governors and mayors have to cope with the complexities of a chief executive's job but gain no experience in the foreign and defense policy areas which have consumed the bulk of recent presidents' time and energy. Senators may have an acquaintanceship with national and international problems and policies that governors and mayors do not, but this exposure can be superficial and

6. See Ralph Miliband, *The State in Capitalist Society* (Basic Books, 1969), p. 100.

the Senate provides no executive experience. Cabinet officers, especially the more important ones, may develop savvy about bureaucratic politics in Washington and considerable knowledge of that segment of public policy with which their departments deal, but most of them have had no significant electoral experience.

The lopsided experience that these offices provide might be compensated for by service in more than one of them. But save between the Senate and the vice presidency, there is little lateral mobility between these offices and not much prospect of encouraging more without basic change in the political opportunity structure. The truth of the matter seems to be that all presidents, without regard to their prior experience, have to learn a very great deal on the job.

Moreover, their previous office-holding experience is not a clear guide to the qualifications of would-be presidents. All those who hold the same office do not emerge from it with the same skills. Some governors are poor administrators, some senators would make good ones. And the personal qualities and skills required to be a successful president are not always the same. Without the Great Depression, Herbert Hoover might have been a successful president. Given all these complexities and ambiguities, it would be absurd to conclude that all governors were better qualified for the presidency than all senators, or vice versa. There is a greater diversity of presidential talent within each of these groups than there is between them.

What then can be said about the relationship between the opportunity structure and presidential performance? No matter how a presidential "success" is defined, only the winner of a national election can be one. A president, be he of the laissez faire or activist variety, must be able to represent and lead millions of people and to inspire their confidence and trust. While he enjoys massive power, the president works within extraordinary political and legal constraints found only in government. Previous experience in high elective public office is not absolutely essential in order to do these things well nor is it a guarantee of adequate performance. Most of the time, though, some experience helps.

For still another reason, previous service in high elective office is desirable for presidential candidates: it increases the opportunity for voters to make an informed judgment about their capacities. A well-publicized career in public office may or may not equip a man for the rigors of the presidency, but it gives the electorate a better chance of making a wise judgment of him either way. The amount of information available to the American electorate is not great under the best of circumstances. To ask voters to judge men without public records (no matter how dissimilar the offices they have held are to the presidency) is to reduce the information level still further.

A presidential system of government in which future chief executives need serve no apprenticeship in comparable office is a risky venture.[7] But a system of leadership selection requiring a long period of training and testing in a prescribed set of offices has problems, too—the dangers of stagnation, of inflexibility in changing times and circumstances, and of development of a self-perpetuating elite. The American system for selecting presidents is something of a compromise between these two extremes. While the presidency is formally open to anyone who meets a few constitutionally imposed qualifications, only a few experienced public officials have much chance of ever becoming president. Sometimes this pool of potential presidents contains no one with much appeal, or a bright and attractive new figure emerges who is able to gain a major party nomination without previously demonstrating any political accomplishment at all. Despite the risk (the voters can know less about the man; the chances that he will prove inept are higher), it seems wise not to rule out the possibility of lateral entry directly into presidential contention.

Recently the vice presidency—once viewed as political dead end —has become the most likely source of presidents. If the office were filled as other offices are through an open competition for popular favor, the growing presidential opportunities of vice presidents should tend to increase the qualifications of its normal incumbent. Now, of course, vice presidential nominations are, in effect, decided by presidential nominees and their intimate advisers within a few

---

7. For a comparison of the American system with the British apprenticeship mode of recruitment, see Hugh Heclo, "Presidential and Prime Ministerial Selection," in Donald R. Matthews, ed., *Perspectives on Presidential Selection* (Brookings Institution, 1973), chap. 2.

hours of their convention victory. Not only is this decision made hurriedly by a few tired men, it is also made without a prior opportunity to view the various possible candidates competing against one another in an open campaign. The president's running mate, understandably enough, is selected on the basis of his probable contribution to electoral victory in November. A certain plausibility as a successor is needed, of course, if a man is considered for a vice presidential nomination. But which of the fairly numerous persons meeting this minimum standard is chosen depends heavily on quite arbitrary electoral considerations. And whether a vice presidential nominee becomes vice president depends almost entirely on the relative popularity of two other people—the presidential candidates. Under these circumstances, the presidential opportunities associated with the office of vice president can increase without an improvement in the capacity of its incumbents to serve as president of the United States. The risks involved in placing a man selected in this fashion so close to the presidency—whether the president serves out his full term or not —are grave. Unless the office can be made into a real apprenticeship or filled in a more reasonable way, it ought perhaps to be eliminated altogether.[8]

The character and personality of potential presidents are as important as their experience, though both are exceedingly difficult to evaluate. In his effort to identify personal qualities associated with presidential behavior, Barber concluded that the nominating process has served badly in recent years.[9] Yet even though he suggests how to identify the kinds of personalities that can do the most good and the most harm in the White House, we see no way of changing selecting procedures to insure that the good will win out.

8. It is unlikely that the office can be made into an effective means of training prospective presidents. Few recent presidents have had the time or inclination to groom a successor. A mandatory delay of several weeks in the presidential nominee's choice of a running mate with ratification by the national committee would be an improvement in the choice process.

9. James David Barber, *The Presidential Character: Predicting Performance in the White House* (Prentice-Hall, 1972). See also Alexander L. George, "Assessing Presidential Character," *World Politics*, vol. 26 (January 1974), pp. 234–82.

## *Who Is a Presidential Possibility?*

Only a limited number of people can be considered remotely realistic presidential possibilities. Who among them become serious candidates depends on access to publicity and to financial support.

### THE NUMBER OF PRESIDENTIAL POSSIBILITIES

The number of Americans who actually are considered for a presidential nomination is very small. If the possibilities are confined to
persons favored for a presidential nomination by 1 percent or more
of their fellow partisans in Gallup polls, only 62 Democrats and 47
Republicans qualified between 1936 and 1972. Some years, very few
did so; both a string of national victories and crushing defeats at the
ballot box can leave a party almost no one with sufficient public
prominence to contest for the presidency. New faces appear only
slowly among this group of presidential possibilities. Moreover, almost all of those who do achieve presidential prominence are elective
public officials, mostly incumbents or recent incumbents of three
offices—vice president, U.S. senator, or governor of one of the larger
states.

Certainly more than these 109 persons have been qualified to serve
as president of the United States since 1936—no matter how qualifications are defined. A large number of qualified potential presidents
have not been considered at all.

It does not necessarily follow, however, that the more presidential
possibilities the better. The Democrats' unusually large number of
candidates in 1972, for example, severely strained the nominating
procedures. It is hard to imagine what might have ensued if there had
been two or three times more. The principal alternative to present
procedures—a direct national presidential primary—seems no more
able to handle the problem of majority choice between numerous
candidates satisfactorily. In either system, numerous candidates make
it difficult to aggregate the broad-ranging support needed to win the
nomination and subsequent general election. Indeed, under either
present institutional arrangements or a national primary, too many

candidates in the race can disadvantage those seeking a broad coalition of supporters in favor of those appealing to highly motivated and active party minorities. Given the nature of the coalitions needed to win general elections in America, this scarcely seems desirable.

Thus, an informal and unofficial process that narrows down the serious contenders is essential to a well-functioning formal nominating process. This does not mean that a more vigorous and far-reaching search for presidential possibilities should not take place well in advance of convention time. The formal choice process is hampered by too many candidates, but the person finally selected cannot be better than the raw materials.

Presidential ambition may well be more widespread than the limited number of presidential possibilities who have been identified in recent years. Though many well-qualified persons may prefer to avoid the awesome burdens of the office, the presidency does represent the ultimate political achievement in the United States. As Schlesinger has argued,[10] political ambitions are heavily affected by political opportunities. If realistic chances to win the office were more widely dispersed, the circle of ambitious self-starters in presidential politics would surely also enlarge.

THE GREAT MENTIONER

The principal agency involved in identifying the group of presidential possibilities, communicating their characteristics, and rating their relative chances is the media of mass communications. Other actors are also engaged in screening and handicapping, of course, but as the nominating process has become more plebiscitary in nature, the media have taken on a central role.

Their discretion and their influence on nominating politics are least when the formal contest is at its height and the media are most active in covering it. The procession of state primary elections, the struggle for delegates at state conventions, and the national conventions themselves are events that reporters must cover; selectivity and interpretation are required if they are to make sense to the audience.

10. Joseph A. Schlesinger, *Ambition and Politics: Political Careers in the United States* (Rand McNally, 1966).

Yet the possibilities for independent media influence on nomination outcomes at this stage of the process are slight compared to the opportunities at earlier stages. Then there are few programmed events which must be covered; the newsman's discretion is large. The press's chance to affect nominating outcomes is at its peak before the formal selection process begins.[11]

The mass media of communications, of course, are not monolithic. Political reality as depicted by the *Manchester Union Leader*, the *Washington Post*, and CBS News is likely to differ substantially. And yet the coverage of presidential nominating politics is dominated by a relatively small number of reporters and news organizations under conditions that encourage consensus among them. No matter what their intentions, their reporting of the presidential nominating process is seldom even-handed in its consequences.[12] Usually, the net effects of this bias seem to favor established political figures over newcomers; anticipated winners over long shots; politicians located in Washington, D.C., over state and local leaders; big-state, urban, and eastern figures over others. The 1972 nomination of George McGovern, who possessed few of these attributes, illustrates that the biases can be overcome. But it does not negate the point that the media are not, and cannot be, merely neutral observers of a nominating process in which they play such a central role.

Nonetheless, "the press still sees itself as a mirror of events, rather than an independent analyst of the political scene and an adviser to the public."[13] This self-conception provides a handy defense against attack—and the media have been under heavy siege in recent years—and a plausible excuse not to accept the heavy burden of responsi-

11. See William R. Keech, "The Mass Media in the Presidential Nominating Process" (paper presented at the Syracuse University Media Politics Conference, Nov. 16–18, 1972; processed).

12. See Paul H. Weaver, "Is Television News Biased?" *Public Interest*, no. 26 (Winter 1972), pp. 57–74; Marc F. Plattner and James R. Ferguson, *Report on Network News Treatment of the 1972 Democratic Presidential Candidates* (Bloomington, Ind.: Alternative Educational Foundation, Inc., 1972); Edward J. Epstein, *News from Nowhere* (Random House, 1973); and James M. Perry, *Us and Them: How the Press Covered the 1972 Election* (Clarkson N. Potter, 1973).

13. Doris Graber, "The Press as Opinion Resource During the 1968 Presidential Campaign," *Public Opinion Quarterly*, vol. 35 (Summer 1971), p. 182.

bility that would accompany an alternative role. It also leaves the American people less well informed about potential and actual presidential candidates than they might be.

The myth of objective reporting leads to political news that focuses attention on what candidates do—often meaningless events staged for the benefit of the media—and what they say. Speculation about who is ahead and what will happen tomorrow too often passes for analysis. The nation would be better served if the media made more, rather than less, self-conscious and explicit efforts to scrutinize the qualifications of candidates and critically to evaluate potential presidents.[14]

### THE ROLE OF MONEY

The costs of contesting a presidential nomination have been enormous, and even with the newly enacted expenditure limitations and partial public funding, competition for presidential nominations is necessarily confined to those who can raise millions of dollars (or who look as if they can).

Two interrelated features of the system tend to counteract the biasing effects of nomination financing, however. The goal of the nominating game is the accumulation of 50 percent plus one of convention delegate votes; money is merely a means to that end. Presidential aspirants who look like winners attract the financial resources they need with relatively little difficulty. Of course no candidate, no matter how favorable his prospects, has as much money as he would like. A leading candidate's ability to raise money is a fragile thing; a bad mistake, a couple of primary defeats, a sag in his poll standings can cause the financial foundation of his campaign to collapse. Such uncertainty is not conducive to overconfidence or tranquillity; even for front-runners, raising money takes place in an atmosphere of permanent crisis. But this scarcely suggests that having more money than the opposition has can alone assure victory.

Secondly, the entire budget of a presidential nominating campaign

14. See Doris Graber, "Personal Qualities in Presidential Images: The Contribution of the Press," *Midwest Journal of Political Science*, vol. 16 (February 1972), pp. 46–76.

need not be in hand in order to begin. The long period of active campaigning, especially the series of primaries stretching from March into June, gives outsiders without access to great wealth a fighting chance. If they can raise a small fraction of the total costs of the campaign to pay start-up expenses, then a strong early showing in the primaries and the polls can lead to more new money, this money can lead to new triumphs, and so on and on to victory. It can be done, as George McGovern demonstrated in 1972. But the outside challenger must win or quickly face political bankruptcy; front-runners need only avoid losing.

Taken together, these two characteristics of presidential nominations open up the process to more candidacies than might be expected, given the huge costs involved, and the partial public funding for presidential primaries provided for in the Federal Election Campaign Act Amendments of 1974 will make it easier for challengers with modest means to raise enough money to compete. Scarcely any presidential possibilities since 1936 could be called poor, but the difference between those who were rich and those who were merely comfortable is not of great consequence for nominating outcomes. Of course, campaigns that can afford to divert more resources to winning votes and less to raising money are better off.

The alarming feature of the high cost of nominating campaigns is much less the effect on who wins and who loses than on the winner's obligations. It would be difficult to show that money was the crucial factor in determining any of the twenty nominations between 1936 and 1972, even though the winners usually had superior financial resources. What is disturbing is the possibility that obligations the winner incurred in the process of financing the campaign affected his stand on public issues. Where a candidate's early money comes from is critically important to an understanding of his behavior thereafter. The suspicion prevails, intermittently reinforced by scandals and exposés, that large and early contributors to winning presidential campaigns receive more than invitations to White House dinners and autographed photos in return. The newly enacted limitations on contributions and expenditures should mitigate this problem, however.

Some of the most serious unsolved problems in American politics concern the financing of political campaigns. While limits on expenditures or public financing may go a long way toward solving these problems for general elections, there are special problems involved in regulating nominating campaign funding. There is no fixed and limited number of candidates in nominations and some candidates begin the contest far ahead of others. Limiting expenditures reinforces the advantages of the early leaders relative to their challengers. Public subsidy of nominating campaigns will probably do the same thing unless subsidies are to be unequal and compensatory. And any allocation scheme that gave more money to the weaker candidates would be politically unacceptable. Thus, efforts to reform nominating campaign funding may well further reduce the presently limited and lopsided competition for presidential nominations.[15]

## *The Early, Informal Nominating Stage*

The three-year period before the first primaries is one of the most important stages in the choice process. Thirteen of the twenty nominees in the last ten elections were clearly identified by the beginning of the nominating year as the front-runner, the candidate to beat. Two more contests were structured as two-candidate races before the first primaries, and one of the two won both times. In only five of the twenty nominations was the preprimary prognosis misleading or unenlightening about the likely winner, and only Willkie was not identifiable before the primaries as a presidential possibility by this standard.

That so much happens so early is a very important fact for those who seek to improve the process. Remarkably conclusive developments take place at a time when the rules of the nominating process have virtually no direct effect (though they are anticipated). If the party is able to agree on a candidate early, the rules have only a slight impact. They become more important as the parties find it harder to reach consensus.

15. The campaign finance reform act of 1974 may advantage candidates favored by groups who can provide large sums through numerous contributors. See Joseph Alsop, "The Effects of Campaign Finance Reform," *Washington Post*, Nov. 25, 1974.

Two formal features of the nominating system have especially significant effects by anticipation—though they may work at cross purposes. One is the absolute majority rule. By requiring the winner to have more convention votes than all his opponents combined, this rule discourages candidates unable or unlikely to attract a broad base of support. The other is the system of state primaries. A little-known candidate with limited resources can invest them in one or a few primaries where he might do well enough to attract the publicity, support, and money he needs in order to become a serious candidate, if not a winner. Though the primaries have had limited effects on nominating outcomes, the system does provide a glimmer of hope to the ambitious but relatively obscure. The recent proliferation of primaries and other rules changes have provided still more hope. This and the resulting proliferation of candidates will surely reduce the importance of the early, informal nominating stage.

The most consequential developments of the preprimary period are difficult to control. Some are seemingly random: Nelson Rockefeller remarries; Edward Kennedy is involved in a tragic accident. Who makes the news is crucial, for preprimary nominating politics is mostly carried on in the media. Opportunities to make the news in a presidential context tend to center around previous conventions and presidential contests, and around midterm elections. The Democratic midterm convention may provide further opportunities for the emergence of presidential possibilities in a setting less concerned with immediate electoral considerations.

## The Formal, Legal Nominating Process

The United States has the most elaborate, complex, and prolonged formal system of nominating candidates for chief executive in the world. The selection of delegates to the national party conventions is spread over several months. The states decide when and how this is to be done, with few limitations on their discretion imposed by the national parties or federal law.[16] Not only is there a great complexity

---

16. The Democratic party, however, has been moving steadily in the direction of national standards for delegate selection. See Commission on Party Structure and

and variety in the methods of selecting delegates but also in the terms of their commitment to support specific presidential candidates at the convention.[17] The winning candidate must somehow attract the votes of 50 percent plus one of these delegates, chosen under fifty different sets of laws and political arrangements. This elaborate machinery is not so consequential, however, as some other features of the system.

## THE PRIMARIES

In spite of their reputation as "the road to the White House,"[18] the primaries rarely have much independent effect on nomination outcomes. From 1936 to 1972, thirteen of the fourteen front-runners before the primaries won nomination. The primaries left Dewey in 1948 and Ike in 1952 roughly where they had been beforehand; they were as much a hindrance as a help to Goldwater. Willkie, Stevenson, and Humphrey won nominations without competing in primaries at all. Only once were the primaries instrumental in the demise of a candidate who was likely to win nomination before they started. Only once were they instrumental in the emergence of a nominee who was otherwise unlikely to win nomination. Both events occurred in 1972 when McGovern was nominated by the Democrats.[19]

A system that grew up without central planning or coordination, the presidential primaries usually either reinforce what is already known (that candidate $X$ is the choice of his party) or produce such mixed and ambiguous results that their aggregate effect on the competitive situation is slight. Turnout in presidential primaries tends to

Delegate Selection, *Mandate for Reform*, Report to the Democratic National Committee (April 1970); Democratic National Committee, "Delegate Selection Rules for the 1976 Democratic National Convention" (March 1, 1974; processed); and "Democratic Party Charter," *Congressional Quarterly*, Dec. 14, 1974, pp. 3334–36.

17. See Paul T. David, Ralph M. Goldman, and Richard C. Bain, *The Politics of the National Party Conventions* (Brookings Institution, 1960), chaps. 10 and 11; and Richard D. Hupman and Robert L. Thornton, comps., *Nomination and Election of the President and Vice-President of the United States, Including the Manner of Selecting Delegates to National Political Conventions* (Government Printing Office, 1972).

18. James W. Davis, *Presidential Primaries: Road to the White House* (Crowell, 1967).

19. The uniqueness of the 1972 nomination is analyzed in Chapter 5.

be low;[20] they are held at different times and places under widely differing sets of rules. Rarely are all candidates on the ballot and, when they are, not all of them campaign equally hard. Only the first choices of voters are counted; this means that when more than two candidates are involved in the race, the most popular candidate overall does not necessarily get the most votes. Often the voters' preferences among the presidential candidates are not well reflected by the delegates selected; the extent to which the delegates are bound by primary results varies from state to state. Who won a single state presidential primary is often unclear. Small wonder that the overall meaning of a long series of such contests is often so ambiguous.

Nonetheless, the states increasingly have turned to the presidential primary; by far the bulk of the delegates to the two major party conventions are now selected in states that use the device. The apparent motivations of the state legislatures have been several, including no doubt a desire to democratize the selection of American presidents. But other more mundane considerations have also been persuasive. A presidential primary can focus national publicity on a state. It can attract a number of candidates, reporters, and miscellaneous political operatives whose free-spending ways give a boost to the local economy. In 1972 it allowed state Democratic parties to separate the selection of national convention delegates from the remainder of party affairs and thus escape the organizational and procedural strictures of the McGovern-Fraser commission. When they are viewed from a national perspective, however, nothing in the historical record suggests the wisdom of proliferating state presidential primaries.

On the other hand, the primaries provide the best available arena in which to challenge front-runners. The chances of destroying the initial leader are forlorn. But there is some chance, the costs of trying to do so are not prohibitive, and the potential pay-offs of an unex-

20. See Austin Ranney, "Turnout and Representation in Presidential Primary Elections," *American Political Science Review*, vol. 66 (March 1972), pp. 21–37; Harvey Zeidenstein, "Presidential Primaries—Reflections of 'The People's Choice'?" *Journal of Politics*, vol. 32 (November 1970), pp. 856–74; and Malcolm E. Jewell, "A Caveat on the Expanding Use of Presidential Primaries," *Policy Studies Journal*, vol. 2 (Summer 1974), pp. 279–84.

pectedly strong showing are very large. The primaries thus provide some testing—no matter how weak and imperfect—of the front-runner's ability to survive a challenge to his greatest asset, the presumption of victory. And the primaries, despite all their blemishes, are the most effective of the existing means of involving the populace in the presidential nominating system.

ABSOLUTE MAJORITY RULE

Both parties have used an absolute-majority-decision rule since 1936. The rule seems a reasonable response to the problems of reaching a fair and democratic agreement when there may be more than two options, and it reflects the judgment that wanting *not* to have someone should count for as much as wanting *to* have someone.[21]

Even though the absolute-majority rule is a high standard of agreement, neither party has had much difficulty in meeting it since 1936. Table 7-1 indicates not only that most nominees have easily reached an absolute majority on the first ballot, but also that about three-fourths of them could have won even under the more rigorous two-thirds rule.[22]

Some candidates who did not gain two-thirds of the delegates' votes might have done so if necessary. For example, Governor Stevenson appears the most marginal nominee on the list with his 50.2 percent on the third ballot in 1952. Yet he was clearly the most widely acceptable compromise choice available, and his total vote on the third ballot remained low because the presiding officer did not recognize Senator Kefauver who was seeking to withdraw in favor of Stevenson. Surely Stevenson would have been able to pick up the small handful necessary to reach two-thirds in 1956 as well, if he had had to in order to win. Similarly, Richard Nixon probably could have risen above his marginal first-ballot win in 1968 if necessary. He was certainly a more likely and more broadly acceptable compromise

---

21. See Douglas W. Rae, "Decision-Rules and Individual Values in Constitutional Choice," *American Political Science Review*, vol. 63 (March 1969), pp. 40–56.

22. Of course, under a two-thirds rule, opponents might have had an incentive to mobilize against a leader whom they found it futile to unite against under majority-rule conditions.

TABLE 7-1. *Presidential Nominees' Percentage of Delegate Votes on the Decisive Ballot*

| | | Decisive vote | |
|---|---|---|---|
| Nominee | Election year | Ballot | Percentage |
| Roosevelt | 1936 | First | 100 |
| Eisenhower | 1956 | First | 100 |
| Johnson | 1964 | First | 100 |
| Dewey | 1948 | Third | 100[a] |
| Nixon | 1972 | First | 99.9 |
| Dewey | 1944 | First | 99.7 |
| Nixon | 1960 | First | 99.2 |
| Landon | 1936 | First | 98.1 |
| Roosevelt | 1944 | First | 92.3 |
| Roosevelt | 1940 | First | 86.0 |
| Truman | 1948 | First | 75.0[b] |
| Eisenhower | 1952 | First | 70.1[c] |
| Goldwater | 1964 | First | 67.5 |
| Humphrey | 1968 | First | 67.1 |
| Stevenson | 1956 | First | 66.0 |
| Willkie | 1940 | Sixth | 65.5[d] |
| McGovern | 1972 | First | 56.8[e] |
| Kennedy | 1960 | First | 53.0 |
| Nixon | 1968 | First | 51.9 |
| Stevenson | 1952 | Third | 50.2[f] |

Source: Computed from Richard C. Bain and Judith H. Parris, *Convention Decisions and Voting Records* (2d ed., Brookings Institution, 1973).

a. Dewey had 39.7 percent and 41.1 percent on the first two ballots.
b. This rose to 76.8 percent after shift.
c. After shift; Eisenhower's figure before shift was 49.3 percent.
d. Willkie rose from 10.5 percent on first ballot to 99.8 percent on shift after sixth.
e. This rose to 61.8 percent after shift.
f. Stevenson had 22.2 percent and 26.4 percent on the first two ballots.

choice than either of his leading opponents, Governors Reagan and Rockefeller.

The two nominees least likely to have been able to reach two-thirds were John Kennedy and George McGovern. While both led in first-choice preferences, each seemed to be relatively close to his peak potential strength, and neither seemed to have much strength among the delegates supporting their opponents. In each case there were other candidates available who would have found it easier to unite a broad majority of the convention.

Two nominations since 1936 would have turned out differently if a simple plurality rule had been employed. Thomas Dewey led on the first ballot of the 1940 Republican convention with 36 percent of the votes, and Estes Kefauver led on the first ballot of the 1952 Democratic convention with 27.6 percent. Both were subsequently passed by another candidate who went on to win nomination, but if more delegates than any other single opponent had been the standard of victory, Dewey would have been Roosevelt's opponent in 1940 and Kefauver would have been the Democratic nominee in 1952.[23]

To sum up, the absolute-majority rule has not had a striking direct impact on recent nominations. While the 50 percent plus one requirement may have had some indirect consequences, in most recent nominations it probably has produced the same nominee who would have been chosen if the convention rule had been a simple plurality, an absolute majority, or a two-thirds majority. The absolute-majority rule discourages candidates who cannot mobilize broad coalitions, but it did not stop the Republicans in 1964 and the Democrats in 1972 from choosing nominees with unusually narrow bases of support.

23. Six other first-ballot leaders failed to win nomination in earlier absolute-majority-rule conventions: Whig candidate Fillmore lost to Scott (who was nominated on the fifty-third ballot) in 1852; and Republican candidates Seward lost to Lincoln (fourth ballot) in 1860, Blaine to Hayes (seventh ballot) in 1876, Grant to Garfield (thirty-sixth ballot) in 1880, Sherman to Harrison (eighth ballot) in 1888, and Wood to Harding (tenth ballot) in 1920. In Democratic two-thirds-rule conventions, seven first-ballot leaders failed to win nomination: Van Buren lost to Polk (who won on the ninth ballot) in 1844, Cass to Pierce (forty-ninth ballot) in 1852, Pendleton to Seymour (twenty-third ballot) in 1868, Bland to Bryan (fifth ballot) in 1896, Clark to Wilson (forty-sixth ballot) in 1912, McAdoo to Cox (forty-fourth ballot) in 1920, and McAdoo to Davis (one hundred and fourth ballot) in 1924. In fact Wilson would have lost in 1912 and Polk in 1844 under absolute-majority rule, for both Clark and Van Buren reached 50 percent of the vote. Three first-ballot leaders moved up from a plurality to a winning vote in previous absolute-majority conventions: Hughes won on the third ballot in the 1916 Republican convention, Blaine on the fourth in the 1884 Republican convention, and Taylor on the fourth in the 1848 Whig. First-ballot leaders who won on later ballots in two-thirds-rule conventions were Democrats Roosevelt (in 1932), Cleveland (in 1884), and Cass (in 1848). The size of their vote on the first ballot does not appear to be what distinguishes first-ballot leaders who go on to win from those who go on to lose in absolute-majority conventions: the losers had an average of 35 percent with a range from 27.5 percent (Sherman) to 44.9 percent (Fillmore), the winners an average of 36.5 percent with a range of 25.7 percent (Hughes) to 49.3 percent (Eisenhower). Calculated from Richard C. Bain and Judith H. Parris, *Convention Decisions and Voting Records* (2d ed., Brookings Institution, 1973).

The major cost of absolute-majority rule is the risk of convention deadlock. Efforts to block the front-running candidate short of a majority occur at all contested conventions but rarely have succeeded in recent decades. Since 1936 the record number of ballots has been six and none of the conventions has been effectively deadlocked. But so long as the rule remains in effect, the possibility that a blocking coalition will succeed is inescapable. The fact that the ultimate winner would be hard to predict is cause for apprehension.[24] Willkie and Stevenson won nomination after an early leader was blocked. So did Warren Harding. New Democratic party rules prohibiting winner-take-all primaries and imposing proportional representation in caucuses and conventions may make a deadlock more likely in the future.[25]

Since 1936 the risks of deadlock have been greatest when no single leader with imposing strength and broad appeal emerges well before the convention. Since 1936 all the preprimary front-runners who survived the primaries have won on the first ballot; the multiballot conventions have occurred only when there was not a strong, single candidate to beat. Multiballot conventions have been a symptom rather than a cause of lack of consensus.

THE APPORTIONMENT OF DELEGATES

In general elections, the adult citizenry chooses representatives on a one-man-one-vote basis. In the selection of delegates to national party conventions, however, parties face many other issues. Should states be represented according to their voting populations and their vote potential, or should they be represented according to their past party loyalty? Should convention delegates be chosen directly by the party rank and file or should they be chosen by party leaders or other groups a step or more removed from the party rank and file? Should

24. But see Eugene B. McGregor, Jr., "Rationality and Uncertainty at National Nominating Conventions," *Journal of Politics*, vol. 35 (May 1973), pp. 459–78; William A. Gamson, "Coalition Formation at Presidential Nominating Conventions," *American Journal of Sociology*, vol. 68 (September 1962), pp. 157–71; and Steven J. Brams and G. William Sensiba, "The Win/Share Principle in National Party Conventions" (Department of Political Science, New York University, September 1971; processed).

25. See *Washington Post*, March 31, 1974.

delegates mirror the demographic characteristics of the party rank and file (or the general public), or should they mirror the presidential preferences of the rank and file, or some combination of both?

That the answers to these questions can affect convention results was most dramatically demonstrated by the Republican convention of 1912. President Taft defeated former President Roosevelt in that contest, with the help of votes cast by delegates from the southern states, which were represented in proportion to their population even though the number of voting Republicans in the region was minuscule.[26]

Because the proportion of the presidential vote a party can expect varies from state to state, as does the strength of candidates for the nomination, both parties have since 1912 recognized the desirability of basing representation at national party conventions on more than population alone. Their apportionment schemes in recent years have taken into account past voting patterns, partly to reward party loyalty, partly to avoid rotten boroughs, and partly to anticipate where the party's potential vote is.[27]

The formula for apportioning delegates among the states was the hottest issue at the otherwise harmonious Republican convention of 1972. Liberals proposed a scheme for the distribution of seats at the 1976 convention based heavily on state population, while the more conservative Republicans supported a system rewarding those states voting with the party in 1972. Each side, of course, hoped that its scheme would favor its kind of candidate four years later. The conservative faction won the skirmish, though the party's landslide victory the following November may have made it a hollow victory.

How often has apportionment affected convention outcomes? For three conventions that seem to have been exceedingly close affairs—the Kennedy and McGovern nominations, which seem to have been won by genuinely small margins, and Eisenhower's nomination in 1952, which hinged on a crucial procedural vote—simulated votes

26. The issue was complicated of course by the numbers of disenfranchised black Republicans.

27. See Judith H. Parris, *The Convention Problem* (Brookings Institution, 1972), chap. 2; and David, Goldman, and Bain, *Politics of National Party Conventions*, chaps. 8 and 9.

under three different apportionment schemes show that none of the outcomes would have been changed (see Table 7-2). The pro-Eisenhower position on the crucial Brown amendment would have won whether apportionment had been based on state electoral college strength, state population, or Republican vote in the previous presidential election. Even though Eisenhower did best on the first ballot under the existing apportionment scheme, he did lead Taft under all three simulated schemes. Kennedy's first-ballot vote would have been strengthened rather than weakened under each of the alternative schemes. McGovern would have won the crucial California challenge vote under each alternative, though his margin would have been smaller under two of them. Thus apportionment seems not to have affected the outcomes of these three closest contests, and probably none of the other outcomes since 1936.

### DELEGATE SELECTION PROCEDURES
### AND CANDIDATE PREFERENCES

Presidential primaries are popularity contests; but they are also a means of selecting convention delegates by direct vote of the party membership.[28] Even after the recent multiplication of presidential primaries, many national convention delegates are still selected by indirect party processes—precinct caucuses and county, district, and state conventions. It seems plausible that national convention delegates chosen by local caucuses and state conventions should favor presidential candidates supported by party leaders and party regulars while delegates from primary states should favor candidates popular among the party rank and file. It takes a far greater commitment to party or candidate to attend party meetings than to vote in primary elections. Delegate selection in nonprimary states is thus ordinarily left in the hands of the faithful few who regularly attend party meetings. While turnout in presidential primaries is not large when compared to that in general elections, delegates are still chosen by a far

28. See Austin Ranney, "Changing the Rules of the Nominating Game," in James David Barber, ed., *Choosing the President* (Prentice-Hall, 1974), pp. 75–77, for a discussion of alternative participants in the choice process.

TABLE 7-2. *Possible Effects of Various Apportionments of Delegate Votes on Critical Roll Calls at the Three Closest Conventions since 1936*

Percent of total votes

| Convention and vote | Actual vote | Simulated vote based on | | |
|---|---|---|---|---|
| | | Electoral college[a] | State population[b] | Party voting[c] |
| 1952 Republican; against Brown Amendment re credentials contests | 54.6 | 52.9 | 53.0 | 61.0 |
| 1952 Republican; for Eisenhower on first ballot before switches | 49.3 | 46.2 | 46.6 | 49.2 |
| 1960 Democratic; for Kennedy on first ballot | 53.0 | 54.4 | 54.2 | 58.2 |
| 1972 Democratic; in favor of minority report of credentials committee on California delegation | 53.7 | 52.2 | 52.0 | 55.0 |

Source: Computed from Bain and Parris, *Convention Decisions.*

a. Actual vote weighted according to state's proportional strength in the electoral college.

b. Actual vote weighted according to population.

c. Actual vote weighted according to state's party vote in the previous presidential election.

larger and more representative cross-section of partisans in the primary than in the convention states.

But delegate selection procedures have little effect on who wins and who loses at national party conventions. In consensual nominations, so little opposition develops to the natural choice that delegate selection systems are irrelevant. Roosevelt, Landon, Dewey (in 1944), Truman, Eisenhower (in 1956), Nixon (in 1960 and 1972), and Johnson were supported by almost all convention delegates no matter how they were chosen. Moreover, sharp differences in candidate preferences between party leaders and party rank and file are uncommon. Comparing Gallup's polls of county party chairmen (taken since 1952), as a rough indicator of leadership opinion, with polls of ordinary party adherents, the candidate preferences of party leadership and rank and file diverged only three times (see Table 7-3).

TABLE 7-3. *County Chairman and Rank-and-File Preferences
for Presidential Nominee in the Final Gallup Poll, 1952–72 Elections*

| Elec- tion year | Democratic choice of | | Republican choice of | |
|---|---|---|---|---|
| | County chairmen | Rank and file | County chairmen | Rank and file |
| 1952 | Stevenson | Kefauver | Taft | Eisenhower |
| 1956 | Stevenson | Stevenson | a | Eisenhower |
| 1960 | Kennedy | Kennedy | Nixon | Nixon |
| 1964 | a | Johnson | Goldwater | Goldwater[b] |
| 1968 | Humphrey | Humphrey | Nixon | Nixon |
| 1972 | Humphrey | McGovern | a | Nixon |

Source: American Institute of Public Opinion, Gallup releases, various dates.

a. No poll, ostensibly because there was no doubt as to whom they preferred.

b. Tied with Nixon, at 22 percent each; Lodge had 21 percent and Scranton 20 percent.

In 1952, Kefauver was the clear first choice of the Democratic party's membership but very unpopular among party leaders. As might be expected, the Tennessee senator ran strongly in most primaries and very poorly in the caucus and convention states. But Kefauver's primary victories did not yield many Kefauver delegates except in states like California, South Dakota, Wisconsin, Maryland, and Oregon where votes for Kefauver automatically resulted in delegates pledged to vote for him. In primary states like Illinois, Nebraska, New Jersey, and Pennsylvania, primary votes do not invariably translate into delegate support. Where the selection of delegates has been separated from the presidential popularity poll, organizational strength is required to contest races for delegate seats. Kefauver did not have this organization; the party regulars did. Thus Kefauver could sweep these states' popularity contests but still gain few delegate votes. More than mass popularity is required to win delegates in many primary states.

The GOP experienced a similar division within the party in 1952 —the rank and file preferred Eisenhower while the party leadership was pro-Taft. Ike might thus have been expected to win the primaries while Taft carried the convention and caucus states. The general did do better in the primary states than Taft, but narrowly so.[29] And Eisenhower won more delegate votes in the nonprimary states than Taft despite the contrary preferences of party leaders. Taft picked up most of his primary state delegates in the Midwest, where his mass popularity was greater than Ike's; Republican governors were overwhelmingly for Eisenhower and proved to have more influence over their delegations than lower level party officialdom. Finally, pro-Eisenhower amateurs flooded the precinct caucuses and state conventions in some nonprimary states, capturing control over those delegations from the party professionals.

The McGovern campaign of 1972 was a classic illustration of how amateur enthusiasts can be a powerful resource in both primary and nonprimary campaigns. The small band of dedicated followers with whom McGovern began his bid for the presidency were welded into a grass-roots campaign organization of surprising effectiveness. The large number of active presidential candidates in 1972 plus traditionally low turnout in the primaries placed an unusually heavy premium on getting out the vote, which the McGovern organization did exceedingly well. They even captured a large number of delegates in primary states that their candidate lost. And McGovern earned 41 percent of the delegate votes—more than any of his competitors—in the nonprimary states despite opposition to his candidacy by most established state and local party leaders.

The general point to be drawn from these three cases—and a number of others could be cited to the same effect—is that the impact of various delegate selection procedures can have very different consequences for nomination outcomes depending on the nature of the candidates and the competitive situation.

The growing prominence and power of dedicated amateurs, whose primary allegiance is to presidential candidates more than to the party, is sometimes viewed with alarm. Experienced party regulars, it is argued, are hardheaded and realistic men and women; amateurs tend to be ideological, extremist, and unrealistic.[30] But the data

29. Without the New York delegation, which is selected in primaries that have been highly responsive to leadership control, Taft would have won more primary state delegates than Eisenhower.

30. See James Q. Wilson, *The Amateur Democrat* (University of Chicago Press, 1966); Nelson W. Polsby and Aaron B. Wildavsky, *Presidential Elections* (3rd ed.,

on the last ten presidential elections suggest that these characteriza-
tions are subject to serious question.

Republican county chairmen were lined up solidly behind Taft in
1952 and Goldwater in 1964 despite overwhelming evidence that
neither was the strongest available leader against the Democrats. The
Democratic county chairmen backed Stevenson over Kefauver in
1952, Humphrey over McCarthy in 1968, and Humphrey over
McGovern in 1972. In each case the Gallup organization's trial-heat
polls showed that the local leaders' first choice would not run as well

---

Scribner, 1971), pp. 35–59; Aaron Wildavsky, "The Goldwater Phenomenon: Pur-
ists, Politicians and the Two-Party System," *Review of Politics*, vol. 27 (July
1965), pp. 386–413; Aaron Wildavsky, *Revolt Against the Masses* (Basic Books,
1971), chap. 13; John W. Soule and James W. Clarke, "Amateurs and Professionals:
A Study of Delegates to the 1968 Democratic National Convention," *American
Political Science Review*, vol. 64 (September 1970), pp. 888–98; Edward Costantini,
"Intraparty Attitude Conflict: Democratic Party Leadership in California," *Western
Political Quarterly*, vol. 16 (December 1963), pp. 756–72; C. Richard Hofstetter,
"The Amateur Politician: A Problem in Construct Validation," *Midwest Journal of
Political Science*, vol. 15 (February 1971), pp. 31–56; and John D. May, "Up with
Dick Daley," *Intellectual Digest*, March 1973, pp. 85–87. Sidney Verba and Norman
H. Nie, *Participation in American Democracy and Social Equality* (Harper
and Row, 1972), pp. 224–28 and 292–98, find that policy preferences motivate political activity more strongly among Republicans than Democrats. The conservative
political beliefs associated with this disproportionately high participation exaggerate
the already conservative bias of higher status people, who are the group most likely
to be politically active. They find that Republican activists' preferences differ more
from those of less active Republicans than Democratic activists' preferences differ
from those of less active Democrats. In fact, the preferences of inactive Republicans
are more like those of both active and inactive Democrats than they are like those of
active Republicans. David Nexon, "Asymmetry in the Political System: Occasional
Activists in the Republican and Democratic Parties," *American Political Science
Review*, vol. 65 (September 1971), pp. 716–30, found in national samples taken in
1956, 1960, and 1964 that higher proportions of Republicans than Democrats are
active in campaigns. On issues polarizing the two parties, Republican activists were
more conservative than the general membership of their party, while Democratic
activists held views that were similar to those of the rank and file of their party.
Herbert McCloskey, Paul J. Hoffman, and Rosemary O'Hara, "Issue Conflict and
Consensus Among Party Leaders and Followers," *American Political Science Review*, vol. 54 (June 1960), pp. 406–27, compared the policy preferences of delegates
to the 1956 Democratic and Republican conventions with the preferences of a sample of the national electorate. While the delegates are different from the Nexon and
Verba-Nie activists, the results are comparable. Republican leaders differed more
from their followers than Democratic leaders did from theirs, and Republican followers were more similar to Democratic leaders and followers than they were to
Republican leaders.

in November as the man they opposed. Perhaps the leaders were right and the trial heats wrong in some or all of these instances. But in five nominations since 1952 the party professionals were willing to defy the hardest evidence available on the prospects of victory or didn't seem to care whether they won in November or not.

The candidates who have stimulated the most activity by amateur enthusiasts since 1936 were Willkie, Eisenhower (in 1952), and Goldwater among the Republicans and Stevenson (in 1952 and 1960), McCarthy, and McGovern for the Democrats. They are a mixture of probable winners and losers. Goldwater, McCarthy, and McGovern were all relatively ideological or extremist candidates; Willkie, Eisenhower, and Stevenson could scarcely be considered either one. But all of them stimulated significant amateur movements.

The truth of the matter seems to be that neither the party professionals nor political amateurs are invariably hardheaded or impractical, ideological or pragmatic, extremist or middle of the road. A rather wide variety of candidates can appeal to each group—or repel them. Both groups have rather mixed records.

## Reform

"Opaque as the future may seem," Austin Ranney recently stated, "one forecast, at least, seems safe: for some time to come Americans of many different persuasions will continue to seek changes in the rules of the nominating game."[31] But these rules make much less difference about who wins, who loses, or who is even considered for the presidency than other less controllable variables. The same formal procedures can have good or bad results depending on the potential candidates and the competitive situation. These, in turn, are shaped by events and processes that normally occur during the first three years of the presidential selection cycle rather than during the relatively few months of official campaigning when the rules are operating. And no set of nominating rules and procedures can guarantee favorable results every time.

31. "Changing the Rules of the Nominating Game," p. 93.

Yet, today, the sense that American political institutions and processes have failed is so widespread and strong that Ranney's hunch about the future is undoubtedly correct. The formal, legal rules of the presidential nominating process can be self-consciously manipulated—by the parties themselves, by the Congress and state legislatures, by the courts—but the critical early stages of the nominating process are not easily changed. Though the effects of rules changes may not be large—certainly they are often unpredictable—changes should be considered.

Many of the recent changes in nominating procedures seem to encourage the proliferation of candidates. For example, the Democratic party's effort to assure all its voters "full meaningful and timely opportunity to participate in the delegate selection process"[32] encourages candidates who expected to do poorly under older procedures. The increase in the number of primaries encourages potential candidates to think that their campaign may catch on in one of them. The promise of public subsidies for nominating campaigns encourages candidates with limited resources to hope that they can overcome that obstacle. Recent moves in the direction of proportional representation of rank-and-file preferences in delegate selection encourage candidates who can mobilize minority support in a variety of states without winning in many.

These changes may bring better qualified candidates into the contest. But a large number of candidates is not desirable for its own sake. Indeed, too many alternatives can make the final choice more difficult and possibly more capricious. The greater the number of candidates arriving at the convention with sizable blocs of pledged delegates, the greater the likelihood of multiballot conventions, of deadlock, and of unpredictable results. Herman Finer has observed that "the selection and election of the President is a gamble on folly, genius, and all the stations between."[33] Increasing the number of candidates and postponing the elimination of alternatives until convention time increases the risk unnecessarily. While a system that gives outsiders and

32. *Mandate for Reform*, p. 9.
33. *The Presidency: Crisis and Regeneration* (University of Chicago Press, 1960), p. 300.

marginal challengers a chance is desirable, many proposed reforms give insufficient attention to the problems of narrowing the alternatives down to one fairly chosen winner. One systematic way to do this is a national primary, the most widely discussed and apparently the most popular alternative to the existing nominating system.[34]

### A NATIONAL PRIMARY

Compared to the complexities of contemporary procedures, a direct choice of a nominee by a single, nationwide primary would have the merit of simplicity. And it seems to promise a quick, timely, unambiguous, and authoritative measure of the relative popularity of all bona fide contenders. Since presidential nominations have become increasingly like mass popularity contests in recent decades in any event, why not go all the way? Although turnout for a national primary would surely be lower than that for the November election, participation would certainly be much higher than it is for the present combination of state primaries and local caucuses. The disproportionate influence of intense minorities—party leaders, party activists, candidate and issue enthusiasts—would be correspondingly reduced. A national primary would force all those seeking a presidential nomination to compete, eliminating the possibility of the last-minute choice of a nonparticipant. The measurement of the relative popularity of the contestants would be made on a single day, not spread over several months during which popular preferences and political conditions can and do change.

The major claim to superiority of the national primary rests on the view that such a system would quickly and automatically designate the party's most popular candidate; but even when judged on this basis, its advantage over the present mixed system is relative. The period of formal campaigning for presidential nominations might indeed be shortened under a national primary system. But so long as the United States has calendar elections—and hence presidential nominations made at fixed intervals—aspirants will actually begin to campaign for the presidential nomination whenever they choose.

34. It is favored by some 72 percent of Americans. See *Congressional Quarterly Weekly Report*, July 8, 1972, p. 1651.

The only practical way to limit the length of presidential nominating contests is to shorten the president's term or to hold presidential elections at irregular and unpredictable intervals. But short campaigns are not wholly desirable anyway, since they provide tremendous advantages to initial front-runners.

Nor would the most popular candidate automatically win a presidential primary. Nomination by a simple plurality, while standard practice in primary elections outside the South, could result in presidential nominees supported by small minorities, especially if the field of contenders were large. This in turn could lead to weak presidential candidates unable to build the broad-ranging support needed to win in November. Thus most national primary proposals require a specified proportion of the total votes cast, usually 40 percent, in order to win and provide for a run-off between the two leading contenders in the event that no one achieves this figure at the first balloting.

However, there is no guarantee that the candidate with the most overall support (for example, in terms of first-plus-second-choice votes) gets into the run-off election. The top two candidates in the first primary might be quite unacceptable to everyone but their first-choice supporters, whereas the most broadly appealing candidate might have substantially less first-choice support. This risk is inescapable so long as the single first-choice vote is used in primaries; none of the proposed run-off provisions eliminates it. If a large number of candidates routinely entered the presidential primary, this sort of outcome might prove to be common.

Voters could be required to rank their preferences, with the candidate who stands highest in the voters' average preferences being declared the winner. Such a voting technique would obviate the need for a run-off, though it could lead to distorted results if voters misrepresented their preferences in order to enhance the prospects of their first choice. But even though such a voting procedure might substantially improve national primary results, it is unlikely that it would be politically acceptable.

Thus, even when judged on its strongest grounds, a national presidential primary poses some problems as acute as those of the existing system. It still seems, however, a more straightforward way of measuring mass preferences and hence more likely to come up with the most popular person in the party as the presidential candidate. But the cumbersome existing system has done this with remarkable regularity since 1936, too. The two systems would probably result in the same winner most of the time when confronted with the same set of alternative candidates.[35]

In addition, a national presidential primary would probably restrict the number of plausible contenders for the presidency to an even smaller number than have participated in recent decades. Unless free television time were made available, it would almost certainly be more expensive than the existing system. Expenditure limitations and public subsidies could reduce dependence on large contributors, but either of these policies is more likely to reinforce the competitive advantage of prominent politicians and initial front-runners than to reduce it. Without a series of state primaries, in which a relatively unknown candidate might dramatically demonstrate his growing popularity and appeal, it would be most difficult to come from far behind and win nomination. Established, well-known politicians would have an even stronger advantage over spokesmen for new groups and new ideas than they have had.

Thus, ironically, a national primary could more accurately and predictably reflect voter preferences among the candidates at the same time that it narrowed the variety of plausible candidates from whom voters could choose. There seems to be no way of reconciling the susceptibility of the present system to insurgency with the systematic responsiveness to popular preferences that the national primary would ideally achieve. The choice between the two systems eventually boils down to the question of which of these conflicting values is to be preferred.

IMPROVING THE EXISTING SYSTEM

Many of the recent changes in nominating procedures have helped to make the existing system more open and public. But some of them

35. See William R. Keech, "Anticipating the Consequences of a National Presidential Primary," *Policy Studies Journal*, vol. 2 (Summer 1974), pp. 274–79.

have had unfortunate side-effects, and further changes are in order.

Efforts to improve representation of minority groups among delegates to national conventions are commendable, but they should not
become an end in themselves. National party conventions are instru-
ments for choosing the nation's top political leaders, and they will be
most legitimate when they are representative of their party's rank
and file. But too much attention to the demographic characteristics of
the delegations can obstruct and distort the representation of candidate preferences. Surely it is far more important that the preferences
of a demographic group be reflected in the enduring consequences
of the choice of a potential president than in the very temporary payoff of having a specified proportion of the delegates at a given convention. The preservation of demographic mixes ought not be permitted to interfere with the representation of political preferences.[36]

One of the disturbing responses to new national guidelines for
state delegate selection systems has been the establishment of new
primaries. If each primary had no more consequence than the selection and instruction of the delegates from a single state, the situation
would be different. In fact, because of the attention focused on them,
state primaries are commonly national events with national consequences on the fortunes of the individual candidates campaigning in
them. It is because a victory in a closely watched primary can make a
marginal candidate viable, and because a loss can do the reverse that
primaries receive so much attention.

But if state primaries are so consequential, it does not make sense
to allow any state to have a primary at almost any time. The result
is a chaotic system that puts excessive burdens on a candidate who
wants to demonstrate a broad national following. This is a cost associated with the advantage given to marginal challengers. But there
must be limits to the number of opportunities given to such challengers, because it is also the task of the nominating process to narrow
the range of alternatives to one. There is little reason to believe that

36. See Carl Baar and Ellen Baar, "Party and Convention Organization and
Leadership Selection in Canada and the United States," in Matthews, ed., *Perspectives*, chap. 3, for a discussion of Canadian experience with direct representation of
various segments of their parties.

multiballot conventions could do this in a fair, open, and publicly accountable way.[37] Therefore, ways must be found to limit the proliferation of primaries and to coordinate them into a national system that may first broaden but will subsequently narrow the alternatives. Congressman Morris Udall's suggestion of a limited number of dates on which all primaries must be held is a step in the right direction.[38] In order to make the initial primaries most open to marginal challengers and the later primaries more difficult for all but the most serious candidates, smaller states should be encouraged to have primaries early and larger states later. In this regard, the New Hampshire to California sequence makes far more sense than the reverse would. Uniform standards of access to the ballot would make it harder for candidates to reap the benefits of winning primaries where they are strong while avoiding the consequences of losing primaries where they are weak. Perhaps candidates removing themselves from one primary ballot should be removed from all.

Efforts to insure proportional representation in the nominating process are similar to other efforts to broaden the alternatives, and they have the same drawbacks. They merely postpone the decisions to narrow the alternatives to one. There may be good reason for a legislative body to mirror the fractionalized preferences of those who select it, because of the variety of decisions that must be made over a long period of time. But there is far less to be said for a national party convention that mirrors fractionalized preferences on its major decision, the choice of a presidential nominee. Since the final choice of the nominee is a winner-take-all decision, delegate selection systems might follow the same rule.

The complexity of the procedures for selecting delegates in non-primary states and the attendant lack of publicity make them relatively inaccessible to those who are not intensely interested in and highly informed about politics. Ways should be sought to lessen the vulnerability of these systems to unrepresentative minorities, espe-

---

37. See ibid. for a discussion of the Canadian low-man-out and secret-ballot procedures for convention voting.

38. See Jules Witcover, "Revising Our Political Primary System," *Washington Post*, Jan. 22, 1975.

cially if primaries are to be discouraged. Uniform and simple national procedures for party caucuses and conventions would facilitate publicity and participation. Furthermore, if each stage took place on a uniform date in every state, the attendant nationwide publicity might increase participation still further.

Efforts to improve the nominating process must not stop with the mechanical procedures, which are relatively easy to change. Knowledge about the skills, experience, and personality traits associated with successful presidential behavior needs to be broadened, and ways should be found to identify those characteristics in potential candidates.

The mass media, in the information they transmit about candidates, should include analyses of the performance of presidential candidates in lower office. The quality of a candidate's performance as a senator, governor, or administrative official is relevant information for the selection process. While it may not have the journalistic appeal of stories about who is winning and how candidates adjust their positions to the demands of the campaign, such analysis deserves more attention than it has received.

More than any other office, the vice presidency has become a source of presidential nominees. Yet in some respects it provides less training, experience, and responsibility than other positions. Improvement of the vice-presidential selection process and an upgrading of the responsibilities of the office would make it a more reasonable training ground for the presidency. Postponement of the designation of the vice president until after the nominating convention would give more time for search, scrutiny, and public discussion of alternatives. Ratification of a more carefully chosen candidate by a representative national party committee would be preferable to the ratification by the convention of a more hasty and ill-considered choice. Such a change would be easy to implement.[39] Unless recruitment for the vice presidency and the responsibilities of the office can

39. This would involve essentially the same procedures used by the Democrats in 1972 when Sargent Shriver was selected to replace Thomas Eagleton, the candidate chosen at the convention.

be made more appropriate to the requirements of the presidency, abolishment of the office should be considered.[40]

Finally, more lateral mobility should be encouraged among offices in the national executive and Congress, in state government, and perhaps elsewhere, to broaden the experience of potential presidents. Presidents should be urged to appoint more members of Congress to administrative posts. And the Congress might count such executive experience toward seniority—or at least not erase most of the seniority of such persons.

Improving both the process and the outcomes of presidential nominations will require far more than changed party organization and formal, legal rules. For the qualities of the persons who win presidential nominations are shaped by America's social and economic structure; by the values and beliefs of its citizens and the issues they think are of paramount importance; by modern communications technology; by political reporters and their definitions of "news"; by the shifting distribution of power, prestige, and opportunities for self-advancement within the governmental structure itself. Many of these things are not easily changed simply because they may stand in the way of a more rational choice of chief executives. Improvement in the choosing of American presidential candidates is not solely a matter of party reform.

40. See Elijah Ben-Zion Kaminsky, "The Selection of French Presidents," in Matthews, ed., *Perspectives*, chap. 4, for a discussion of relevant French experience.

# Index

Chester, Lewis, 51n, 109n, 125n, 165n, 197n
Chisholm, Shirley, 87
Civil rights, effect on presidential nominations, 41, 43
Clarke, James W., 157n, 159n, 198n, 240n
Clark, Jim, 206n
Clausen, Aage R., 193n
Coll, Edward, 145
Collins, Nancy J., 109n, 198n
Congressmen, 18–25, 29–30, 218–19, 220
Congress, U.S., 24, 30, 35, 249
Connecticut, 175
Consensual nomination, 160–61, 212, 237
Constitution, U.S., 22nd Amendment, 34, 41–42, 47
Contested delegations, 161n, 182–84, 211
Conventions, national, 6, 8, 55; control of, 91; credentials disputes in, 161n, 182–84, 211; decision by, 157–213; representative nature of, 234–36, 242, 247; risk of deadlock in, 234; rules changes in, 4, 161n, 182. *See also* Delegate selection
Conventions, state and local, 178–81, 187, 197–98, 208–09, 236; reforms in, 53, 87, 210, 234
Converse, Philip E., 193n
Coolidge, Calvin, 33n, 166n
Costain, Anne Nicholas, 158n, 159n
Costantini, Edward, 240n
Cottin, Jonathan, 208n
County chairmen, 240; Gallup polls of, 76, 162n, 166n, 177n, 193, 201–02, 237–38, 240–41
Credentials disputes, 161n, 182–84, 211
Crespi, Irving, 8n, 155n, 202n
Crouse, Timothy, 12n

Dauer, Manning J., 92n
David, Paul T., 33n, 73n, 74n, 76n, 92n, 95n, 157n, 168n, 179n, 182n, 188n, 190n, 191n, 229n, 235n
Davis, James W., 98n, 229n
Davis, Kenneth S., 43n
Dawes, Robyn M., 109n, 198n
Deadlocked conventions, risk of, 234
Delegate selection, 87, 92–95, 186–88, 192, 195–98, 202, 206, 208–11, 228–30, 234–42; minority representation in, 246–47. *See also* Caucuses, precinct; Conventions, state and local; Primaries
Delegates, 157–58; credentials contests re, 161n, 182–84, 211; pledged, 93, 172n, 182n, 186, 188, 190, 200, 204, 206, 238
Democratic party, 2, 240n; Dixiecrat rebellion, 190–91; McGovern-Fraser commission, 87, 94–95, 191, 211, 230; midterm convention, 228; nonconsensual nominations, 166n, 185–92, 196–212; presidential possibilities, 15–17, 40; rules changes by, 4, 53, 161n, 210, 234
DeSapio, Carmine, 62
Dever, Paul, 189, 191
Dewey, Thomas E., 16, 54–55, 74, 99n, 179–80, 215–16; *1940* campaign and convention, 8, 77–79, 134–38, 167–72, 233; *1944* campaign and convention, 52, 58–60, 114, 116–17, 161, 237; *1948* campaign and nomination, 71–73, 112–13, 126–30, 156, 166, 172–77, 229
DiSalle, Michael, 164
District of Columbia, 104n, 107, 120n, 152n
Dixiecrat rebellion (*1948*), 190
Domhoff, G. William, 217n
Donahoe, Bernard F., 35n, 36n, 37n, 165n
Douglas, Paul, 68, 100
Douglas, William O., 27, 99n, 100
Driscoll, Alfred, 133, 175
Duff, James, 74

Eagleton, Thomas, 23n, 212, 248n
Earle, George, 35
Eisenhower, Dwight D., 6–7, 9, 17, 22, 34, 59, 63, 84, 143, 218; amateur support for, 194, 241; illness of, 45–47; refusal to run (*1948*), 40, 72, 99–100, 162–63; *1952* campaign, 53, 61, 74–77, 113, 130–34, 216, 229, 238–39; *1952* nomination, 166, 177–85, 235–36; *1956* campaign and convention, 98, 161, 237
Eisenhower, Milton, 15n, 17
Elections, midterm, 55, 62, 64, 75, 228
Elective-office experience, need for, 219–20
Epstein, Edward J., 224n
Epstein, Leon D., 2n, 193n
Evans, Rowland, 86n, 89n

Factionalism, 158–60, 166, 170, 175–77, 183, 190–91, 213
Fair play amendment (*1952* Republican convention), 182
Family life, of presidential candidates, 6
Farley, James, 36, 38
Farmers Alliance, 92
Fauntroy, Walter, 152n
Federal Election Campaign Act, 226–27
Fenno, Richard F., Jr., 28n
Ferguson, James R., 14n, 155n, 224n
Field poll (*1972*), 153